Digital Control
using
Microprocessors

PAUL KATZ

Technion—Israel Institute of Technology

Prentice/Hall PHI International

Englewood Cliffs, New Jersey · London · New Delhi
Sydney · Toronto · Tokyo · Singapore · Wellington

Library of Congress Cataloging in Publication Data

Katz, Paul, 1934–
  Digital control using microprocessors.

  Bibliography: p.
  Includes index.
  1. Microprocessors. 2. Digital control systems.
I. Title.
TJ223.M53K37   629.8'95   80-27234
ISBN 0-13-212191-3

British Library Cataloguing in Publication Data

Katz, Paul
  Digital control using microprocessors.
  1. Digital control systems
  I. Title
  629.8'3   TJ216

  ISBN 0-13-212191-3

ISBN 0-13-212191-3

PRENTICE-HALL INTERNATIONAL, INC., *London*
PRENTICE-HALL OF AUSTRALIA PTY., LTD., *Sydney*
PRENTICE-HALL CANADA, INC., *Toronto*
PRENTICE-HALL OF INDIA PRIVATE LIMITED, *New Delhi*
PRENTICE-HALL OF JAPAN, INC., *Tokyo*
PRENTICE-HALL OF SOUTHEAST ASIA PTE., LTD., *Singapore*
PRENTICE-HALL, INC., *Englewood Cliffs, New Jersey*
WHITEHALL BOOKS LIMITED, *Wellington, New Zealand*

Printed in the United States of America

10 9 8 7 6 5 4 3 2 1

Contents

PREFACE   vii

1 ANALYTICAL BACKGROUND   1

   1.1 Introduction   1
   1.2 Linear, Time-invariant, Discrete Systems   2
   1.3 The Calculus of Finite Differences   5
   1.4 The z-transform   10
   1.5 The Inverse Transformation   14
   1.6 Discretization of a Continuous System   15
   1.7 Properties of Discrete and Discretized Linear Systems   24
   1.8 Converting Discrete Signals to a Continuous Control Signal   29
   Appendix 1A   Overview of Classical Sampled Data Theory   33
   Exercises   36

2 DIGITAL CONTROL DESIGN VIA CONTINUOUS DESIGN   38

   2.1 Introduction   38
   2.2 Continuous Design and Discretization of the Compensation
       Network   39
   2.3 Digital Filter Properties, Frequency Response, Aliasing   41
   2.4 Methods of Discretization of Analog Filters   47
   2.5 Comparison of the Various Discretization Methods   57

2.6 Design Example   64

Appendix 2A   Design of Filters Using Lowpass Filter, Bilinear
        Transformation and Frequency Prewarping   68

Exercises   69

3 DISCRETE DESIGN OF DIGITAL CONTROL   70

3.1 Introduction   70
3.2 Analytical Design   71
3.3 Design on the z-plane   79
3.4 Design on the w-plane and the w'-plane   84
3.5 Compensation Design Using the Frequency Response on the
    w-plane   89
3.6 Example of w and w'-plane Design Method   96

Exercises   101

4 MULTIVARIABLE DIGITAL CONTROL,
  STATE SPACE APPROACH   104

4.1 Introduction   104
4.2 State Space Approach; Pole Placement, Observer Design   105
4.3 Observer Design   113
4.4 Optimal Control Based on Quadratic Synthesis   122
4.5 Optimal Filtering in the Presence of Noise   125
4.6 Model Following Methods   128

Exercises   132

5 MECHANIZATION OF CONTROL ALGORITHMS ON
  MICROCONTROLLERS   135

5.1 Introduction   135
5.2 Iterative Computation via Parallel, Direct, Canonical and Cascade
    Mechanization   135
5.3 Properties of Microcomputers   143
5.4 Stabilization of an Antenna Dish. Example of Microcontroller
    Design   148

Exercises   162

6 ANALYSIS OF THE IMPLEMENTATION OF THE NUMERICAL
  ALGORITHM   163

6.1 Introduction
6.2 Binary Arithmetic with a Finite Word Length, Types of Numerical
    Errors and Their Generation in Various Forms of Representation   164
6.3 Generation and Propagation of Quantization Noise Through the
    System   169
6.4 Coefficient Errors and Their Influence on the Dynamics of the
    Controller   179
6.5 Nonlinear Properties of the Controller Caused by Quantization,
    Deadband, Limit Cycle   183
6.6 Word Length in A/D Converters, Memory, Arithmetic Unit and
    A/D Converters   190
6.7 Design Example. Microprocessor Implementation of a Digital
    Autopilot   195
Exercises   214

7 SELECTION OF SAMPLING RATE   216

7.1 Introduction   216
7.2 Unmodelled States and Prefiltering of Unwanted Frequencies   217
7.3 The Time Response and the Response to an External Noise—
    Relation to the Sampling Rate   224
7.4 The Roughness of Control Caused by Sampling   229
7.5 Fidelity of the Response and Sampling Rate   234
7.6 Practical Selection of the Sampling Rate   236
Exercises   238

8 DESIGN EXAMPLE 1   239

8.1 Introduction   239
8.2 The Analog Scheme   239
8.3 Discrete Model of the System and an Estimation of the Required
    Computing Capability   242
8.4 The Computing System   248
Exercises   252

9 DESIGN EXAMPLE 2   253

9.1 Introduction   253
9.2 The Control Requirements   253
9.3 Description of the Subsystems   254
9.4 The Controller Design   257
9.5 Selection of A/D and D/A Converters   262
9.6 The CPU   263
9.7 The Controller Program   265
Exercises   267

**Appendix A   OPTIMAL DISCRETE CONTROL, SOME COMPUTATIONAL
TOOLS**   268

A.1 Discretization of a Continuous Cost Function   268
A.2 General Formulation of the Discrete Regulator Problem   269
A.3 Solution of the Optimal Regulator   270
A.4 Solution of the Discrete Riccati Equation by Eigenvector
      Decomposition   272
A.5 Calculation of the Steady State Optimal Filter by Eigenvector
      Decomposition   277
A.6 Algorithm for an Evaluation of the Steady State Response to an
      External Noise   278

Appendix B   THE ROUGHNESS FUNCTION (RF)   281

B.1 Definition of the Roughness Function   281
B.2 The Mean Roughness Function of a Closed Loop System Disturbed
      by an External Noise   283

Appendix C   TABLE OF z-TRANSFORMS AND s-TRANSFORMS   285

REFERENCES   286

INDEX   289

Preface

The design of controllers using microprocessors is a changing and fast growing subject. From my experience young engineers, often freshly graduated, are quickly conquering this field, whereas the mature control engineers experienced in the design of analog controllers, are finding the conversion from the design of analog network circuits to programming of microprocessors a rather uneasy process.

However the experience gained in designing continuous controllers is highly valuable as most controlled plants are continuous. All digital control systems which are actually implemented are based on continuous design. Therefore an additional aim of this book is to help the experienced control designer to convert to digital control.

During the last few years many excellent books on digital processing and digital filters have been published. It must be noted that there is some difference between digital processing of signals and digital control. Processing of signals is not always done in real time and some delays are tolerated. The implementation may include floating point representation and roundoff of numbers. In contrast the processing in microcontrollers is in real time and only fixed point two's complement arithmetic is used, consequently numbers are truncated. Furthermore, the major effort of the designer in practical implementation of digital controllers is concentrated around the subjects of finite word length, selection of sampling rate, clever programming of the algorithm, proper scaling of all variables and coefficients and selection of analog-to-digital and digital-to-analog converters. These topics with appropriate examples are stressed in this book.

The well established graphical aids of root locus and Bode diagrams are still valuable, but it is unnecessary to master all the finesses of an accurate plot, as computer programs for calculating and tracing these plots are now generally available for most computer systems. The major benefit of having skill in quick graphic plots lies in the ability of the designer to formulate a preliminary design of a control system. The basic rules for approximate tracing of the root locus and Bode diagrams are included in this book as they are most useful for the w-plane approach to digital control.

This book is based on my experience and the experience of my colleagues in designing digital controllers using microprocessors. Selection and arrangement of the material is based on my one-semester course on digital control which I am teaching in the Technion, Israel Institute of Technology.

This book is oriented for the final year BS student and for the practical engineer. Detailed proofs of theorems are kept to a minimum, and most of the examples of microcontrollers are actual working systems. In Chapter 1 the theory of discrete, linear, non-time varying systems is surveyed, and the concept of discretized continuous systems is stressed. Chapter 2 describes digital controller design methods based on analog controller design. Various phenomena, such as aliasing, caused by sampling are explained. A comparison is made between all the discretization methods of analog controllers. Chapter 3 deals with design methods which are done in the discrete domain and are not based on a previous design of an analog controller. This does not imply that the design is not based on previous experience of design of analog controllers. Chapter 4 considers the multi-input/multi-output discrete control systems based on state variable representation approach. Simple explanations of pole placement, observer design and linear optimal control are part of this chapter. Theorems and proofs are given in Appendix A. Chapter 5 covers the mechanization of the digital controller on the microcomputer. Various methods of mechanization are described and a general overview of microcomputers and microprocessor development systems is given. Chapter 6 is the most important chapter for the designer. The actual numerical implementation of the algorithm, including all the errors caused by quantization, is the major concern of the practical designer. Incorrect numerical mechanization may destroy the properties of a well designed digital controller. In Chapter 6 all these errors and accompanied numerical phenomena are described. Suggestions for proper mechanization based on theory and experience are topics presented in this chapter. Chapter 7 deals with a subject related to Chapter 6, the selection of sampling rate. Increase in sampling rate demands an increase in word length and for economy the designer aims to reduce both of these. Two new concepts related to sampling rate are introduced; the fidelity of response and the roughness function. In Chapters 8 and 9 design examples are described and explained in detail. These are practical, not classroom examples, where the theories and results of previous chapters are demonstrated. Appendices A and B include detailed explanations and proofs of theorems discussed in Chapters 4 and 7.

Proposed solutions to the exercises can be found in the Teacher's Manual which is available from the publisher.

To SHELLY, ERAN and IDAN

I would like to thank my colleagues and students from whom I learned so much and who contributed their experience and knowledge: in particular, Ytzhak Shenberg for his pioneer work on microcontrollers; Baruch Glick, Nahum Nechemia and Yakor Sharoni for their design of microcontroller systems demonstrated in examples in Chapters 4, 5 and 7; Fred Berkowitz and Avner Ben-Zwi, experienced engineers whose theses provided the basis for Chapters 8 and 9. I should also like to thank Dr. R. J. Simpson for his careful reviewing of the manuscript and many helpful suggestions; Henry Hirschberg, Executive Editor, for his helpful guidance and Ron Decent, Production Manager (both of Prentice-Hall International), for his extraordinary efforts to convert a manuscript into a book in a short time despite the distances between everybody concerned.

Finally, I must thank RAFAEL-Israel MOD, where thousands of scientists generate an unbelievably creative atmosphere, and who provided moral support and typing services.

P.K.

1
Analytical Background

1.1 INTRODUCTION

The material covered in this book describes control problems which may be modelled as linear, time-invariant, discrete systems. Practical examples which accompany the theoretical text may include non-linear elements such as thresholds or limiters, but the system's behavior is assumed to be essentially linear and slow time varying.

Analytical treatment of linear sampled data continuous control systems was developed in the fifties and is covered in several classical text books (see RA-1, JU-1). Independently of sample data theory, the increasing use of digital computers triggered extensive interest in numerical analysis, especially in numerical integration methods, data interpolation, extrapolation and filtering, matrix treatment of n-dimensional systems as states spaces and discrete modelling of continuous systems. Many of the methods and theories of numerical analysis and linear algebra, developed by mathematicians during the last two hundred years were rediscovered during the fifties and sixties by control engineers and computer scientists.

In order to separate somehow the classical single-input-single-output sampled data theory from multivariable digital control, we will use throughout the book the name 'discretization' instead of sampling.

The mathematical theory for discrete or digital control is similar to sampled data theory with the addition that pure discrete systems are included. Furthermore, multivariable systems are easily handled with the linear state space approach.

For these reasons this chapter is divided into three areas:

(i)   Linear discrete systems formulated by linear differences equations.
(ii) z-transform representation of linear discrete systems.
(iii) Discretization (sampling) of linear continuous system, properties of discretized systems and relations between the s-plane and the z-plane.

For educational purposes an overview of sampled data theory is given in Appendix 1A at the end of this chapter.

1.2   LINEAR, TIME-INVARIANT, DISCRETE SYSTEMS

It is assumed that the reader is familiar with the basic concepts of linear system theory.

The discrete dynamic systems we are interested in may be modelled or represented by:

(i)   Discrete (or difference) equations,
(ii) Impulse response,
(iii) Transfer function.

1.2.1   The System

The system, S, transforms an input u to an output x. This may be represented in block diagram form as Fig. 1.1.

Fig. 1.1   The discrete system

The input u is a string of numbers $u = \{u_0, u_1, \ldots u_i\}$, and the output x is a string of numbers $x = \{x_0, x_1, \ldots x_i\}$. For a multidimensional system u and x are vectors.

Generally, the relation is given by

$$x = S(u) \tag{1.1}$$

where S is the transformation which defines the system.

We will define linearity, time-invariance and an impulse response. The concept of transfer function will be presented in the section on z-transforms.

1.2.2 Linearity

The system transformation, S, is linear if it follows the principle of superposition, i.e.

$$x = S(au + bu') = aS(u) + bS(u') \tag{1.2}$$

In this case x is a linear function of u, in other words, S is a linear operator.

1.2.3 Time-invariance

The system S is time-invariant if its response is independent of the moment of application of the input u.

If i and k represent non-dimensional time instances, then:

For all $k \geqslant 0$

$$S(u_{i-k}) = x_{i-k} \tag{1.3}$$

where

$$u_{i-k} = 0 \text{ for } i = 0, 1, 2, \ldots, k-1.$$

1.2.4 Impulse Response

Let h_i be a response of S to a unit impulse at $i = 0$. In the input-output nomenclature, if $u_0 = \{1, 0, 0, \ldots, 0\}$

then

$$x = S(u_0) = \{h_0, h_1, \ldots, h_i\} \tag{1.4}$$

the impulse response, h_i, is a property of S which defines the system. This may be given in an analytical or empirical form.

The input-output relation is based on the principle of linear superposition. The output is a summation of influences of the individual impulses

$$x_i = \sum_{k=0}^{i} h_k u_{k-i} \qquad u = \{u_0, u_1, \ldots, u_i\} \tag{1.5}$$

x is a linear convolution of u.

Example:

$$h_i = (0.1)^i$$

$$u_i = 1, 1, 1, \ldots 1,$$

$$x_i = \sum_{k=0}^{i} (0.1)^k = \frac{1 - (0.1)^{i+1}}{1 - 0.1}$$

1.2.5 The Discrete Time System

Nomenclature: t — time,
   i — integers $(0, 1, 2, \ldots)$,
   T — time interval between samples,
   f_s — sampling rate,
   ω_s — sampling frequency.

The variables are related as follows

$$i = \frac{t}{T}$$

$$\omega_s = \frac{2\pi}{T} \text{ (rad/s)} \right\} \quad\quad (1.6)$$

$$f_s = \frac{1}{T} \text{ (Hz)}$$

We will describe $f(i)$, a function of discrete time, by means of an example:

$f(i)$ — function of discrete time $f(t)$ — time function
   $i = 0, 1, 2 \ldots$ t — continuous variable

$$f(i) = 0.5i^2 + 2i$$ $$f(t) = \frac{0.5}{T^2}t^2 + \frac{2}{T}t$$

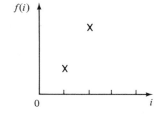   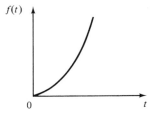

Fig. 1.2 $f(i)$ — function of discrete time,
$f(t)$ — function of continuous time

$f(i)$ is given by
    analytical expression, e.g. $f(i) = 0.5i^2 + 2i$

table, e.g.

i	0	1	2	3	4
$f(i)$	0	2.5	6	10.5	16

$f(i)$ may be generated by sampling a continuous function, or as a description of a pure discrete phenomenon, e.g. number of accidents per year.

   In this book $f(i)$ is usually generated by sampling a continuous function

$f(t)$, i.e. $f(iT) = f(t)$. We will use a short notation $f(iT) \stackrel{\Delta}{=} f_i$. Other sources use different notation for i, sometimes n or k. Throughout this book n will define the order of an n-dimensional system.

1.3 THE CALCULUS OF FINITE DIFFERENCES

The calculus of finite differences is the analytical machinery which helps to formulate, synthesize and analyze discrete systems, similar to linear differential equations which represent continuous dynamic systems. The methodological structure of this calculus used in the literature is similar to methods of differential equations.

Again, assuming that the reader is familiar with linear differential equations and their s-plane representation, we will always compare the discrete domain to the continuous domain, in order to make the transition more fluent.

1.3.1 The Discrete Equation

As in differential equations, the discrete equation describes the relation between a dependent variable x and an independent variable i. The forcing function u_i and/or initial conditions $x_0, x_1, \ldots,$ excite the system.

The discrete equation definition is shown by equation (1.7), where

$$b_0 x_{i+n} + b_1 x_{i+n-1} + \ldots b_{n-1} x_{i+1} + b_n x_i = u_i \qquad (1.7)$$

where n is the order of the equation (system).

A first order homogeneous discrete equation is of the form,

$$b_0 x_{i+1} + b_1 x_i = 0. \qquad (1.8)$$

Example: x_i is the number of cells in counting i,
    B is the rate of reproduction, A is the dying rate.

The next count gives $x_{i+1} = (B-A)x_i$.

The first order discrete equation is, $x_{i+1} + (A-B) x_i = 0$, where x_0 is the initial condition.

A second order discrete equation is of the form

$$b_0 x_{i+2} + b_1 x_{i+1} + b_2 x_i = u_i. \qquad (1.9)$$

Another example is the total deflection of a floating bridge.

In this case the deflection x_{i+1} of an m-segment floating bridge, at the segment $i + 1$, depends on the load u_{i+1}, on the spring coefficient k and on the deflection of the two neighboring segments (see Fig. 1.3). A is proportional to rotational stiffness.

$$x_{i+1} = 1/k\, u_{i+1} + Ax_i + Ax_{i+2}$$

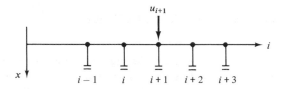

Fig. 1.3   An example of a second order discrete equation. The deflection of a floating bridge

Note: This is an unusual example, the only one in this book where the independent variable i is not time.

An *nth*-order discrete equation, or a set of discrete equations may be represented by n-first order equations.

$$\begin{bmatrix} x_1 \\ \vdots \\ x_n \end{bmatrix}_{i+1} = \begin{bmatrix} b_{11} \cdots \\ \vdots \\ & b_{nn} \end{bmatrix} \begin{bmatrix} x_1 \\ \vdots \\ x_n \end{bmatrix} + \begin{bmatrix} g_1 \\ \vdots \\ g_n \end{bmatrix} u_i \tag{1.10}$$

This n-order state space system may be simplified to a first order discrete matrix form.

$$\bar{x}_{i+1} = B\bar{x}_i + Gu_i \tag{1.11}$$

For example, consider α-β radar tracking.

$$\left. \begin{array}{l} \tilde{y}_i = y_{i-1} + T_{i-1} v_{i-1} \\[2mm] y_i = \tilde{y}_i + \alpha(u_i - \tilde{y}_i) \\[2mm] v_i = v_{i-1} + \dfrac{\beta}{T}(u_i - \tilde{y}_i) \end{array} \right\} \quad \begin{array}{l} \text{set of} \\ \text{first order} \\ \text{difference} \\ \text{equations} \end{array}$$

where:

y_i — the range at i,

$\tilde{y}_i$ — prediction of y_i at $i-1$ measurement,

v_i — estimate of velocity at i, $(v = \dot{y})$,

u_i — noise contaminated measurement of range.

This may be written in a state variable form as:

$$\begin{bmatrix} \tilde{y} \\ y \\ v \end{bmatrix}_i = \begin{bmatrix} 0 & 1 & T \\ 1-\alpha & 0 & 0 \\ -\dfrac{\beta}{T} & 0 & 1 \end{bmatrix} \begin{bmatrix} \tilde{y} \\ y \\ v \end{bmatrix}_{i-1} + \begin{bmatrix} 0 \\ \alpha \\ \dfrac{\beta}{T} \end{bmatrix} u_i$$

1.3.2 The Difference Equation

Another approach to formulate a discrete equation is to analyze the behavior of the differences between two successive values of the dependent variable. The first forward difference $\Delta x_i \triangleq x_{i+1} - x_i$ transforms the discrete equation to a difference equation.

$$a_0 \Delta^n x_i + a_1 \Delta^{n-1} x_i + \ldots a_{n-1} \Delta x_i + a_n x_i = u_i \tag{1.12}$$

Higher differences are defined similarly to the first difference, i.e.

$$\Delta^n x_i \triangleq \Delta(\Delta^{n-1} x_i) \tag{1.13}$$

The second forward difference, following the definition, is given by:

$$\Delta^2 x_i \triangleq \Delta(\Delta x_i) \tag{1.14}$$

$$= \Delta x_{i+1} - \Delta x_i$$

$$= x_{i+2} - 2x_{i+1} + x_i$$

Example:

A non-linear heat accumulation may be approximated using three last measurements.

$$Q_i = K_1(T_i - T_{i-1}) + K_2[(T_i - T_{i-1}) - (T_{i-1} - T_{i-2})]$$

$$Q_i = K_1 \Delta T_i + K_2[\Delta T_i - \Delta T_{i-1}]$$

$$Q_i = K_1 \Delta T_i + K_2 \Delta^2 T_i$$

Some useful properties are:-

(i) The first forward difference of the product of two discrete functions is:−

$$\Delta(f_i g_i) = f_{i+1} \Delta g_i + g_i \Delta f_i \tag{1.15}$$

Proof.

$$\Delta(f_i g_i) = f_{i+1} g_{i+1} - f_i g_i$$
$$= f_{i+1} g_{i+1} - f_{i+1} g_i + f_{i+1} g_i - f_i g_i$$
$$= f_{i+1} (g_{i+1} - g_i) + g_i (f_{i+1} - f_i) \tag{1.16}$$

(ii)   Relating discrete equation to difference equations:

$$\left. \begin{array}{l} b_k = \displaystyle\sum_{p=0}^{k} (-1)^{k-p} \, C_{k-p}^{\,n-p} \, a_p \\[20pt] a_k = \displaystyle\sum_{p=0}^{k} C_{k-p}^{\,n-p} \, b_p \end{array} \right\} \tag{1.17}$$

Eqn. (1.17) relates the coefficients of the difference equation to coefficients of the discrete equation and vice versa.

1.3.3   Solution of Linear, Time-invariant, Discrete or Difference Equations

The classical methods for the solution of discrete equations are similar to the methods of differential equations.

Solution of the Homogeneous Equation

Classical solution (homogenous equation).

Given

$$b_0 x_{i+n} + b_1 x_{i+n-1} + \ldots b_n x_i = 0$$

and assuming $x_i = \lambda^i$ is a solution, then:

$$x_{i+n-k} = \lambda^{i+n-k}$$

for all $k, 0 \leqslant k \leqslant n$

$$\underbrace{\lambda^i \, [b_0 \lambda^n + b_1 \lambda^{n-1} + \ldots + b_n]}_{} = 0 \tag{1.18}$$

the characteristic equation.

The general solution is a linear combination of solutions, based on the roots (λ's) of the characteristic equation.

For example,

$$x_{i+2} - 3 x_{i+1} + 2 x_i = 0$$

The characteristic equation in this case is

$$\lambda^2 - 3\lambda + 2 = 0 \Rightarrow \lambda = 2, 1$$

and the solution is:

$$x_i = C_1 2^i + C_2$$

Note: λ^i plays the same role in discrete equations as $e^{\lambda t}$ in linear, time-invariant differential equations.

The values of the roots λ's describe the natural behavior of the solution x_i. Assuming that one of the roots is real

$$x_i = C^i \tag{1.19}$$

The numerical behavior of x_i is summarized in tabular form below.

λ	value of x_i for $i = 0, 1, 2 \ldots$
$\lambda > 1$	increasing
$\lambda = 1$	constant
$0 < \lambda < 1$	decreasing
$-1 < \lambda < 0$	decreasing, alternating sign
$\lambda = -1$	alternating value between $+C$ and $-C$
$\lambda < -1$	increasing, alternating sign.

Complex or imaginary roots always occur in conjugate pairs and give a solution of the form of eqn. (1.20).

$$x_i = C_1 \lambda + C_2 \lambda' \tag{1.20}$$

where:

$$\lambda = a + jb, \lambda' = a - jb.$$

Similarly to continuous systems, the behavior of x_i is described by a combination of two sinusoids, damped or undamped, and for the case of a conjugate imaginary pair it is a pure oscillation.

Multiple real roots generate behavior which consists of the terms $i\lambda^i$.

The graphical description of the natural behavior of the homogeneous equation, which is important to control engineers, is given in the section on the z-plane.

Two important methods for finding the particular solution to linear discrete equations with constant coefficients are (i) the method of undetermined coefficients, and (ii) the method of variation of parameters. Both of these require the prior determination of the homogeneous solution x_i.

A practical method for solving the discrete or difference equation is to use the z-transform approach. This is the subject of the next section.

1.4 THE Z-TRANSFORM

The z-transform is a highly valuable approach for formulating, analyzing and solving problems in the time-invariant, linear, discrete domain. Similar to the advantages of the Laplace transformation in the continuous time domain, the major benefit is in the reduction of the complexity of handling difference equations to relatively simple methods of algebraic equations.

1.4.1 Definition of the z-transform

The basic z-transform (one-sided) may be defined as:-

$$Z[f_i] \triangleq F(z) = \sum_{i=0}^{\infty} f_i z^{-1} \tag{1.21}$$

$$i < 0 \Rightarrow f_i = 0$$

The one-sided z-transform satisfies most engineering applications.
The property of convergence must be satisfied, this states that

$$Z[f_i] \text{ exists if } \lim_{k \to \infty} \sum_{i=0}^{k} f_i z^{-i} \text{ exists.}$$

Example:

$$f_i = a^i$$

$$Z[a^i] = \sum_{i=0}^{\infty} a^i z^{-i} = \frac{z}{z - a}$$

Some properties of z-transforms are:-
  (i)   Superposition.

$$Z[af_i + bg_i] = a Z[f_i] + b Z[g_i] \tag{1.22}$$

  (ii)   Real forward translation (shift theorem).

$$Z[f_{i+k}] = z^k F(z) - \sum_{i=0}^{k-1} f_i z^{k-1} \tag{1.23}$$

Example:

$$Z[a^{i+1}] = z \left(\frac{z}{z - a} \right) - a^0 = \frac{z^2}{z - a} - 1$$

1.4.2 Solving Discrete Equations

Using the definition of the z-transform and its properties, we may formulate an approach for solving a discrete equation.

Consider the discrete equation.

$$b_0 x_{i+n} + \ldots b_n x_i = f_i$$

We will transform every term in both sides of the equation

$$Z\{f_i\} = F(z) \tag{1.24}$$

This result may be obtained by using the definition, or directly by using tables of z-transforms.

$$Z\{b_n x_i\} = b_n x(z) \tag{1.25}$$

Using the shift theorem gives

$$Z\{b_{n-1} x_{i+1}\} = b_{n-1} z x(z) \tag{1.26}$$

and the last term will be

$$Z\{b_0 z_{i+n}\} = b_0 z^n x(z) \tag{1.27}$$

The transformed equation is therefore

$$(b_0 z^n + b_1 z^{n-1} + \ldots + b_n) x(z) = F(z) \tag{1.28}$$

For simplicity, the terms which include the initial conditions have been omitted. Eqn. (1.28) may be written as

$$x(z) = \frac{F(z)}{b_0 z^n + \ldots + b_n} \tag{1.29}$$

where $b_0 z^n + \ldots + b_n$ is the characteristic polynomial. The roots of the characteristic polynomial are the roots, λ's, of the homogeneous solution.

Example:

$$x_{i+2} - 3x_{i+1} + 2x_i = 4^i$$

The transformed equation is

$$(z^2 - 3z + 2) x(z) - z^2 x(0) - zx(1) + 3zx(0) = \frac{z}{z-4}$$

The solution of $x(z)$ is

$$x(z) = \frac{\left(\dfrac{z}{z-4}\right) + z^2 x(0) + zx(1) + 3zx(0)}{z^2 - 3z + 2}$$

The method used to find the explicit solution x_i will be described in the section on the inverse transformation.

1.4.3 The Transfer Function

The concept of transfer function may be developed independently by using the discrete equation formulation of the system, or using the system's impulse response and convolution.

(i)   The system is formulated by a discrete equation.

$$b_0 x_{i+n} + \ldots b_n x_i = u_i$$

In this case z-transformation yields,

$$(b_0 z^n + \ldots + b_n) x(z) = u(z),$$

$$\frac{x(z)}{u(z)} = \frac{1}{b_0 z^n + \ldots + b_n} \tag{1.30}$$

Hence the transfer function is given by:-

$$H(z) = \frac{1}{b_0 z^n + \ldots + b_n} \tag{1.31}$$

(ii)   The system is defined by its impulse response h_i

$$x_i = \sum_{k=0}^{i} h_i u_{i-k} \tag{1.32}$$

In this case z-transformation of eqn. (1.32) gives:-

$$x(z) = Z \left\{ \sum_{k=0}^{i} h_i u_{i-k} \right\} \tag{1.33}$$

It may be proven that the z-transform of the right-hand side is:-

$$x(z) = Z \{ h_i \} \ Z \{ u_i \}$$

$$x(z) = Z \{ h_i \} \ u(z) \tag{1.34}$$

The transfer function $H(z)$ is defined as

$$H(z) \triangleq Z \{ h_i \} \tag{1.35}$$

The block diagram description of a transfer function in the z-domain is the same as in the s-domain.

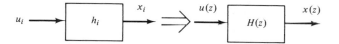

Fig. 1.4 The block diagram of $H(z)$

1.4.4 The Transfer Function of Connected Linear Discrete Systems

If several discrete systems are connected each to the other, the output of one of the systems serves as the input to others.

Fig. 1.5 The open loop discrete system

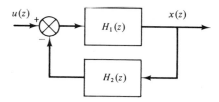

Fig. 1.6 The block diagram of the closed loop system

The transfer function of the closed loop system is given by eqn. (1.36).

$$\frac{x(z)}{u(z)} = \frac{H_1(z)}{1 + H_1(z)H_2(z)} \tag{1.36}$$

Additional useful properties of z-transforms:

(iii) Initial value theorem (IVT).

$$\lim_{i \to 0} f_i = \lim_{z \to \infty} F(z) \tag{1.37}$$

(iv) Final value theorem (FVT).

If $(z - 1)\, F(z)$ is analytic for $z \geqslant 1$, i.e., all derivatives of $(z - 1)\, F(z)$ exists for all $z \geqslant 1$, then

$$\lim_{i \to \infty} f_i = \lim_{z \to 1}(z - 1)F(z) \tag{1.38}$$

Example:

$$f_i = \sum_{k=0}^{i} a^k$$

$$\mathbf{Z}[f_i] = \frac{z^2}{(z-1)(z-a)}$$

$$\lim_{i \to \infty} f_i = \lim_{z \to 1} (z-1) \frac{z^2}{(z-1)(z-a)} = \frac{1}{1-a}$$

1.5 THE INVERSE TRANSFORMATION

The purpose of the inverse transformation is to obtain the explicit behavior of the discrete system, i.e., the solution in the time domain of the difference equations.

As in Laplace transformation applications in control theory, the actual time solution is not the main objective. The transform representation helps us to analyze the behavior of the controlled system. The discrete time solution is usually obtained by a digital simulation.

Three methods will be described. Contour integration based on Cauchy's residue theorem, power series expansion by long division, and a practical way using tables of transforms.

Method 1. Contour Integration

As we are interested only in one-sided transforms ($i \geqslant 0$), and assuming that $F(z)$ is analytic in annular domain $R_1 < |z| < R_2$ and C is any simple closed curve separating R_1 from R_2, then

$$f_i = \frac{1}{2\pi j} \oint_C F(z) z^{i-1} dz \tag{1.39}$$

Example:

$$F(z) = \frac{1}{(1 - z^{-1})(1 - e^{-aT} z^{-1})}$$

$$f_i = \text{Res}\,[F(z) z^{i-1}, 1] + \text{Res}\,[F(z) z^{i-1}, e^{-aT}]$$

$$f_i = \frac{1}{1 - e^{-aT}} + \frac{e^{-(i+1)aT}}{e^{-aT} - 1}$$

Method 2. Power Series Expansion by Long Division

From the definition of the z-transform we have

$$F(z) \triangleq \sum_{i=0}^{\infty} f_i z^{-i} \tag{1.40}$$

Therefore long division of the rational function $F(z) = (\sum_l a_l z^l)/(\sum_k b_k z^k)$ will generate the power expansion

$$F(z) = \frac{\sum\limits_l a_l z^l}{\sum\limits_k b_k z^k} = f_0 z^0 + f_1 z^{-1} + f_2 z^{-2} + \ldots \qquad (1.41)$$

$$f_i = f_0, f_1, f_2, \ldots \qquad (1.42)$$

Example:

$$F(z) = \frac{z^3 + 2z^2 + z + 1}{z^3 - z^2 - 8z + 12}$$

$$= 1 + 3z^{-1} + 12z^{-2} + 25z^{-3} + \ldots$$

$$f_i = 1, 3, 12, 25, \ldots$$

Method 3

In this method we use partial-fraction expansion and search in tables.

Example:

$$F(z) = \frac{z^2 + 2z}{3z^2 - 4z - 7}$$

$$F(z) = \left(\frac{13}{30}\right)\frac{z}{z - 7/3} - \left(\frac{1}{10}\right)\frac{z}{z + 1}$$

from z-transform tables we obtain

$$f_i = \frac{13}{30}\left(\frac{7}{3}\right)^i - \frac{1}{10}\left(-1\right)^i$$

1.6 DISCRETIZATION OF A CONTINUOUS SYSTEM

In a completely discrete environment, digital control theory may be developed without even mentioning sampling, discretization and other subjects related to discrete observation or discrete control of continuous signals and systems (CA-1). Actually there are branches of control theory dealing with pure discrete phenomena, e.g., control of industrial processes (BI-1), but most of the controlled plants are continuous, and a wealth of experience has been accumulated in the design of continuous compensation networks. Therefore proper sampling (discretization) is the key to a successful digital control design.

A thorough knowledge of discretization is required for two different purposes:-

(i)   Transformation of analog compensation networks to digital algorithms (see Chapter 2 for details).
(ii) Formulation of discrete models of continuous plants. This discretization is required for digital simulation and analysis of the whole digitally controlled system.

1.6.1   The Fundamental Problem of Discrete Processing

(i)   The sampling process

This consists of sampling a continuous signal $f(t)$ every T seconds. Usually this is an electrical signal, but optical, mechanical and other forms of signals are possible. During this sampling process the continuous time function is converted to a discrete time sequence f_i. In classical sampled data theory consideration is given to the width and energy content of the impulses generated through the sampling process, but for practical purposes the sequence f_i is a string of numbers and f_i is considered to be exactly equal to $f(iT)$. The inconsistency of the energy contents is handled through an appropriate scaling and gain adjustment of the whole digitally controlled loop.

(ii)   The Sampling Theorem

The well-known sampling theorem as developed by Shannon and Nyquist states that a sampled continuous signal may be reconstructed from its samples if, and only if, the frequency contents of the signal is lower than $\omega_s/2$.

Unfortunately, in the discrete control of continuous plant, time delays occur and these must be considered together with the Shannon theorem.

We are interested in the sampling theorem with respect to the properties of digital filters. A complete proof is given in Chapter 2.

(iii)   What is the Fundamental Problem of Discrete Processing?

The input-output waveforms of a continuous system are depicted in Fig. 1.7.

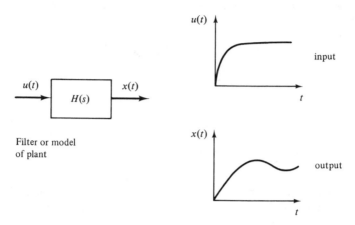

Fig. 1.7 A continuous system showing input and output signals

The input-output signals in a discretized system are depicted in Fig. 1.8.

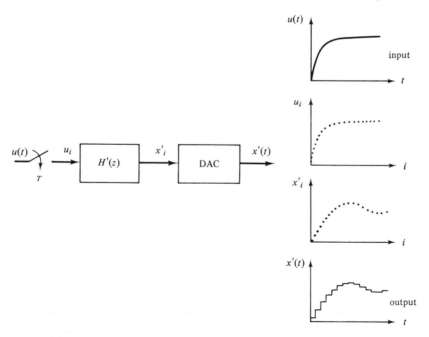

Fig. 1.8 The input-output signals of a discretized system

The results are compared in Fig. 1.9.

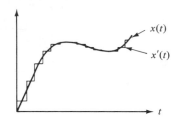

Fig. 1.9 Comparison of the output of the continuous
system and its discretized version.

The fundamental problems of discrete processing of analog signals is how to
choose $H(z)$ and the digital-to-analog converter (DAC) in order to get $x'(t) \simeq x(t)$.

There are various criteria and methods which compare the analog processing
with the discrete processing, e.g. the time response, the frequency response,
roughness of the output and others (see details in Chapters 2 and 7).

Intuitively it seems that by increasing the sampling rate ($T \to 0$), the discrete
processing will asymptotically convert to an analog output.

This assumption is not correct because it will require an infinitely long word
length.

Example:

$$\text{Let} \quad x_i = \frac{A}{u_i - u_{i-1}}$$

as $T \to 0$ (increasing the sampling rate) the difference between two successive
samples u_i and u_{i-1} is very small and we may run to a singularity problem.
Increasing the sampling rate almost always demands increasing the word length.

1.6.2 Pulse Transfer Function (z-transform) of a Continuous System

As mentioned earlier, the purpose of discretization is to observe and to analyze
the behavior of continuous systems in discrete instances. Several different
mathematical methods may be used. The classical sampled data theory uses the
Laplace transform approach to calculate the response of a continuous system to
equally spaced impulses. In Appendix 1A we will overview this approach. The
z-transform formulation gives directly the impulse response of the continuous
system, but the output is known only at the sampling points. Therefore the
z-transform formulation of an input-output system is also called the pulse transfer function. To a sampled input the z-transform gives an exact solution.

Description of the Method

Given a continuous model or filter, $H(s)$, we may write:

$$\frac{x(s)}{u(s)} = H(s) = \frac{A_1}{s + a_1} + \frac{A_2}{s + a_2} + \ldots + \frac{A_n}{s + a_n} \tag{1.43}$$

By sampling the input u, x is the response to a train of impulses, i.e., the solution after time iT.

For one impulse u_0 at $t = 0$ ($i = 0$), the response is

$$x_{iT} = u_0(A_1 e^{-a_1 iT} + \ldots + A_n e^{-a_n iT}) \tag{1.44}$$

whereas for a train of impulses it is

$$x_{iT} = \sum_{k=0}^{i} u_k(A_1 e^{-a_1(i-k)T} + \ldots + A_n e^{-a_n(i-k)T}) \tag{1.45}$$

Using the z-transform of a convolution we have

$$x(z) = \left(\frac{A_1}{1 - e^{-a_1 T} z^{-1}} + \ldots + \frac{A_n}{1 - e^{-a_n T} z^{-1}} \right) u(z) \tag{1.46}$$

$$x(z) = H(z)u(z) \tag{1.47}$$

The z-transform representation of a pulse transfer function is summarized in tables for various transfer functions $H(s)$, but complicated forms of $H(s)$ require partial fraction expansion.

Example:

$$H(s) = \frac{K}{(s + a)(s + b)}$$

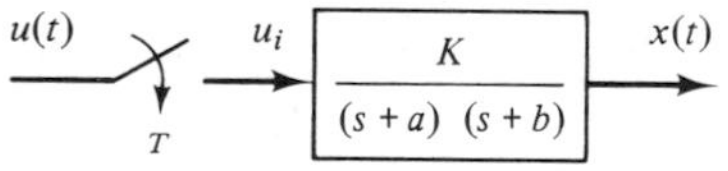

Fig. 1.10 The block diagram of the sampled system

$$x(t) = \frac{K}{b - a}(e^{-at} - e^{-bt})$$

$x(t)$ is the response to an impulse at $t = 0$ (zero initial condition).

By looking on $x(t)$ at $t = iT$ instances we obtain the response of $x(iT)$ to an impulse at $t = 0$.

$$x_i = \frac{K}{b-a}(e^{-aTi} - e^{-bTi})$$

Using the convolution theorem we will sum up the response to inputs in different times

$$\frac{x(z)}{u(z)} = \sum_{i=0}^{\infty} \frac{K}{(b-a)}(e^{-aTi} - e^{-bTi})z^{-i} \triangleq H(z) \tag{1.48}$$

This yields the transfer function

$$H(z) = -\frac{K}{b-a}\frac{z(e^{-aT} - e^{-bT})}{(z - e^{-aT})(z - e^{-bT})} \tag{1.49}$$

We have transformed eqn. (1.48) to eqn. (1.49). This may be shown diagrammatically by Fig 1.11.

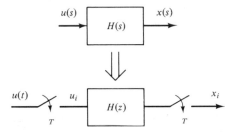

Fig. 1.11   Transforming s-representation to z-representation

1.6.3   Some Useful Rules for Discretizing (Impulse Response Sampling) Continuous Systems

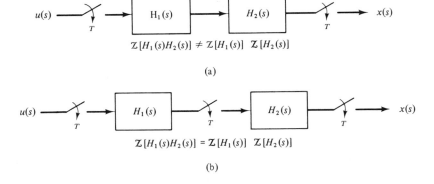

Fig. 1.12   Block diagrams for sampled linear systems in
series (open loop)

In Fig. 1.12a we see probably the most common mistake of the beginner. The
z-transform of two systems, H_1 and H_2, without a sampler between is
$Z\,[H_1\,(s)\,H_2\,(s)]$. A similar rule for a closed loop system is depicted in Fig. 1.13.

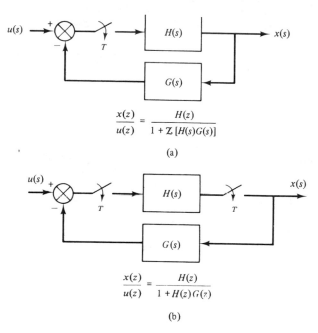

(a)

(b)

Fig. 1.13   The z-transform of two sampled linear systems
in series (closed loop)

Example:

The discretization of an open loop continuous system is given in Fig. 1.14. What
is the time response to a unit step function, given that $T = 1s$?

Fig. 1.14   An open loop discretized system

$$G(s) = \frac{1 - e^{-sT}}{s} \cdot \frac{1}{s(s + 1)}$$

$$G(z) = (1 - z^{-1})\, Z \left[\frac{1}{s^2(s + 1)} \right]$$

$$= (1 - z^{-1})\mathbf{Z}\left[\frac{1}{s^2} - \frac{1}{s} + \frac{1}{s+1}\right]$$

$$= (1 - z^{-1}) \left(\frac{Tz}{(z-1)^2} - \frac{z}{z-1} + \frac{z}{z - e^{-T}}\right)$$

$$G(z) = \frac{0.368z + 0.264}{(z-1)(z-0.368)} \quad \text{the open loop transfer function}$$

For a unit step function $\rightarrow u(z) = \dfrac{z}{z-1}$

$$x(z) = G(z)u(z) = \frac{(0.368z + 0.264)z}{(z-1)(z^2 - z + 0.632)} \quad \text{the discrete output}$$

What is the steady state value of the output? Appling FVT gives

$$x(\infty) = \lim_{z \to 1}(z - 1)x(z) = \frac{0.368 + 0.264}{1 - 1 + 0.632} = 1$$

The description of the discrete output may be written as:

$$x(z) = 0.368z^{-1} + 1.00z^{-2} + 1.399z^{-3} + 1.399z^{-4} + 1.147z^{-5} + \ldots$$

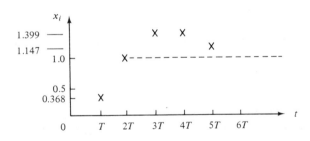

Fig. 1.15   The discrete output of the system described in
example

The same results may be obtained using Laplace transforms only, but the calculations will be much more cumbersome. The z-transform simplifies the handling
of the discretized system.

1.6.4   Discretization of State Space Representation of a Continuous System

A discretized state space system is depicted in Fig. 1.16, where x is a n-dimen-
sional state vector.

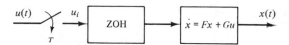

Fig. 1.16 Schematic representation of a discretized state
space system

The continuous system may be written in the form:

$$\dot{x} = Fx + Gu \tag{1.50}$$

Its discretized version is

$$x_{i+1} = \Phi(T)x_i + \int_{iT}^{(i+1)T} \Phi[(i+1)T - \tau]Gu(\tau)d\tau \tag{1.51}$$

If $F \neq F(t)$ (time invariant)

$$x_{i+1} = \Phi(T)x_i + \int_0^T \Phi(\tau)Gu(\tau)d\tau \tag{1.52}$$

Where $\Phi(\tau)$, the transition matrix, is given by

$$\Phi(\tau) \triangleq e^{F\tau} = 1 + F\tau + \frac{F\tau^2}{2!} + \ldots \tag{1.53}$$

For $u(\tau)$ = constant, during T

$$x_{i+1} = \Phi(T)x_i + \Gamma(T)u_i \tag{1.54}$$

$$\Gamma(T) = \int_0^T \Phi(\tau)Gd\tau \tag{1.55}$$

The z-transform of a state space representation is given by

$$x_{i+1} = \Phi x_i + \Gamma u_i,$$

and the z-transform of the system, using the shift theorem yields

$$zx(z) = \Phi x(z) + \Gamma u(z).$$

Rearranging the terms we obtain

$$[I - \Phi z^{-1}] x(z) = \Gamma z^{-1}u(z)$$

and solving for x gives

$$x(z) = [I - \Phi z^{-1}]^{-1}\Gamma z^{-1}u(z) \tag{1.56}$$

Example:

We shall apply this approach to a discretized model of an integrator (see Fig.
1.17).

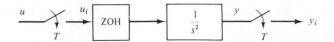

Fig. 1.17   The discretized version of an integrator

The state space model of the integrator is

$$\dot{y} = v$$
$$\dot{v} = u.$$

The matrix notation of the system is

$$\begin{bmatrix} \dot{y} \\ \dot{v} \end{bmatrix} = \begin{bmatrix} 0 & 1 \\ 0 & 0 \end{bmatrix} \begin{bmatrix} y \\ v \end{bmatrix} + \begin{bmatrix} 0 \\ 1 \end{bmatrix} u$$

Using eqns. (1.53) and (1.55) gives

$$\Phi = \begin{bmatrix} 1 & 0 \\ 0 & 1 \end{bmatrix} + \begin{bmatrix} 0 & 1 \\ 0 & 0 \end{bmatrix} T + \begin{bmatrix} 0 & 1 \\ 0 & 0 \end{bmatrix} \begin{bmatrix} 0 & 1 \\ 0 & 0 \end{bmatrix} \frac{T^2}{2!} = \begin{bmatrix} 1 & T \\ 0 & 1 \end{bmatrix}$$

$$\Gamma = \int_0^T \begin{bmatrix} 1 & \lambda \\ 0 & 1 \end{bmatrix} d\lambda G = \begin{bmatrix} T & T^2/2 \\ 0 & T \end{bmatrix} \begin{bmatrix} 0 \\ 1 \end{bmatrix} = \begin{bmatrix} T^2/2 \\ T \end{bmatrix}$$

Applying the results to eqn. (1.56) yields,

$$x(z) = \left\{ \begin{bmatrix} 1 & 0 \\ 0 & 1 \end{bmatrix} - \begin{bmatrix} 1 & T \\ 0 & 1 \end{bmatrix} z^{-1} \right\}^{-1} \begin{bmatrix} T^2/2 \\ T \end{bmatrix} z^{-1} u(z).$$

Solving for x we obtain

$$\frac{y(z)}{u(z)} = \frac{T^2/2 \,(1 + z^{-1}) z^{-1}}{(1 - z^{-1})^2} \; ; \; \frac{v(z)}{u(z)} = \frac{T z^{-1}}{1 - z^{-1}}.$$

1.7 PROPERTIES OF DISCRETE AND DISCRETIZED LINEAR SYSTEMS

1.7.1 Stability

A discrete or discretized system is stable if all its poles are located inside the unit circle on the z-plane.

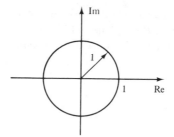

Fig. 1.18   The z-plane

If the poles of the system are located at $a_1, a_2, \ldots$, then the response of the system to an impulse is given by:-

$$x(z) = \frac{b_1}{z - a_1} + \frac{b_2}{z - a_2} + \ldots$$

Its discrete time representation is

$$x(iT) = b_1 a_1^{i-1} + b_2 a_2^{i-1} + \ldots$$

and for $|a| < 1$, we can see that x converges to zero.

Tests for Stability

There are two methods:-

(i)   The direct test which checks the stability of the z-transfer function (see JU–1).

(ii) The application of the Routh-Hurwitz criterion using a bilinear transformation

$$z = \frac{w + 1}{w - 1} \tag{1.57}$$

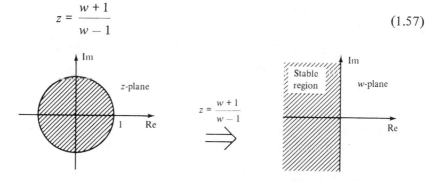

Fig. 1.19   The bilinear transformation

The bilinear transformation transforms the complex z-plane to another complex plane, very similar to the s-plane, which we shall call the w-plane. The unit circle is transformed to the left-hand side of the w-plane (see Fig. 1.19).

Example:

Given $\qquad H(z) = \dfrac{1}{z + 0.1}$,

$$H(w) = H(z) \Big|_{z = \frac{w+1}{w-1}} ,$$

$$H(w) = \frac{w - 1}{1.1w + 0.9} .$$

The stable pole at $z = -0.1$ is relocated on the left-hand side of the w-plane at $w = -0.9/1.1$.

1.7.2 Relationship between the z-plane and the s-plane

During the continuous control system design process the location of the poles (and the zeros) on the s-plane helps the designer to understand the dynamic behavior of the system. In order to help to acquire the same necessary experience for discrete or discretized systems, the location of the poles on the z-plane is compared to the location of the poles of a continuous (and sampled) system on the s-plane.

Let a discretized system be represented by a transfer function given in partial fraction form as

$$H(z) = \frac{A_1(z)}{z + a_1} + \frac{A_2(z)}{z + a_2} + \dots \tag{1.58}$$

The individual terms on the z-plane describe an exponential decay on the s-plane during the sampling interval. The variable z^{-1} actually represents a shift on the z-plane, or a pure delay (e^{-sT}) in the s-plane.

$$z^{-1} = e^{-sT} \tag{1.59}$$

The relationship of eqn. (1.59) is a transformation between the s-plane pole locations and between the z-plane locations.

The complex variable s may be written as $s = \sigma + j\omega$, hence

$$z = e^{(\sigma + j\omega)T} = e^{\sigma T} e^{j\omega T} \tag{1.60}$$

or $\qquad |z| = e^{\sigma T} ; \angle z = \omega T$

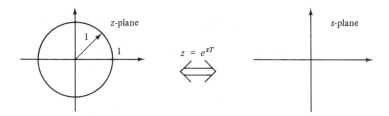

Fig. 1.20 The $z = e^{sT}$ transformation

This relationship is correct for an impulse response sampling only (z-transform method of discretization). For a pure discrete system or for any other methods of discretization (see section on digital filters) this is only a fair approximation. Furthermore, this is not a one-to-one correspondence as there is an ambiguity in phase as illustrated by eqns. (1.60) and (1.61).

$$z = e^{sT} = e^{\sigma T} e^{j(\omega T + 2\pi k)} \qquad (1.61)$$

From (1.61) we may see that poles on the s-plane, whose frequencies differ in integral multiples of the sampling frequency, are transformed to the same position on the z-plane.

The fundamental frequency poles ($k = 0$) are located on the so-called 'primary strip'. This property is depicted in Fig. 1.21.

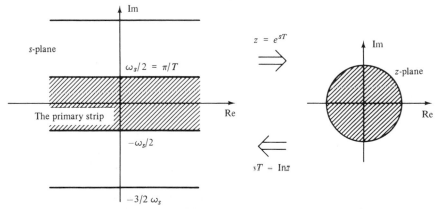

Fig. 1.21 Graphic representation of the primary strip in impulse response transformation

Specific patterns on the s-plane are transformed by the $z = e^{sT}$ transformation to characteristic patterns in the z-plane. In Fig. 1.22 we may compare the geometrical position of various common patterns.

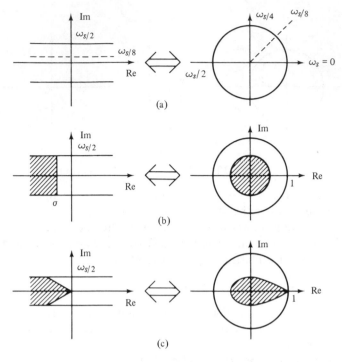

Fig. 1.22 Geometrical characteristic of poles having some
common property
(a) the same ω,
(b) the same σ,
(c) the same damping coefficients.

Most helpful is the graphic description of complex poles,

i.e. $z = e^{sT}$

where,

$$s = \zeta\omega_n \pm \sqrt{1 - \zeta^2}\ \omega_n \qquad\qquad (1.62)$$

For ζ = constant the pattern on the z-plane is a logarithmic spiral (see Fig. 1.22 (c)). In Fig. 1.24 the patterns are traced for various frequencies and various damping coefficients.

Caution: The location of the poles on the z-plane depends on T. This is the difference between the s-plane locations and the z-plane locations of poles.

For poles clustered around $z = 1$ corresponding to fast sampling or short time constants, the exponential expression $z = e^{(\sigma + j\omega)T}$ may be approximated by eqn. (1.63),

$$z \cong 1 + \sigma T + j\omega T \tag{1.63}$$

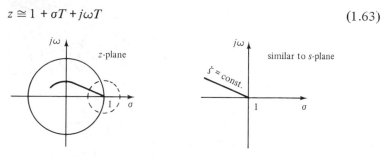

Fig. 1.23   Enlargement of the area near $z = 1$

As depicted in Fig. 1.23 the geometrical patterns of the poles near $z = 1$ are very similar to patterns of poles on the s-plane.

1.8 CONVERTING DISCRETE SIGNALS TO A CONTINUOUS CONTROL SIGNAL

The output of the control computer is a string of numbers which consists of one or more control sequences. Every sampling interval, T, eight or more binary digits should be converted to a physical control command.

We do not always convert the discrete signal to an analog quantity. For example: On-off control may be activated using only three logic outputs; Pulse width modulation, which is essentially a linear control, translates the amplitude to a number of impulses; Stepper motors combined with digital synchros actually represent a whole pseudodiscrete environment. However in many of the digital control applications the command activates an electro-mechanical actuator which is basically a continuous device. Therefore the sequence of numbers should be converted in real time to a continuous signal.

Reconstruction of the analog signal from discrete data is usually done using a polynomial extrapolation or other related methods.

1.8.1 The Zero Order Hold (ZOH)

The most common reconstruction polynomial extrapolator is the zero order hold in which the signal is held constant during the interval T. See Fig. 1.25.

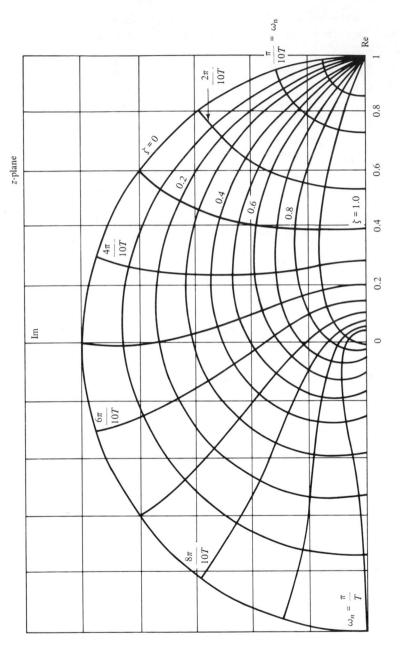

Fig. 1.24 Template no. 1 $z = e^{sT}$

$$s = -\zeta\omega_n \pm \sqrt{1 - \zeta^2}\,\omega_n$$

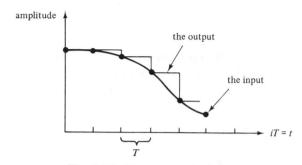

Fig. 1.25 The zero order hold

The transfer function of the ZOH is given by:-

$$H(s) = \frac{1 - e^{-sT}}{s} \qquad (1.64)$$

and its frequency response is given by substituting $s = j\omega$ in eqn. (1.64),

$$H(j\omega) = \frac{1 - e^{-j\omega T}}{j\omega} = Te^{-j\omega T/2}\frac{\sin \omega T/2}{\omega T/2} \qquad (1.65)$$

The zero order hold generates approximately a delay of $T/2$ seconds.

1.8.2 The First Order Hold and Correction

The first order hold is a polynomial extrapolator using the last two data points. See Fig. 1.26.

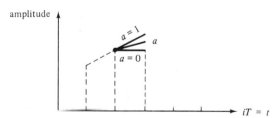

Fig. 1.26 The first order hold and correction

In this case

$$u(t) = u_i + a\frac{u_i - u_{i-1}}{T}\tau \quad \text{for } 0 \leqslant \tau < T \qquad (1.66)$$

where

$$0 \leqslant a \leqslant 1.$$

For $a = 0$ this is a zero order hold and for $a = 1$ it is a first order hold.

The transfer function of the first order hold + correction is given by:-

$$H(s) = \frac{1}{s}(1 - e^{-sT})\, [1 - ae^{-sT} + \frac{a}{sT}(1 - e^{-sT})] \qquad (1.67)$$

and the frequency response is

$$H(j\omega) = T\, \frac{\sin\dfrac{\omega T}{2}}{\omega T/2}\, [1 - a + a(1 + j\omega T)\frac{\sin\dfrac{\omega T}{2}}{\omega T/2}\, e^{-j\omega T/2}\,] \qquad (1.68)$$

The choice of transfer function depends on the frequency contents of the signal and on the sampling interval T.

1.8.3   Trapezoidal Reconstruction Schemes

Trapezoidal data reconstructions are sometimes called triangular holds or linear point connectors. The characteristic is depicted in Fig. 1.27.

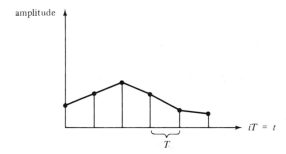

Fig. 1.27   The triangular hold (linear point connector)

This hold is actually an interpolation and the reconstruction scheme is unrealizable in a real time procedure. However it is realizable if a delay of one sample is allowable.

1.8.4   State and Velocity Predictor

Reconstruction holds based on a parallel computer output may generate a smooth output with a low time delay.

Different schemes are possible, e.g., state and velocity predictor. In the case where state control is required and velocity state is available, the reconstruction scheme generates the following signal:-

$$u(t) = u_i + \dot{u}_i \tau \quad 0 \leqslant \tau < T \tag{1.69}$$

See Fig. 1.28.

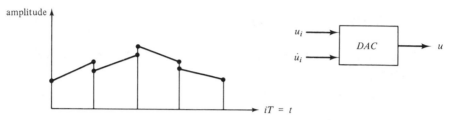

Fig. 1.28 Hold based on state and velocity predictor

1.8.5 Summary

We have seen in the previous sections that several different reconstruction schemes may be used to convert a discrete output to a form suitable for digital control. In practice, however, the zero order hold is used almost exclusively.

APPENDIX 1A. OVERVIEW OF CLASSICAL SAMPLED DATA THEORY

(i) The Sampling Process

Let us consider a continuous time function, $f(t)$, to be sampled every T seconds by using a switch to produce a sampled time function $f^*(t)$. The analytical expression for this sampling process may be thought of as being the result of multiplying a sampling function, $p(t)$, by the original time function, $f(t)$.

This 'modulation' process may be represented by the equation

$$f^*(t) = f(t)p(t) \tag{1 A 1}$$

Assuming an infinitely small duration for the sampling, the switching process $p(t)$, may be represented by a sequence of Dirac delta functions

$$p(t) = \sum_{i=-\infty}^{\infty} \delta(t - iT) = \delta_T(t) \tag{1A.2}$$

The switching function $\delta_T(t)$ is called the impulse train.

(ii) The Laplace Transformation of the Impulse Sequence

We are interested in $f(t)$, only at the instances iT, therefore:

$$f^*(t) = f(iT)\delta_T(t) \qquad i = 0, 1, \ldots$$

$$f^*(t) = \sum_{i=0}^{\infty} f_i \delta(t - iT) \tag{1A.3}$$

The Laplace transform of eqn. (1A.3) is a summation of the transformations of the individual terms

$$\mathcal{L}[f_i \delta(t - iT) = f_i e^{-isT} \tag{1A.4}$$

i.e.

$$F^*(s) = \mathcal{L}[f^*(t)] = \sum_{i=0}^{\infty} f_i e^{-isT} \tag{1A.5}$$

Example:

For f_i, a unit step function,

$$F^*(s) = \frac{1}{1 - e^{-sT}}$$

An alternative form of $F^*(s)$ is obtained using Fourier series and Poisson summation rule. Since $\delta_T(t)$ is a periodic function

$$f^*(t) = \frac{1}{T} \sum_{i=-\infty}^{\infty} f(t) e^{ji\omega_s t} \tag{1A.6}$$

where

$$\omega_s = \frac{2\pi}{T}$$

and the Laplace transform of eqn. (1A.6) is

$$F^*(s) = \frac{1}{T} \sum_{i=-\infty}^{\infty} F(s + ji\omega_s) \tag{1A.7}$$

(iii) Deriving the z-transform $F(z)$ of Sampled Time Function f_i from its Laplace Transform $F(s)$ or $F^*(s)$

The Laplace transform of the product of two signals is the convolution of their Laplace transformation

$$\mathcal{L}\left\{f(t)g(t)\right\} = \frac{1}{2\pi j} \int_C F(s)G(s-p)dp \qquad (1A.8)$$

The integration is carried out along a path C parallel to the imaginary axis. The poles of $G(s-p)$ lie to the right and the poles of $F(s)$ lie to the left of the path C.

Applying this rule to $f^*(t)$ by defining

$$g(t) = \sum_{i=-\infty}^{\infty} \delta(t - iT) \qquad (1A.9)$$

and its s-transform

$$G(s) = \sum_{i=0}^{\infty} e^{-iTs} = \frac{1}{1 - e^{-sT}} \qquad (1A.10)$$

we obtain,

$$F^*(s) = \frac{1}{2\pi j} \int_C \frac{F(p)}{1 - e^{-(s-p)T}} \, dp \qquad (1A.11)$$

Evaluating this integral on the p-plane by using Cauchy's residue theorem (see Fig. 1A.1) we obtain the result

$$F^* = \sum_{\substack{\text{poles} \\ \text{of} \\ F(p)}} \text{Res}\left[\frac{F(p)}{1 - e^{-(s-p)T}}\right] \qquad (1A.12)$$

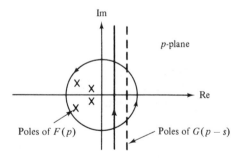

Fig. 1A.1   Evaluating $F(z)$ using Cauchy's residue theorem

By defining $z = e^{sT}$ eqn. (1 A.12) becomes

$$F(z) = \sum \text{Res}\left[\frac{F(p)}{1 - e^{-pT} z^{-1}}\right] \qquad (1A.13)$$

EXERCISES

1.1 Find the homogeneous solutions to each of the following linear difference
equations

(i) $x_{i+2} - 2x_{i+1} + x_i = f_i$

(ii) $x_{i+3} - 3x_{i+2} + 3x_{i+1} - x_i = f_i$

1.2 Find the z-transform of the following functions of discrete time i

(i)

i	0	1	2	3	4	5	6	7	8	...
f_i	1	2	3	2	1	1	0	0	0	...

(ii)

i	0	1	2	3	4	5	6	7	8	...
f_i	1	2	1	0	-1	0	0	0	0	...

For f_i in (i) and (ii) find the z-transform of f_{i+3}.

1.3 Prove that

$$\mathbf{Z}[if_i] = -z \frac{dF(z)}{dz} \quad \text{for } |z| > 1.$$

1.4 Determine the z-transform of the discrete ramp function

$$f_i = \begin{cases} i & \text{for } i \geqslant 0 \\ 0 & \text{for } i < 0 \end{cases}$$

1.5 Determine $f(i)$ for

$$F(z) = \frac{-3z^3 + z^2}{z^3 - 4z^2 + 5z - 2} \quad \text{for } |z| > 2.$$

1.6 Find the z-transform of the ramp function

$$f(t) = t \text{ for } t > 0.$$

1.7 Find the z-transform of ZOH .

1.8 Discretize

$$\begin{vmatrix} \dot{x}_1 \\ \dot{x}_2 \end{vmatrix} = \begin{bmatrix} 0 & 1 \\ -2 & -3 \end{bmatrix} \begin{bmatrix} x_1 \\ x_2 \end{bmatrix} + \begin{bmatrix} 0 \\ 1 \end{bmatrix} u(t)$$

Assume $T = 1$, and u = constant through $0 \leqslant t \leqslant T$.

1.9 Trace the response to a step input of the following open loop system.

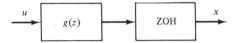

The transfer function $g(z)$ is characterized by a pole-zero configuration on the z-plane. Consider the seven different cases.

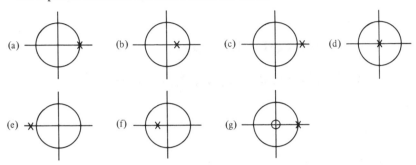

1.10 Given $y_{i+2} - 4y_{i+1} + 4y_i = u_i + 2u_{i+1}$

   (i)   Find the state space representation (you may use the following trans-
           formation: $w_{i+2} - 4w_{i+1} + 4w_i = u_i$).
  (ii) Describe the response to initial conditions y_0 and y_1.

1.11 Given an impulse response of a finite length memory system

$$h_i = \delta_i - 2\delta_{i-1} + 0.5\delta_{i-2} + 0.5\delta_{i-3}$$

   (i)   Find state space representation;
  (ii) Find transfer function in z;
 (iii) Describe a realization of the system with lag elements (z^{-1}).

1.12 Find $y(t)$ as a function of $x(t)$ for the following network.

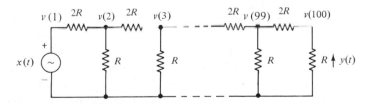

Hint. Use the difference equations for current i in R (node i).

2

Digital Control Design
via Continuous Design

2.1 INTRODUCTION

During recent decades analog control methods have been refined and a large body of knowledge accumulated.

This experience may be directly applied to designing digital controllers. Design methods described in this chapter are based on the conventional classical design of the analog compensation network, using the well-known techniques of root locus and Bode plot. The additional knowledge required is the conversion of the controller's continuous transfer function to a digital filter. Digitizing the continuous filter creates various new phenomena not encountered in the continuous design. The major property required of the digitized filter is the fidelity of the impulse and frequency response of the original analog filter.

This fidelity depends on the sampling rate and on the particular method of discretization. Various methods of discretization are described, some more complicated and more accurate than others. Their common properties are that by lowering the sampling rate, the fidelity and accuracy of the discretized filter are decreased. Therefore these methods are sometimes called the approximate methods, compared to the 'exact' methods (Chapter 3) which generate stable systems even for slow sampling rates. However methods which use the discretized version of the well designed analog controller are highly practical and actually the design of a digital controller generally starts with an analog design. Probably in the future, when enough experience in digital control design has been accumulated, the background of an analog design will be unnecessary.

2.2 CONTINUOUS DESIGN AND DISCRETIZATION OF THE COMPENSA-TION NETWORK

The procedure is based on the fact that the analog controller has been well designed or at least is in the stage of being designed using a continuous compensation network. It is necessary to be familiar with the design rationalities involved because the conversion to discrete filter will introduce time lags. Furthermore, finite word length (as discussed in Chapter 6) will influence the dynamics, thus a complete understanding of the design objectives is a prerequisite.

We start with the continuous control system as shown in Fig. 2.1.

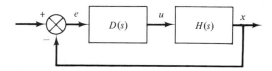

Fig. 2.1   The continuous control system

Our objective is to transform the compensation network $D(s)$ to $D(z)$ so that we obtain the discretely controlled system shown in Fig. 2.2, which will behave as similar as possible to the continuous system.

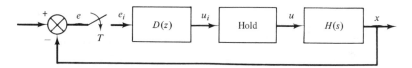

Fig. 2.2   The discretely controlled system

This objective will be accomplished in a four-step procedure.

Step 1:   Check the behavior of the continuous system when a hold is inserted (hold causes delays). If necessary, correct $D(s)$, i.e., check the behavior of the continuous system modified by the approximated time lag of the ZOH.

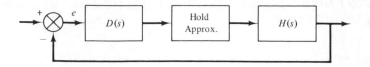

Fig. 2.3 The continuous control system with a hold approximation

The hold should be approximated by rational expressions like Padé expansions. For a ZOH the expansion is:-

$$\frac{1 - e^{-sT}}{s} \cong \frac{T}{1 + \dfrac{sT}{2}} \; , \; \frac{T}{1 + \dfrac{sT}{2} + \dfrac{(sT)^2}{2!}} \; , \; \ldots \tag{2.1}$$

The selection of appropriate sampling interval T is discussed in detail in Chapter 7.

Step 2:   Transform $D(s)$ to $D(z)$.

            Six different methods of transformation will be described in Sec. 2.4.

Step 3:   Check the behavior of the discretely controlled closed loop system depicted in Fig. 2.4.

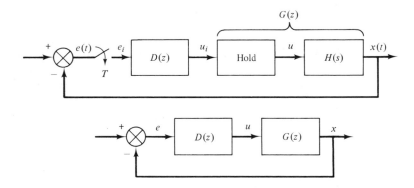

Fig. 2.4 z-transform representation of the discretely controlled closed loop system

Step 4:   Convert $D(z)$ to a numerical algorithm (described in detail in Chapter 5). An example at the end of this chapter will demonstrate the procedure.

2.3 DIGITAL FILTER PROPERTIES, FREQUENCY RESPONSE, ALIASING

2.3.1 A Short Overview

The design of digital filters is well established and extensively covered in the literature. The name itself refers to a whole field of methods for the digital processing of signals. Several classifications are possible:

— Recursive and non-recursive filters.

Discrete linear filters may be represented by a rational pulse transfer function of the form

$$\frac{u(z)}{e(z)} = D(z) = \frac{a_1 + a_2 z^{-1} + \ldots + a_k z^{-k}}{1 + b_1 z^{-1} + \ldots + b_n z^{-n}} \quad k \leqslant n. \tag{2.2}$$

This is a recursive filter, i.e., the previous outputs of the filter $(u_i, u_{i-1}, \ldots)$ are processed in the next calculation.

If the filter output is a linear continuation of the inputs

$$\frac{u(z)}{e(z)} = a_1 + a_2 z^{-1} + \ldots + a_k z^{-k} \tag{2.3}$$

then it is a non-recursive filter, sometimes called Finite-duration Impulse Response filter (FIR), and also known as Moving Average or Transversal filters.

— Another classification is based on methods of design. Some of the methods, based on placement of poles and zeros in the z-plane, will be covered in Chapter 3. Other methods are based on the conversion of analog filters to digital algorithms, and this is the subject of this chapter. All methods are centered around the subject of the sampling theorem, i.e., the relation between the bandwidth of the processed continuous signal and the sampling rate.

2.3.2 The Frequency Response

The z-transforms of discrete or discretized systems define the response to an impulse. The impulse response alone does not characterize sufficiently the behavior of compensation networks (filters) and more information about their frequency response is needed.

The frequency response, i.e., the response to periodic signals, is characterized by four properties, namely

(i)   Amplitude response
(ii) Phase response
(iii) Magnitude square response
(iv) Group delay

All four properties are based on the well-known fact that a linear system which transmits a periodic signal, preserves the frequency, but changes the amplitude and the phase of the signal.

When a discrete system, represented by a transfer function $D(z)$, is excited by a periodic input signal $e(z)$, we may obtain an expression for the output $u(z)$ from the relationship

$$\frac{u(z)}{e(z)} = D(z).$$

For a periodic input $e_i = \sin(\omega iT)$ where $i = 0, 1, 2, \ldots$, the output u is given by

$$u_i = M \sin (\omega iT + \theta) \tag{2.4}$$

The proof is the same as for continuous systems. How do we calculate it?

By definition: $z = e^{sT}$, and if we replace s by $j\omega$, for a steady state periodic input, the output is:

$$u(e^{j\omega T}) = D(e^{j\omega T})e(e^{j\omega T}) \tag{2.5}$$

Using eqn. (2.4) we may define the four properties:

(i)   Amplitude response.

$$|M| = |D(e^{j\omega T})| \tag{2.6}$$

(ii)   Phase response.

$$\theta = \measuredangle\left\{D(e^{j\omega T})\right\} \tag{2.7}$$

$$\theta = \tan^{-1}\left\{\frac{\text{Im}\,[D(z)]}{\text{Re}\,[D(z)]}\right\}_{z\,=\,e^{j\omega T}}$$

$$\theta = \frac{1}{2j}\,\ln\left\{\frac{D(z)}{D(z^{-1})}\right\}_{z\,=\,e^{j\omega T}} \tag{2.8}$$

(iii)   Magnitude square response.

$$|D(e^{j\omega T})| = |D(z)D(z^{-1})|_{z\,=\,e^{j\omega T}} \tag{2.9}$$

(iv)   Group delay.
The group delay measures the average delay of the filter as a function of the frequency.

$$\tau_g(e^{j\omega T}) \triangleq -\frac{d\theta(e^{j\omega T})}{d(\omega T)} = -jz\,\frac{d\theta}{dz}\bigg|_{z\,=\,e^{j\omega T}} \tag{2.10}$$

$$\tau_g(e^{j\omega T}) = -\operatorname{Re}\left\{ z\ \frac{dD(z)/dz}{D(z)} \right\}_{z\,=\,e^{j\omega T}} \tag{2.11}$$

$$\tau_g(e^{j\omega T}) = -\operatorname{Re}\left\{ z\ \frac{d}{dz}\ [\ln D(z)] \right\}_{z\,=\,e^{j\omega T}} \tag{2.12}$$

Example. Consider the frequency response of a first order filter. The continuous filter is $1/s + a$, its impulse transfer function is given by its z-transform

$$D(z) = \frac{z}{z - e^{-aT}}\ .$$

(i) Amplitude response.

$$M = |D(e^{j\omega T})|$$

$$M = \frac{|e^{j\omega T}|}{|e^{j\omega T} - e^{-aT}|}$$

$$M = \frac{1}{\sqrt{1 - 2\cos(\omega T)e^{-aT} + e^{-2aT}}}$$

(ii) Phase response.

$$\theta = \sphericalangle\left\{ D(e^{j\omega T}) \right\}$$

$$\theta = \omega T - \tan^{-1}\frac{\sin \omega T}{\cos \omega T - e^{-aT}}$$

(iii) Amplitude square response.

$$M^2 = |D(e^{j\omega T})|^2$$

$$M^2 = \frac{1}{1 - 2\cos(\omega T)e^{-aT} + e^{-2aT}}$$

This is the same result as

$$\left\{ D(z)D(z^{-1}) \right\}_{z\,=\,e^{j\omega T}} = \frac{z}{z - e^{-aT}}\ \cdot\ \frac{z^{-1}}{z^{-1} - e^{-aT}}\ \bigg|_{z\,=\,e^{j\omega T}}$$

$$= \frac{1}{1 - 2e^{j\omega T}e^{-aT} + e^{-2aT}}$$

$$M^2 = \frac{1}{1 - 2\cos(\omega T)e^{-aT} + e^{-2aT}}$$

(iv) Group delay.

$$\tau_g(e^{j\omega T}) = -\frac{d\theta}{d\omega T}$$

$$= -\left\{\frac{d}{d\omega}\left[T\omega - \tan^{-1}\frac{\sin \omega T}{\cos \omega T - e^{-aT}}\right]\right\}$$

$$\tau_g(e^{j\omega T}) = -T\left(\frac{2 - 3\cos \omega T e^{-aT}}{1 - 2\cos (\omega T)e^{-aT} + e^{-2aT}}\right)$$

2.3.3 Folding of Frequencies or Aliasing

Aliasing is an important property related to the sampling of continuous periodic signals. The main consequence of aliasing is that we cannot distinguish between two periodic signals whose frequencies differ in integral multiples of the sampling rate.

Explanation:

Typical frequency spectra of band-limited continuous signals (Ω) are depicted in Figs 2.5 and 2.6. The signals in both cases, are considered to be sampled at the frequency ω_s, but Fig. 2.5 has a higher value of ω_s than Fig. 2.6.

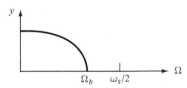

Fig. 2.5 Frequency contents of a period signal. High sampling frequency.

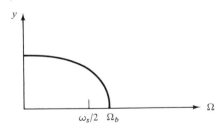

Fig. 2.6 Frequency contents of a periodic signal, low sampling frequency.

Case I. (as Fig. 2.5). ~ $\qquad \Omega_b < \dfrac{\omega_s}{2}$ $\qquad\qquad\qquad\qquad$ (2.13)

The sampling rate is at least twice as high as the highest frequency contained in the signal. This case does not present sampling problems.

Case II (as Fig. 2.6). $\qquad \Omega_b > \dfrac{\omega_s}{2}$ $\qquad\qquad\qquad\qquad$ (2.14)

We will show that in this case it is impossible to differentiate between two sampled sinusoids whose sum or difference of frequencies is an integral multiple of ω_s.

(e.g. $\qquad \Omega_1, \Omega_1 + \omega_s, \Omega_1 + 2\omega_s \ldots)$

For all $\qquad \Omega \Rightarrow 0 < \Omega < \Omega_b$

let $\qquad \Omega = \Omega_1 + \omega_s k$ $\qquad\qquad$ where $k = 0, 1, 2, \ldots$ $\qquad$ (2.15)

then $\qquad y(t) = \sin(\Omega t)$

$\qquad\qquad y(t) = \sin(\Omega_1 + \omega_s k)t$ $\qquad\qquad\qquad\qquad\qquad$ (2.16)

$\qquad\qquad y_i \ = \sin(\Omega i T)$

$\qquad\qquad y_i \ = \sin(\Omega_1 + \omega_s k)iT$ $\qquad$ where $\omega_s = \dfrac{2\pi}{T}$

$\qquad\qquad y_i \ = \sin(\Omega_1 iT + 2\pi i k)$ $\qquad (ik = 0, 1, 2, \ldots)$ $\qquad$ (2.17)

$\qquad\qquad y_i \ = \sin(\Omega_1 iT) = \sin(\Omega iT)$ $\qquad\qquad\qquad\qquad$ (2.18)

The consequences are:-

(i) We cannot reconstruct (detect) a signal whose frequency is higher than $\omega_s/2$. This frequency is called the Nyquist frequency.

(ii) All the signals whose frequencies are higher than $\omega_s/2$ look like signals of a frequency between zero to $\omega_s/2$. The higher frequency signals are *folded* to the interval $0 < \Omega < \omega_s/2$.

We may visualize this by making reference to Fig. 2.7. In part (a) of Fig. 2.7 the frequency spectrum of the signal and the sampling rate are depicted.

In part (b) we see that the sampled frequency spectrum is repeated in $\omega_s/2$ intervals.

Part (c) shows the superposition of the signals. The slow sampled case contains distortion due to the superposition of frequency components.

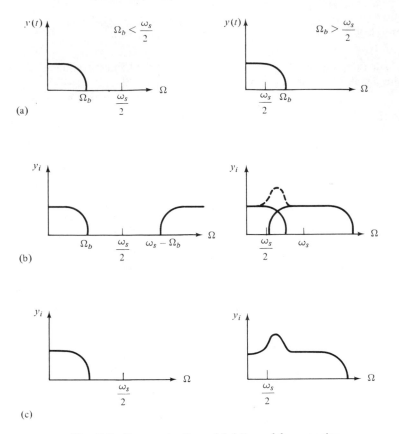

Fig. 2.7   Demonstration of folding of frequencies

A practical illustration of the problem is to be found in the case of a rate gyro, as used to measure aircraft pitch rate, when the rate signal is contaminated by various noises. Typical signal and unwanted frequencies are depicted in Fig. 2.8.

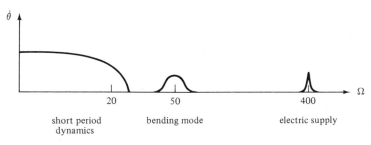

Fig. 2.8   Signal contents of aircraft rate gyro

It is necessary to filter out the 400 Hz frequency and use of a sampling rate higher than 400 Hz is unpractical. If the pitch rate $\dot{\theta}$, is sampled at a slower rate ($\omega_s/2 < 400$ Hz) the high frequency will be folded in and appear as a low frequency.

2.4 METHODS OF DISCRETIZATION OF ANALOG FILTERS

There are many methods of discretization of analog filters and new methods are being developed all the time. The most used methods are the following:

(i)   Impulse invariant transformation (z-transform).
(ii)   Impulse invariant transformation and artificial holds.
(iii) Mapping of differentials.
(iv)   Bilinear transformation.
(v)   Bilinear transformation and frequency prewarping.
(vi)   Matched z-transform.

Proper selection of a discretization method for the analog compensation network is a rather confusing task. The designer has to ask himself what he is expecting from the discretized control algorithm, compared to the analog filter performance.

The most used properties which characterize the compensation filter are:-

(a) the number of poles and zeros
(b) the bandwidth, the crossover frequency
(c) the DC gain
(d) the phase margin
(e) the gain margin
(f) step overshoot
(g) peak closed loop frequency response (MP)

It is highly probable that not all these properties will be preserved during the discretization process and the designer has to compromise.

In Sec. 2.4.1 to 2.4.6 the various discretization methods are described in some detail, and in order to help the reader the most important properties of the methods are listed.

However the most valuable information on the topic is included in Sec. 2.5, where results of an extensive piece of work on the comparison of various discretization methods is summarized. This research, undertaken by Avner Ben-Zwi and Meir Preiszler, is a valuable contribution to the digital control field.

2.4.1 Impulse Invariant Transformation (z-transform)

This method was described in Sec. 1.6.2 where we showed that a continuous filter and its pulse transfer function may be represented in the form of eqns. 2.20 and 2.21.

$$\frac{u(s)}{e(s)} = D(s) \tag{2.19}$$

$$D(s) = \frac{A_1}{s + a_1} + \frac{A_2}{s + a_2} + \dots \tag{2.20}$$

$$D(z) \triangleq Z[D(s)] = \frac{A_1 z}{z - e^{-a_1 T}} + \frac{A_2 z}{z - e^{-a_2 T}} + \dots \tag{2.21}$$

A summary of the properties of the z-transform method are given in (i) to (v) below.

(i) $D(z)$ has the same impulse response as $D(s)$.
(ii) If $D(s)$ is stable so is $D(z)$.
(iii) $D(z)$ does not preserve the frequency response of $D(s)$.
(iv) $D(z)$ transforms frequencies which are multiples of ω_s to the same frequency on z-plane hence aliasing may occur.
(v)   If $D(s)$ is a complicated transfer function, the z-transform is probably not tabulated and requires partial fraction expansion.

Using the z-transform method for conversion of an analog filter, $D(s)$, to a discrete filter seems to be a straightforward procedure, but the major problem encountered in this approach is the folding of high frequencies into the desired bandwidth (aliasing). As a result of aliasing, the frequency response of the discretized filter will be a poor approximation to the desired analog filter.

To solve the aliasing problem, a low-pass filter $H(s)$ can be cascaded with $D(s)$, resulting in new modified filter $D_1(s) = H(s)D(s)$. The filter $H(s)$ is often called a guard filter. However, this method has two major drawbacks;

(i)   the guard filter, $H(s)$, introduces a time lag which may cause some degradation in performance, and may require a redesign of the control loop.
(ii) the modified discrete filter $D(z) \triangleq Z\{H(s)D(s)\}$ is more complicated and requires more coefficients for its realization.

Another approach to reduce the aliasing problem is to increase the sampling rate, ω_s, much higher than the cutoff frequency, Ω_b of the filter. In most cases this results in an unpractical or uneconomical hardware realization.

2.4.2 Impulse Invariant Transformation and Hold

This method was demonstrated for the case of discretization of the state space formulation of a system. In that case the hold was a model of a D/A converter. Now, in the discretization of a filter, the hold is an analytical part of the method and not a model of hardware.

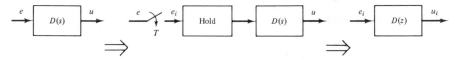

Fig. 2.9 Impulse invariant transformation and artificial hold

For a zero order hold

$$D(z) \triangleq Z \left[\frac{1 - e^{-sT}}{s} D(s) \right] \tag{2.22}$$

Example: Given, $D(s) = \dfrac{a}{s + a}$

$$\frac{u(z)}{e(z)} = D(z) = \frac{z^{-1}(1 - e^{-aT})}{1 - e^{-aT} z^{-1}} \tag{2.23}$$

$$u_i = e^{-aT} u_{i-1} + (1 - e^{-aT}) e_{i-1} \tag{2.24}$$

From eqn. (2.24) we can see that u_i is influenced by e_{i-1} and u_{i-1}, and not by e_i.

For a triangular hold

$$D(z) \triangleq Z \left[\frac{e^{sT} - 2 + e^{-sT}}{Ts^2} D(s) \right] \tag{2.25}$$

Example: Given, $D(s) = \dfrac{a}{s + a}$

$$\frac{u(z)}{e(z)} = D(z) = \frac{A_1 + A_2 z^{-1}}{aT(1 - e^{-aT} z^{-1})} \tag{2.26}$$

$$u_i = \frac{1}{aT} (aT e^{-aT} u_{i-1} + A_1 e_i + A_2 e_{i-1}) \tag{2.27}$$

From eqn. (2.27) we see that u_i is influenced not only by e_{i-1} (as in ZOH) but also by the recent value of e_i.

Properties of the z-transform and hold method are:-

(i)   If $D(s)$ is stable so is $D(z)$.
(ii) If $D(z)$ is not tabulated it requires partial fraction expansion.
(iii) $D(z)$ does not preserve the impulse and frequency response of $D(s)$.

2.4.3 Mapping of Differentials

(i)   Backwards difference:

$$\text{Given } \frac{u(s)}{e(s)} = D(s) \tag{2.28}$$

we replace all derivatives by a first order approximation, i.e. replace s by d/dt

$$\frac{de}{dt} \simeq \frac{e_i - e_{i-1}}{T} \quad ; \quad \frac{du}{dt} \simeq \frac{u_i - u_{i-1}}{T} \tag{2.29}$$

The z-transform of the backwards difference is,

$$\mathcal{Z}[s] = \frac{1 - z^{-1}}{T} \tag{2.30}$$

and this yields

$$D(z) \triangleq D(s) \Bigg|_{s = \frac{1-z^{-1}}{T}} . \tag{2.31}$$

For example. $D(s) = \dfrac{a}{s+a}$ yields

$$D(z) = \frac{u(z)}{e(z)} = \frac{a}{\dfrac{1 - z^{-1}}{T} + a} = \frac{aT}{1 + aT - z^{-1}}$$

$$u_i = \frac{1}{1 + aT}(u_{i-1} + aTe_i)$$

Properties of the backward difference transformation are:-

(a)   It is easy to apply and does not require factorization of the transfer function.
(b)   A stable $D(s)$ transforms to a stable $D(z)$.
(c)   Does not preserve the impulse and frequency response of $D(s)$.

The transformation

$$s = \frac{1 - z^{-1}}{T}$$

highly distorts the frequency response. We may see it in the mapping of the $j\Omega$ axis on the s-plane to the z-plane. See Fig. 2.10.

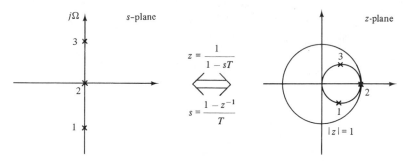

Fig. 2.10 Mapping of differentials (backward difference) between s-plane and z-plane

(ii) Forward difference. This approach generates unstable filters.
(iii) Higher order differences, i.e.

$$s = \frac{1}{T} \sum_k \alpha_k (z^k - z^{-k})$$ (2.32)

By proper choice of α a desirable filter characteristic may be preserved, but it is difficult to select proper values for α.

2.4.4 Bilinear Transformation

This transformation is also called the Tustin transformation and trapezoid integration method.

Given that $\dfrac{u(s)}{e(s)} = D(s)$

the bilinear transformation, as defined in Chapter 1, substitutes for values of s in terms of z, as given by eqn (2.33)

$$s = \frac{2}{T} \frac{1 - z^{-1}}{1 + z^{-1}}$$ (2.33)

This yields the transformed system, i.e.,

$$D(z) \triangleq D(s) \Bigg|_{s = \frac{2}{T} \frac{1-z^{-1}}{1+z^{-1}}}$$ (2.34)

Example: $\dfrac{u(s)}{e(s)} = D(s) = \dfrac{1}{s}$

$$\frac{u(z)}{e(z)} = \frac{T}{2} \frac{1+z^{-1}}{1-z^{-1}}$$

$$u_i = u_{i-1} + \frac{T}{2}(e_i - e_{i-1})$$

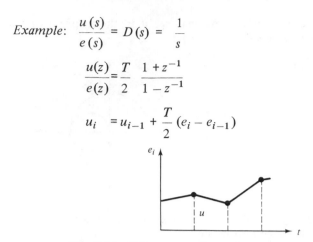

Fig. 2.11 Bilinear transformation as a trapezoidal integration

As seen from Fig. 2.11, u is a trapezoid integration of e.

The properties of the bilinear transformation are:-

(i)   It is easy to apply.
(ii) It transforms the whole left-hand side of s-plane into unit circle in the z-plane, hence no aliasing effect.
(iii) If $D(s)$ is stable so is $D(z)$.
(iv) It does not preserve impulse and frequency response.

2.4.5 Bilinear Transformation and Frequency Prewarping

Given that $\dfrac{u(s)}{e(s)} = D(s)$

$$D(z) \overset{\Delta}{=} D(s) \Bigg|_{s = \frac{2}{T} \frac{1-z^{-1}}{1+z^{-1}}}$$ (eqn. (2.34) repeated)

It does not preserve the frequency response.

What is the frequency response of $D(z)$ as compared to $D(s)$?

We will compare $D(j\Omega)$ to $D(e^{j\omega T})$ where $D(j\Omega)$ is the frequency response of the continuous system $D(s)$, and $D(e^{j\omega T})$ is the frequency response of the discrete system $D(z)$.

We will replace s by $j\Omega$ and z by $e^{j\omega T}$ in the bilinear transformation:

$$s = \frac{2}{T} \frac{1 - z^{-1}}{1 + z^{-1}}$$ (eqn. (2.33) repeated)

$$j\Omega = \frac{2}{T} \frac{1 - e^{-j\omega T}}{1 + e^{j\omega T}} \tag{2.35}$$

Using De Moivre's theorems

$$\Omega = \frac{2}{T} \tan \frac{\omega T}{2} \tag{2.36}$$

Equation (2.36) reflects the distortion between Ω and ω.

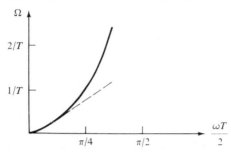

Fig. 2.12 Relationship between Ω and ω.

Using eqns. (2.34) and (2.36) we obtain

$$|D(s)|_{s=j\Omega} = |D(z)|_{z=e^{j\omega T}} \qquad \text{if } \Omega \frac{2}{T} \tan \frac{\omega T}{2} \tag{2.37}$$

The amplitude of $D(s)$ at frequency Ω equals the amplitude of $D(z)$ at frequency ω where $\Omega = 2/T \tan \omega T/2$.

The main consequence is that the bilinear transformation distorts the frequency response. This distortion, depicted in Fig. 2.13, may be taken into account in our design of the compensation network.

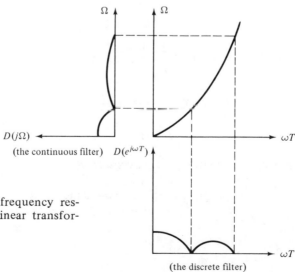

Fig. 2.13 Distortion of frequency response caused by the bilinear transformation

As seen in Fig. 2.13, the bilinear transformation compresses the continuous frequency $0 < \Omega < \infty$ to a limited digital range $0 < \omega T < \pi$.

In the compensation design process the continuous breakpoints should be adjusted to new values. The bilinear transformation will place them back to the desired breakpoints in the discrete domain. The adjustment wil be done in a two-step procedure. This is illustrated below and in an example.

Step 1: For all desired poles and zeros $(s + a)$ replace a by a',

$$s + a \Rightarrow s + a' \Bigg|_{a' = \frac{2}{T}\tan\frac{aT}{2}} \tag{2.38}$$

Step 2: Transform $D(s, a')$ to $D(z, a)$

$$D(z, a) \triangleq D(s, a') \Bigg|_{s = \frac{2}{T}\frac{1 - z^{-1}}{1 + z^{-1}}} \tag{2.39}$$

Note: The amplitude scaling is not automatically satisfied and must be considered separately. If DC gain should be 1 (low frequency transmission), we evaluate the filter's constant for $z = 1$ (s.s. gain = 1), whereas for high frequency transmission we evaluate the filter's constant for $z = -1$.

Let us consider the example

$$D(s) = \frac{a}{s + a}$$

Step 1: Prewarp, i.e.

$$D(s, a') = \frac{a}{s + \frac{2}{T}\tan\frac{aT}{2}}$$

Step 2: Substituting $\dfrac{2}{T}\dfrac{1 - z^{-1}}{1 + z^{-1}}$ gives,

$$D(z) = K\frac{a}{\dfrac{2}{T}\dfrac{1-z^{-1}}{1+z^{-1}} + \dfrac{2}{T}\tan\dfrac{aT}{2}}$$

For a required $D(s)_{s.s.} = 1$ we consider

$$\lim_{t \to \infty} D(z) \cdot \frac{1}{z - 1} = \lim_{z \to 1}(z - 1)\frac{1}{z - 1}K\frac{a}{\dfrac{2}{T}\dfrac{1 - z^{-1}}{1 + z^{-1}} + \dfrac{2}{T}\tan\dfrac{aT}{2}}$$

$$= K \cfrac{a}{\cfrac{2}{T}\tan\cfrac{aT}{2}} = 1$$

i.e. $\qquad K = \cfrac{\cfrac{2}{T}\tan\cfrac{aT}{2}}{a}$

The complete digital filter is therefore given by:

$$D(z) = \cfrac{\tan\cfrac{aT}{2}}{\cfrac{1-z^{-1}}{1+z^{-1}}+\tan\cfrac{aT}{2}}$$

which, for organized numerical calculation, may be written in the form:-

$$D(z) = \cfrac{1+z^{-1}}{1+\cot\cfrac{aT}{2}+(1-\cot\cfrac{aT}{2})z^{-1}}$$

Properties of bilinear transformation and frequency prewarping are:-

(i)   It maps the left-hand side (LHS) of the s-plane to unit circle on the z-plane (one-to-one correspondence).
(ii) A stable $D(s)$ transforms to a stable $D(z)$.
(iii) There is no aliasing.
(iv) A wideband sharp cutoff $D(s)$ is transformed to wideband sharp cutoff $D(z)$.
(v)   It matches the frequency response for breakpoints and for zero frequency, and compresses the response at $\Omega = \infty$ to $\omega T = \pi$.
(vi) The impulse response and phase response are not preserved.

2.4.6 Matched z transform

The matched z-transformation maps poles or zeros of $D(s)$ on the s-plane to poles and zeros of $D(z)$ on the z-plane.

$$D(z)\triangleq D(s)\,\big|\,{}_{(s+a)}=(1-z^{-1}e^{-aT}) \tag{2.40}$$

$$(s+a)\to(1-z^{-1}e^{-aT}) \tag{2.41}$$

$$(s+a\pm jb)\to(1-2z^{-1}\,e^{-aT}\cos bT+e^{-2aT}z^{-2}) \tag{2.42}$$

Note:

(i)   The last transformation eqn. (2.42) is easier to program than a separate transformation of the complex form

$$(s + a \pm jb) \rightarrow (1 - z^{-1} e^{-a \pm jb}) \tag{2.43}$$

The complex form requires programming with complex numbers (this depends on realization of the algorithm, see Chapter 5).

(ii) The impulse invariant method transforms the poles of $D(s)$ to the same place as the matched z-transform method, but the method does not place the zeros of $D(s)$ at the same place as the matched z-transform method.

(iii) The gain should be scaled.

(iv) $D(s)$ must be given in a factorized form.

Example:

$$D(s) = \frac{s}{s + a}$$

$$D(z) = K' \frac{1 - z^{-1}}{1 - z^{-1} e^{-aT}}$$

This is a highpass filter so we are asking for a high frequency transmission $(z \rightarrow -1)$.

$$D(z) \Big|_{z=-1} = K' \frac{1 - (-1)}{1 - (-1)e^{-aT}} = 1$$

$$K' = \frac{1 - e^{-aT}}{2}$$

$$D(z) = \frac{1 - e^{-aT}}{2} \frac{1 - z^{-1}}{1 - z^{-1} e^{-aT}}$$

Some difficulties may be encountered with this method. These are:-

(i)   If the analog filter has zeros with frequencies greater than $\omega_s/2$ their z-plane position will be aliased.

(ii) An all-pole transfer function transformed by matched z-transform does not adequately represent the analog filter. It is usual to add artificial zeros at -1 for every excess pole.

This last point has a logical explanation because one of the objectives of the matched z-transform is to cancel the aliasing property of the impulse invariant transformation (the z-transform). This will be achieved if the frequency response of the discretized controller for $\omega \to \omega_s/2$ is similar to the frequency response of the analog filter for $\Omega \to \infty$. Applying the bilinear transformation and frequency prewarping to a single pole or a single zero we obtain

$$s + \sigma \to K \frac{z - e^{-\sigma T}}{z + 1} \tag{2.44}$$

and for complex poles or zero we obtain

$$(s + \sigma)^2 + (\Omega)^2 \ \to \ K \frac{z^2 - 2ze^{-\sigma T}\cos(\Omega T) + e^{-2\sigma T}}{(z + 1)^2} \tag{2.45}$$

Cancellation of $(z + 1)$ terms in the transformed discrete transfer function leaves excessive poles at $z = -1$.

2.5 COMPARISON OF THE VARIOUS DISCRETIZATION METHODS

Extensive work has been done by Avner Ben-Zwi and Meir Preiszler (BEN-1) to compare the performance of a descretized controller to the performance of an analog design. Their results are summarized in this section. Their method of investigation was an experimental search using as a working case the analog design of a general position servo system. Eight different methods of discretization and four different sampling rates were considered.

    Their results are numerical in nature, but their study and conclusions are useful for designers.

2.5.1 The Analog Control Loop

The position servo considered by Ben-Zwi and Preiszler is depicted in Fig. 2.14.

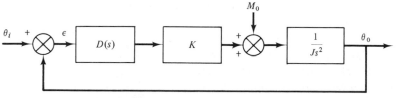

Fig. 2.14   The position servo system

The requirements of the closed loop were considered to be:

The maximum phase lag at ω = 3 Hz should not be more than 13°. The maximum gain, relative to the DC gain, 5dB. The maximum error, ϵ, due to an input disturbing moment of 0.028 Nm should be 0.01 rad.

Careful design resulted in a compensation network $D(s)$, as given in eqn. (2.46).

$$D(s) = \frac{k\left(1 + \dfrac{s}{a}\right)}{\left(1 + \dfrac{s}{b}\right)^2} \tag{2.46}$$

where: k = 3.8
         a = 29.4 rad/s
         b = 294 rad/s

The overall performance of the closed loop is summarized in Table 2.1.

Table 2.1   Performance of the analog closed loop

Phase margin	37°
Gain margin	25 dB
Step overshoot	42%
Damping coefficient of the dominant poles	0.427
Closed loop bandwidth	8 Hz
Closed loop peak frequency response (MP)	4.95 dB at 475 Hz

2.5.2   The Discretization of the Compensation Network

Four different sampling rates were used: 1 KHz, 100 Hz, 50 Hz, 33 Hz.

Eight discretization methods were investigated:
(i)   Mapping of differentials.
(ii)   Impulse response transformation (z-transform).
(iii) z-transform and ZOH.
(iv) z-transform and triangular hold.
(v)   Matched z-transform, excess zeros at $z = -1$.
(vi)   Matched z-transform, excess zeros at $z = 0$.
(vii)   Bilinear transformation.
(viii) Bilinear transformation and frequency prewarping.

Table 2.2 Ben-Zwi and Preiszler's results, comparison of performance, $\omega_s = 1\text{KHz}$

Method	BW of closed loop (Hz)	Damping coefficient of dominant poles	Gain margin (dB)	Phase margin (degrees)	Frequency response Freq. (Hz)	Max. gain (dB)	Phase at 3 Hz (degrees)	Step overshoot (%)
Analog	8.0	0.42	$\simeq 24$	37	4.75	4.94	−12	42
Mapping of differentials	9.76	0.417	$\simeq 23$	36	4.85	5.19	−12	45
Impulse response z-transformation	7.13	0.147	$\simeq 27$	17	4.75	11.6	−1	70
z-transforms and ZOH	8.28	0.41	$\simeq 23$	37	4.75	5.09	−12	45
z-transforms and triangular hold	8.15	0.42	$\simeq 22$	37	4.75	5.09	−12	43
Matched z-transforms ($z = -1$, excess zeros)	7.95	0.417	$\simeq 22$	37	4.75	5.13	−12	44
Matched z-transforms ($z = 0$, excess zeros)	8.08	0.425	$\simeq 24$	37	4.75	4.97	−12	43
Bilinear	8.16	0.42	$\simeq 23$	37	4.75	5.11	−12	43
Bilinear and prewarping	8.16	0.42	$\simeq 22$	37	4.75	5.09	−11.8	43

Table 2.3 Ben-Zwi and Preiszler's results, comparison of performance, $\omega_s = 100$ Hz

Method	BW of closed loop (Hz)	Damping coefficient of dominant poles	Gain margin (dB)	Phase margin (degrees)	Frequency response		Phase at 3 Hz (degrees)	Step overshoot (%)
					Freq. (Hz)	Max. gain (dB)		
Analog	8.0	.41	$\simeq 44$	37	4.75	4.94	−12	42
Mapping of differentials	9.59	.25	$\simeq 11$	23	5.91	9.0	−8.6	71
Impulse response z-transformation	UNSTABLE							
z-transforms and ZOH	UNSTABLE							
z-transforms and triangular hold	9.15	.33	$\simeq 13$	28	5.35	7.2	−10	60
Matched z-transforms ($z = -1$, excess zeros)	9.39	.25	$\simeq 9$	20	5.68	10.13	−7.9	77
Matched z-transforms ($z = 0$, excess zeros)	9.01	.35	$\simeq 15$	30	5.25	6.6	−10.3	55
Bilinear	9.25	.34	$\simeq 12$	27	7.4	7.06	−10	59
Bilinear and prewarping	7.96	.44	$\simeq 15$	39	4.66	4.69	−17.4	40

Table 2.4 Ben-Zwi and Preiszler's results, comparison of performance for $\omega_s = 50$ Hz and 33 Hz

Method	ω_s (Hz)	BW of closed loop (Hz)	Damping coefficient of dominant poles	Gain margin (dB)	Phase margin (degrees)	Frequency response Freq. (Hz)	Max. gain (dB)	Phase at 3 Hz (degrees)	Step overshoot (%)
Analog		8.0	0.12	$\simeq 24$	37	4.7	4.9	-1	42
Mapping of differentials	50	9.07	0.44	$\simeq 2$	5	6.03	22.8	-5	113
z-transforms and triangular hold	50	9.87	0.16	$\simeq 5$	12	6.02	13.4	-7	88
Matched z-transforms ($z=-1$, excess zeros)	50	UNSTABLE							
Matched z-transforms ($z=0$, excess zeros)	50	9.25	0.13	$\simeq 6$	10	5.8	14.15	-6.2	95
Mapping of differentials	33	UNSTABLE							
z-transforms and triangular hold	33	UNSTABLE							
Matched z-transforms ($z=0$, excess zeros)	33	UNSTABLE							
Bilinear	33	10.05	0.85	$\simeq 3$	7	6.03	18.83	5.3	129

All together twenty-four discrete compensators were implemented using a ZOH as the reconstruction hold. The behavior of the closed loop system was plotted on numerous graphs. Its performance is summarized in Tables, 2.2, 2.3 and 2.4

Note:

The phase lag generated by the reconstruction hold influenced the performance, i.e. the analog closed loop was not redesigned for each sampling rate.

2.5.3 Conclusions

After analyzing all the charts and numerical results a long list of conclusions was derived. Obviously some may be questioned by the reader, others may need further verification, but all of them should be noted and considered.

(i) Sampling rate ω_s = 1 kHz
   — For ω_s = 1 kHz more than hundred times the crossover frequency of the analog filter (6 Hz), all discretization methods, except the z-transform, yielded results similar to the analog design.
   — In the matched z-transform method, replacement of $z = 0$ to $z = -1$ did not influence the results.
   — Using the bilinear transformation, prewarping of the critical frequencies was found to be unnecessary.
   — For ω_s = 1 kHz, the performance of the filter was highly sensitive to the word length. (This topic will be discussed in detail in Chapter 6.)

(ii) Sampling rate ω_s = 100 Hz
   — For ω_s = 100 Hz, about fifteen times the analog crossover frequency, the z-transform, and z-transform and ZOH methods degraded the performance of the closed loop.
   — The discrete controller, discretized using the matched z-transform ($z = 0$) yielded better performance than the matched z-transform ($z = -1$). The reason is that the matched z-transform ($z = 0$) generates nearly the same phase lead as the analog filter.
   — The bilinear transformation, the z-transform and triangular hold, and the matched z-transform ($z = 0$) method performed almost as the analog filter. The performance of the closed loop was slightly degraded due to the phase lag generated by the reconstruction hold (ZOH).
   — The prewarping in the bilinear transformation method preserved the location of the critical frequencies, but not their gain and phase.

(iii)   Sampling rates ω_s = 50 Hz, ω_s = 33 Hz
- For slow sampling frequencies (relative to the crossover of 6 Hz), all methods perform poorly.
- The bilinear transformation gave results closest to the analog performance, but the reconstruction hold generated a phase lag at the crossover frequency which resulted in an unsatisfactory phase margin.

(iv)   General conclusions
- The best discretization method was the bilinear transformation. This method performed well even for slow sampling frequencies (five times the crossover frequency).
- If gain is the only criterion, the matched z-transform performed better than the bilinear method.
- The prewarping preserved the locations of the critical frequencies but not their gain and phases. If a pole or a zero in the analog filter is located far away from the frequency we are interested in, then, prewarping is unnecessary.

Finally, the frequency properties of the discretized filters are listed in Table 2.5.

Table 2.5   Comparison of frequency properties of discretized compensation networks. (Ben-Zwi and Preiszler's conclusions)

The discretization method	The transformation	The gain properties	The phase properties
Mapping of differentials	$s = \dfrac{1 - z^{-1}}{T}$	Preserved in low BW of interest even if $\omega_s \sim 6 \times$ crossover frequency. Degraded in high frequencies (even for $\omega_s \sim 15 \times$ crossover frequency	Degraded even for $\omega_s \sim 15 \times$ crossover frequency
Impulse invariant response (z-transform)	$\mathbf{Z}\{D(s)\}$	Not preserved even for $\omega_s \sim 150 \times$ crossover frequency	Not preserved
z-transform and ZOH	$\mathbf{Z}\left\{ \dfrac{1 - e^{-Ts}}{s} D(s) \right\}$	Not preserved even for $\omega_s \sim 15 \times$ crossover frequency	Not preserved even for $\omega_s \sim 15 \times$ crossover frequency
z-transform and triangular hold	$\dfrac{(z + z^{-1} - 2)}{T} \mathbf{Z}\left\{ \dfrac{D(s)}{s^2} \right\}$	Satisfactory up to $\omega_s/2$, even for slow sampling rate	Degradation near $\omega_s = 8 \times$ crossover frequency in BW of interest

Table 2.5 (*contd*)

The discretiza-tion method	The transformation	The gain properties	The phase properties
Matched z-transform ($z = 0$, excess zeros)	$z \to e^{sT}$	Satisfactory performance, even for $\omega_s/2$.	Degradation near $\omega_s = 8 \times$ crossover frequency
Matched z-transform ($z = -1$, excess zeros)	$z \to e^{sT}$	Preserved in BW of interest. $\omega \to \omega_s/2$. $\Omega \to \infty$ Consequently degradation for high frequencies.	Degraded even for $\omega_s = 15 \times$ crossover in BW of interest
The bilinear transformation	$s = \dfrac{2}{T} \dfrac{z-1}{z+1}$	Preserved in BW of interest even for $\omega_s \sim 8 \times$ crossover frequency. Degraded in high frequencies.	Preserved in BW of interest even for $\omega_s \sim 6 \times$ crossover frequency

2.6 DESIGN EXAMPLE

We shall consider a position servomechanism which controls the angular attitude of an optical element forming part of a hybrid simulator. For an all-digital simulation the analog control networks should be converted to a digital algorithm.

The actual analog servo system is shown in Fig. 2.15.

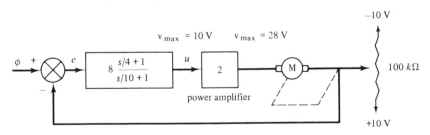

Fig. 2.15 A position servo of an inertial element

In our model the motor and optical system are considered to be represented by a double integrator.

We will follow the design procedure described earlier in this chapter.

In order to obtain an estimation of the time lag caused by a zero order hold, for which the sampling time was chosen as $T = 0.015$ s, the zero order hold (hardware in the simulator) is approximated by a first order Padé expansion. This gives:

$$\frac{1 - e^{-sT}}{s} \simeq k \frac{T}{1 + \dfrac{sT}{2}} = k \frac{2}{s + \dfrac{2}{T}} = \frac{133}{s + 133} \quad .$$

The closed loop system is now in the form shown in Fig. 2.16 and its behavior will be investigated.

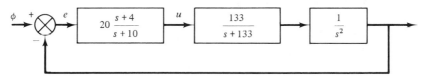

Fig. 2.16   The block diagram of the position servo including an approximation for the ZOH

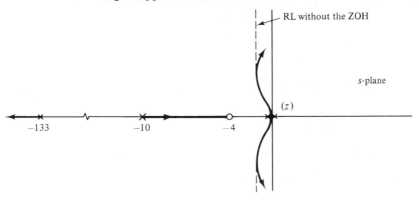

Fig. 2.17   The Root Locus (RL) diagram for the position servo system

Conclusions

(i)   Since the sampling is fast the ZOH has no significant influence on the closed loop dynamics.

(ii) We achieve transformation of the analog controller,

$$D(s) = \frac{s/a + 1}{s/b + 1} \quad a = 4, \quad b = 10$$

to a discrete algorithm by using the matched z-transform. This gives:

$$D(z) = k \frac{z - e^{-aT}}{z - e^{-bT}}$$

$$e^{-aT} = e^{-4 \times 0.015} \cong 0.94$$
$$e^{-bT} = e^{-10 \times 0.015} \cong 0.86$$

$$D(z) = k \frac{z - 0.94}{z - 0.84} .$$

The DC gain of $D(z)$ should be the same as the DC gain of $D(s)$, this condition yields

$$k = \lim_{s \to 0} D(s)/\lim_{z \to 1} D(z),$$

$$k = 8 \frac{1 - 0.86}{1 - 0.94},$$

$$k \cong 19.1.$$

(iii) In the implemented algorithm the variables and coefficients are represented by signed binary fractions:-

$$D(z) = \frac{u(z)}{e(z)} = 19.1 \frac{z - 0.94}{z - 0.84}$$

$$x_i = \frac{19.1}{32} e_i - \left(\frac{19.1}{32} \right) \left(0.94 \right) e_{i-1} + 0.86 \, x_{i-1} \bigg\} \text{ the algorithm}$$

$$u_i = 32 x_i$$

Appropriate scaling and limiters are necessary in order to avoid overflows.

The complete block diagram is depicted in Fig. 2.18.

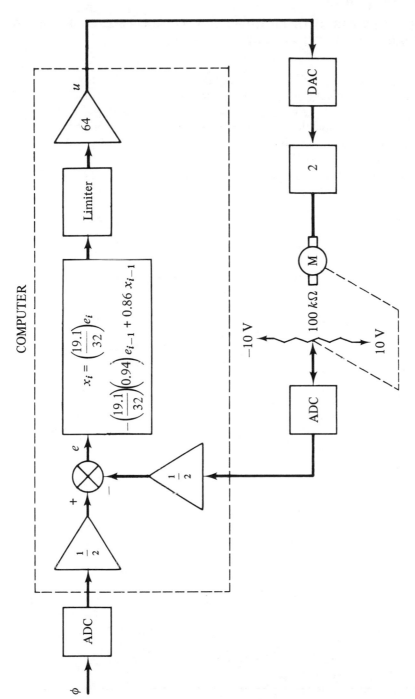

$$x_i = \left(\frac{19.1}{32}\right)e_i$$

$$-\left(\frac{19.1}{32}\right)(0.94)e_{i-1} + 0.86\, x_{i-1}$$

Fig. 2.18 Block diagram of the discrete control system

APPENDIX 2A. DESIGN OF FILTERS USING LOWPASS FILTER, BILINEAR TRANSFORMATION AND FREQUENCY PREWARPING

Transforming a lowpass filter to a highpass, bandpass or bandstop filter is a well-known technique for the continuous filter designer. Constantinides (BOG-1) developed a method to design a digital lowpass, highpass, bandpass and bandstop filter from a continuous lowpass filter transfer function. The method uses the bilinear transformation and frequency prewarping. The useful transformations are given below.

Given a lowpass continuous filter transfer function with cutoff frequency w_c, the required digital filters are given as follows:

Required digital filter	Cutoff frequency	Replace s by:	Where
Lowpass	ω_c	$k\,\dfrac{1 - z^{-1}}{1 + z^{-1}}$	$k = \Omega_c \cot \dfrac{\omega_c T}{2}$
Highpass	ω_c	$k\,\dfrac{1 + z^{-1}}{1 - z^{-1}}$	$k = \Omega_c \tan \dfrac{\omega_c T}{2}$
Bandpass	ω_1, ω_2	$k\,\dfrac{z^{-2} - 2\alpha z^{-1} + 1}{1 + z^{-2}}$	$\alpha = \dfrac{\cos\left(\dfrac{\omega_1 + \omega_2}{2}\right) T}{\cos\left(\dfrac{\omega_1 - \omega_2}{2}\right) T}$
	ω_0 center freq.	$\alpha = \cos \omega_0 T$	$k = \Omega_c \cot\left(\dfrac{\omega_2 - \omega_1}{2}\right) T$
Bandstop	ω_1, ω_2	$k\,\dfrac{1 - z^{-2}}{z^{-2} - 2\alpha z^{\alpha-1} + 1}$	$\alpha = \dfrac{\cos\left(\dfrac{\omega_1 + \omega_2}{2}\right) T}{\cos\left(\dfrac{\omega_1 - \omega_2}{2}\right) T}$
	ω_0 center freq.	$\alpha = \cos \omega T$	$k = \Omega_c \tan\left(\dfrac{\omega_2 - \omega_1}{2}\right) T$

EXERCISES

2.1 Prove, that if s is approximated by the first backward difference,

$$s \cong \frac{\Delta}{T} \quad (\Delta = f_i - f_{i-1}),$$

then, if $H(s)$ is stable so is $H'(z)$, where

$$H'(z) = H(s) \Big|_{s = \frac{\Delta}{T}} .$$

2.2 For a discrete filter H
defined by the equation:-

$$y_{i+1} - ay_i = x_{i+1} - bx_i.$$

Find the values of b such that H is an allpass filter.

2.3 For

$$G(z) = \frac{z}{z - e^{aT}}$$

calculate:-

(i)   the amplitude response,
(ii) the phase response,
(iii) square amplitude response,
(iv) group delay response.

2.4 Analyze the forward difference transformation

$$\frac{de}{dt} \cong \frac{e_{i+1} - e_i}{T}$$

2.5 Given $H(s) = \dfrac{1}{1 + s/\omega_0}$

find $H'(z) = \dfrac{1}{1 + f(z)}$ such that $\begin{cases} \omega = 0 \;\to\; f(1) = 0 \\[2mm] \omega = \pi/T \;\to\; f(-1) = \infty \\[2mm] \omega = \omega_0 \;\to\; f(e^{j\omega T}) = j \end{cases}$

3

Discrete Design of Digital Control

3.1 INTRODUCTION

This chapter deals with the design of single-input control systems in the discrete domain. The controlled plant is represented by either a discrete model, as in the case of certain industrial processes where continuous dynamics is inappropriate, or by a discretized model, i.e., a continuous system observed, analyzed and controlled in discrete instances. The methods of discrete design of the controller assume that a continuous compensation network is not included. Discretization of an analog controller is not considered and theoretically the behavior of the closed loop system is not dependent on the initial choice of the sampling rate. This can be contrasted with discretized controllers, where an increase of the sampling interval changes the dynamics and may lead to destabilization of the closed loop system. Therefore for this reason, discrete design methods are sometimes called the exact methods. Obviously, the exactness is correct only in the linear domain and at the sampling points. Saturation of the controller in practical systems and intersample behavior not detected by z-transform analysis, will quickly destroy the exactness, if a reasonable sampling rate is not chosen.

The experienced designer may have in the back of his mind examples of previous analog controllers and these designs give him his first approximation for a discrete design.

Three different methods will be covered in this chapter:

(i) The so-called analytical method, developed in the fifties, which, by manipulating controller transfer functions attempts to reach a predetermined behavior of the closed loop.

(ii) Pole-zero configurations on the z-plane using familiar root locus techniques.
(iii) The w-plane method which transforms the design problem to a plane similar to the s-plane.

The w-plane method is the most used and many highly successful digital designs have used this approach.

As mentioned in the preface, the classical textbooks on continuous control describe in great detail graphical methods for constructing root loci, Bode plots, Nyquist plots for stability, and various plots for determining transient characteristics. All these are still valuable for obtaining a quick sketch of a preliminary design of a controller. However excellent computer programs for numerical and graphical representations of these techniques are readily available and as they are more accurate, it is not important to remember all the graphical construction rules but rather to understand the meaning of the plots.

3.2 ANALYTICAL DESIGN

Analytical design based on Truxal's method (TR-1) was developed for sampled data control systems. The method is based on the formulation of the desired behavior of the plant and gives an algebraic solution for the controller. Various constraints influence the extent of the solution.

3.2.1 Formulation of the Method

The continuous plant $G(s)$ and the reconstruction hold are transformed to the z-plane and the controlled plant system is shown in Fig. 3.1.

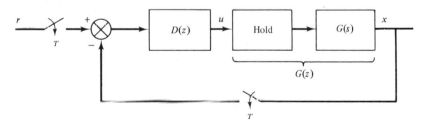

Fig. 3.1 The scheme of the controlled plant

The hold and the plant may be transformed to the z-plane, using any method of discretization, e.g., the impulse invariant method

$$G(z) = \mathbf{Z}\left\{\text{Hold} \times G(s)\right\} \tag{3.1}$$

If other methods are used, we should be cautious with the selection of the sampling rate.

We are looking for $D(z)$ so that the closed loop will behave as the desired plant $K(z)$.

Fig. 3.2 The desired plant

The designer must have the experience to translate the desired behavior to a transfer function $K(z)$.

$$\frac{x(z)}{r(z)} = \frac{D(z)G(z)}{1 + D(z)G(z)} \overset{\triangle}{=} K(z) \tag{3.2}$$

Given $K(z)$ we may solve for $D(z)$, i.e.

$$D(z) = \frac{1}{G(z)} \frac{K(z)}{1 - K(z)} \tag{3.3}$$

Equation (3.3) looks like a simple way to design, but we must be careful in choosing K.

What are the problems? There are two of them; the first one and the simple one is hidden in the discrete modelling of the desired behavior. The translation of engineering objectives such as maximum overshoot or loop stiffness to a discrete transfer function is not a simple task. It is a simple task only in class-room examples. The second, well-known in continuous controllers of non-minimum phase systems, is that it is impossible to compensate an unstable pole in the plant by a zero in the controller, and vice versa; an unstable zero in the plant cannot be compensated by an unstable pole in the controller. It is unrealistic to locate an unstable compensation pole exactly on the right place and to keep it there. The error (difference) will quickly diverge. For these reasons, the design of a controller using an algebraic solution of eqn. (3.2) is highly constrained.

The constraints on $K(z)$, the desired transfer function of the closed loop plant, are discussed below.

(i) Causality of D (physical realizability).

Let $\qquad u_i = a_0 e_i + a_1 e_{i-1} + \ldots + b_1 u_{i-1} + b_2 u_{i-2} + \ldots$

i.e. $\qquad D(z) = \dfrac{a_0 + a_1 z^{-1} + a_2 z^{-2} + \ldots}{1 - b_1 z^{-1} - b_2 z^{-2} - \ldots} = \dfrac{a_0 z^n + a_1 z^{n-1} + \ldots}{z^n - b_1 z^{n-1} - \ldots} \tag{3.4}$

$D(z)$ is realizable (in real time) if the numerator of D has a lower order or the same order of z as the denominator. Otherwise, $u_i = f(i + 1, \ldots)$ i.e., the control at time i depends on future data.

For a physical plant, $G(z)$, has a lower order of numerator than denominator. For example, let us say that $G(z)$ is a transportation lag $\sim z^{-\varrho}$, then in this case $K(z)$ must have, at least, the same lag, i.e.

$$K(z) = z^{-\varrho} K'(z) \qquad (3.5)$$

(ii)   Stability.

If $G(z)$ contains poles or zeros on, or outside the unit circle, $D(z)$ should not cancel them (the closed loop might). How do we avoid cancellation? From eqn. (3.3), repeated here for convenience,

$$D(z) = \frac{1}{G(z)} \frac{K(z)}{1 - K(z)} \qquad (3.3)$$

we can see that we have chosen

$$1 - K(z) = \left[\overset{i}{\Pi}(1 - b_i z^{-1}) \right] F_1(z) \qquad (3.6)$$

such that $1 - K(z)$ must contain as zeros all the poles of $G(z)$ located on or outside the unit circle (b_i). We have also chosen

$$K(z) = \left[\overset{i}{\Pi}(1 - a_i z^{-1}) \right] F_2(z) \qquad (3.7)$$

where $K(z)$ contains all the zeros of $G(z)$ located on or outside the unit circle (a_i).

Note:

F_1 and F_2 do not cancel the a_i's or b_i's.

Example:

Consider

$$G(z) = \frac{(z - 1.1)(z - 0.9)}{(z - 1.2)(z - 0.8)} = \frac{z - 1.1}{z - 1.2} G'(z)$$

using eqn. (3.2) we obtain

$$D(z) = \frac{z - 1.2}{(z - 1.1) G'(z)} \frac{K(z)}{1 - K(z)}$$

In specifying $K(z)$, which will satisfy the stability condition, the following relationships must be satisfied:—

$$K(z) = (1 - 1.1z^{-1}) F_2(z)$$

$$1 - K(z) = (1 - 1.2z^{-1}) F_1(z)$$

These constraints lead to

$$D(z) = \frac{F_2(z)}{G'(z) F_1(z)}$$

$G'(z)$ does not contain unstable poles or zeros.

To formulate $K(z)$ is still difficult. Some help will be given in the following section.

3.2.2   The Design Procedure for Various Requirements

In this section we consider some rules which will help us to formulate the required transfer function to achieve specific performance criteria.

(i)   Zero steady state error to a step function.

We can define the error $e(z)$ as:—

$$e(z) = r(z) - x(z)$$
$$e(z) = r(z)(1 - Kz)$$

(3.8)

Using the final value theorem gives:—

$$\lim_{t \to 0} e(t) = \lim_{z \to 1} (1 - z^{-1}) \frac{1}{(1 - z^{-1})} (1 - K(z)) \to 0$$

where $r(z) = \dfrac{1}{1 - z^{-1}}$ is the unit step function, i.e.,

$$\lim_{z \to 1} e(z) = \lim [1 - K(z)] \to 0$$

Therefore if a zero steady state error to a step input is required we design $K(z)$ so that

$$1 - K(z) = (1 - z^{-1}) F_1(z)$$

(3.9)

where $F_1(z)$ does not contain any poles at the point +1.

(ii)   Zero steady state error to generalized input function.

If a response to an input $r(z) = \dfrac{A(z)}{(1 - z^{-1})^k}$

where a zero steady-state error is desired, then

$$1 - K(z) = (1 - z^{-1})^k F_1(z) \qquad\qquad (3.10)$$

where $F_1(z)$ does not contain multiple poles of order K at the point $+1$.

(iii)   Finite-settling time response (deadbeat).

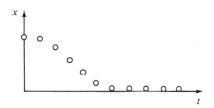

Fig. 3.3   Finite settling response

The output of $K(z)$ should be a polynomial in z^{-1}.

(iv)   Ripple-free response.

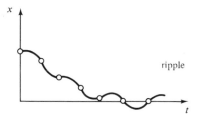 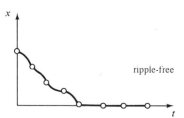

Fig. 3.4   Ripple and ripple-free response

The conditions for a ripple-free output are:—

(a) $\dfrac{u(z)}{r(z)}$ finite settling — otherwise $u(z)$ will excite the plant. Since $\dfrac{u(z)}{r(z)} = \dfrac{K(z)}{G(z)}$, finite settling conditions requires that $\dfrac{K(z)}{G(z)}$ is a polynomial in z^{-1},

i.e. $K(z)$ contains all the zeros of $G(z)$

(b)   Zero steady state error to input.

(c) $G(s)$ is not diverging so that the actual plant is stable.

Example:

Let us consider the system shown in Fig. 3.5 where $G(s) = 1/s^2$.

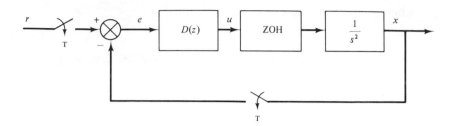

Fig. 3.5 An example for analytical design

Assume the control requirements are:

(i)   Zero steady-state error to a ramp input.
(ii) Finite settling time.

The first step is the discretization of the plant, i.e.,

$$G(z) = \mathbf{Z}\left[\frac{1 - e^{-sT}}{s}\,\frac{1}{s^2}\right]$$

hence $$G(z) = (1 - z^{-1})\,\frac{T^2 z(z + 1)}{2(z - 1)^3}$$

If we assume that $T = 1$s then,

$$G(z) = \frac{z + 1}{2(z - 1)^2} = \frac{(1 + z^{-1})z^{-1}}{2(1 - z^{-1})^2} \tag{3.11}$$

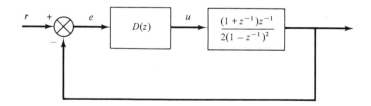

Fig. 3.6 The discretized plant

Following the design procedure discussed we have the following points to consider:

(i) For a zero steady state error to a ramp input we have to satisfy the condition of eqn. (3.10), i.e.

$$1 - K(z) = (1 - z^{-1})^2 F_1(z)$$

(ii) Stability

(a) If we consider the condition given in eqn. (3.6) we have $1 - K(z) = (1 - z^{-1})^2 F_1(z)$, so that the $G(z)$ poles located on the unit circle will not be cancelled. Incidentally, this is the same condition as (i) above.

(b) In order to avoid cancellation of the zeros of $G(z)$ located on the unit circle we must satisfy the condition

$$K(z) = (1 + z^{-1}) F_2(z)$$

(iii) Finite settling time.

This requires that $F_1(z)$ and $F_2(z)$ are finite polynomials in z^{-1}.

We are looking for K, F_1 and F_2 which will satisfy these conditions with a minimal number of terms (i.e. minimal realization).

$$\begin{aligned} F_1 &= (b_0 z^{-1} + 1) \\ F_2 &= (c_0 + c_1 z^{-1}) z^{-1} \\ K &= (a_0 + a_1 z^{-1} + a_2 z^{-2}) z^{-1} \end{aligned} \qquad (3.12)$$

The conditions are summarized in eqns. (3.13)

$$\left. \begin{aligned} 1 - a_0 - a_1 z^{-1} - a_2 z^{-2} &= (1 - z^{-1})^2 (b_0 z^{-1} + 1) \\ a_0 + a_1 z^{-1} + a_2 z^{-2} &= (1 + z^{-1})(c_0 + c_1 z^{-1}) \end{aligned} \right\} \qquad (3.13)$$

By comparing the coefficients of the various power of z^{-1} we may solve for the unknowns a, b and c:

$$\left. \begin{aligned} 1 - a_0 z^{-1} - a_2 z^{-2} - a_2 z^{-3} &= 1 + (b_0 - 2) z^{-1} + (1 - 2b_0) z^{-2} + b_0 z^{-3} \\ a_0 + a_1 z^{-1} + a_2 z^{-2} &= c_0 + (c_1 + c_0) z^{-1} + c_1 z^{-2} \end{aligned} \right\} (3.14)$$

The comparison yields

$$\begin{aligned} -a_0 &= b_0 - 2 & a_0 &= c_0 \\ -a_1 &= 1 - 2b_0 & a_1 &= c_1 + c_0 \\ a_2 &= -b_0 & a_2 &= c_1 \end{aligned}$$

Hence the solution is:

$$\begin{aligned} a_0 &= 1.25 & a_1 &= 0.5 & a_2 &= -0.75 \\ b_0 &= 0.75 & c_0 &= 1.25 & c_1 &= -0.75 \end{aligned}$$

The system $K(z)$ may therefore be expressed as

$$K(z) = 1.25z^{-1} + 0.5z^{-2} - 0.75z^{-3} \tag{3.15}$$

The controller is therefore given by

$$D(z) = \frac{1}{G(z)} \frac{K(z)}{1 - K(z)}$$

$$D(z) = \frac{2(1 - z^{-1})^2}{(1 + z^{-1})z^{-1}} \frac{(1 + z^{-1})(1.25 - 0.75z^{-1})z^{-1}}{(1 - z^{-1})^2(0.75z^{-1} + 1)} \tag{3.16}$$

Simplification of eqn. (3.16) gives

$$\frac{u(z)}{e(z)} = D(z) = 2 \frac{1.25 - 0.75z^{-1}}{0.75z^{-1} + 1} \tag{3.17}$$

Thus the control algorithm is:

$$u_i = -0.75u_{i-1} + 2.5e_i - 1.5e_{i-1} \tag{3.18}$$

The controlled system is depicted in Fig. 3.7.

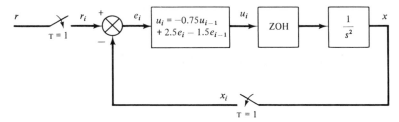

Fig. 3.7 The controlled system

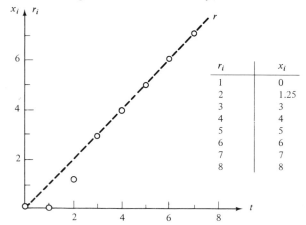

r_i	x_i
1	0
2	1.25
3	3
4	4
5	5
6	6
7	7
8	8

Fig. 3.8 The response to a ramp of the controlled system

The discrete behavior for zero initial conditions and a unit ramp input r_i is given in Fig. 3.8.

3.3 DESIGN ON THE z-PLANE

Design of compensation networks, using the root locus technique, is a well established procedure in continuous control systems. This is essentially a trial and error method using different compensation filters whereby varying the feedback gain the roots of the closed loop plant are relocated to favorable positions.

3.3.1 The Root Locus on the z-plane

For a given system, the model of the plant $G(s)$, including the reconstruction hold, is transformed to the z-plane. The closed loop system is depicted in Fig. 3.9.

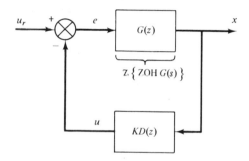

Fig. 3.9 Formulation of the closed loop plant for a root locus analysis

The transfer function relating the input u_r to the output x is given in eqn. (3.19).

$$\frac{x(z)}{u_r(z)} = \frac{G(z)}{1 + KD(z)\,G(z)} \tag{3.19}$$

The 'classical' root locus method helps to trace graphically the roots of the characteristic polynomial $1 + KD(z)G(z) = 0$. Obviously the roots are the poles of the closed loop system.

Despite the fact that computer programs for polynomial factorization are readily available, the skill of an experienced designer to sketch quickly the roots loci for various compensations as a function of gain, is highly valuable and saves time. The roots of the characteristic equation represent the natural modes of the closed loop system, however, the transient behavior and the frequency response are strongly influenced by the location of the zeros.

For these reasons the usual practice is to apply the root locus approach to a preliminary design, i.e. to stabilize the system and to relocate the dominant poles at a desired position. Improvement of the closed loop performance to achieve desired specifications is obtained using a digital simulation.

3.3.2 Description of the Method

The root locus for a discrete system can be generated in the same way as for a continuous system, in both cases it is a graphical procedure for solving an nth-order polynomial. Of course in the discrete domain the root locus must be interpreted relative to the unit circle. Since the root locus method is presented in most classical automatic control textbooks only a summary will be given here.

For simplification, the method will be demonstrated for a unity feedback system with a forward loop gain K. The characteristic equation for such a system has the form

$$1 + KG(z) = 0 \qquad (3.20)$$

Let $K > 0$ and $G(z) = M(z)/N(z)$ where $N(z)$ is polynomial in z with degree n greater or equal to the degree m of polynomial $M(z)$. Eqn. (3.20) can be written in the form

$$N(z) + KM(z) = 0 \qquad (3.21)$$

The locus of the solution of the characteristic equation, as K varies from 0 to ∞, is called the root locus of the system. The number of branches of the root locus is equal to the order of the polynomial $N(z)$.

For $K = 0$ the roots are obviously identical to the poles of the open loop system.

For $K \neq 0$, and using eqn. (3.20), any point on the root locus must satisfy the equations

$$G(z) = -\frac{1}{K} \qquad \measuredangle G(z) = -\pi - 2\pi k \qquad (k = 0, 1, 2, \ldots) \quad (3.22)$$

As K is increased from zero to infinity, the branches of the root locus converge to the zeros of $G(z)$ and the remaining $n\text{-}m$ branches go out to infinity.

There are three basic rules, which greatly help the designer to sketch the root locus as a function of K. These are:

(i) The roots on the locus move from the open loop poles to the open loop zeros as K is increased.

(ii) Excess branches go to infinity. These branches converge asymptotically to straight lines which are symmetrically distributed around the real axis on the complex plane. The asymptotes subtend angles θ to the real axis where θ is given by:

$$\theta = \frac{\pi}{n-m} + \frac{2\pi}{n-m} k \tag{3.23}$$

(iii) The starting point of the asymptotes is the 'center of gravity' (c.g.) of the real part of the open loop poles and open loop zeros, i.e.

$$\begin{array}{c} \text{center of} \\ \text{gravity} \end{array} = \frac{\sum\limits_{n} \text{Real (Poles)} - \sum\limits_{m} \text{Real (Zeros)}}{n-m} \tag{3.24}$$

Example:

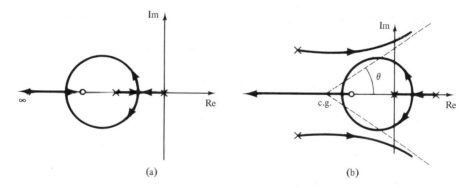

$$(a) \qquad\qquad\qquad\qquad (b)$$

Fig. 3.10 Example showing the basic rules used for a quick tracing of a root locus

3.3.3 The Root Locus for the Non-unity Feedback Case

Continuous systems often use as the control element some combination of PID, i.e. *P*roportional *I*ntegral and *D*erivative control. By changing gains and parameters, the closed loop roots are relocated to favorable positions. We will use the same approach.

The discrete PID control will be:

Proportional control

$$u_i = Ke_i \tag{3.25}$$

which has a transfer function

$$D(z) = K \tag{3.26}$$

Integral control

$$u_i = u_{i-1} + Ke_i \tag{3.27}$$

which has a transfer function

$$D(z) = \frac{K}{1 - z^{-1}} \tag{3.28}$$

Derivative control

$$u_i = K(e_i - e_{i-1}) \tag{3.29}$$

which has a transfer function

$$D(z) = K(1 - z^{-1}) \tag{3.30}$$

A combination of these generates various compensation networks, such as Lead, Lag, Lag-Lead and others.

There are two basic ways to include the controller in the closed loop. These are:
(i)   In the feedback loop as shown in Fig. 3.9
(ii)   In cascade with the plant $G(z)$.
The corresponding closed loop transfer functions are:

case (i) $\dfrac{x(z)}{u_r(z)} = \dfrac{G(z)}{1 + KD(z)G(z)}$ (3.19 repeated)

case (ii) $\dfrac{x(z)}{r(z)} = \dfrac{KD(z)G(z)}{1 + KD(z)G(z)}$ (3.31)

In both cases the closed loop poles are determined by $KD(z)G(z)$ only and not by the location of the controller. However the closed loop zeros and accordingly the closed loop transient and the frequency responses are influenced by the $KD(z)$ position in the control loop.

Furthermore, a combination of a cascade controller and multiloop feedback are possible, the particular choice of a control configuration depends on the designer's preference.

3.3.4 Example

The root locus design method will be demonstrated by the same example as was considered in Sec. 3.2., see Fig. 3.5.

The discretized plant, including the ZOH is given by

$$G(z) = \frac{\frac{T^2}{2}(1 + z^{-1})z^{-1}}{(1 - z^{-1})^2}$$

(3.32)

We shall let $T = 1s$ and we will use the z-formulation

$$G(z) = \frac{\frac{1}{2}(z + 1)}{(z - 1)^2}$$

(3.33)

The design procedure is as follows.

(i) First trial: $D(z) = K$

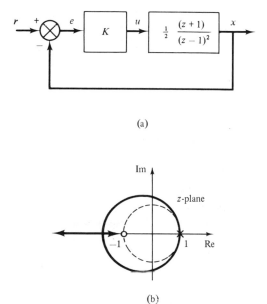

(a)

(b)

Fig. 3.11   First trial where $D(z) = K$.
(a) the plant, (b) the root locus

Result. The system is always unstable as shown by Fig. 3.11(b).

(ii) Second trial: Let $D(z) = K_1 + K_2(1 - z^{-1})$, i.e. proportional and derivative control.

Hence $D(z) = \dfrac{K(z - a)}{z}$ (3.34)

There are two parameters to be considered, the gain K and location of the zero at a.

A zero located at $0 < a < 1$ will 'attract' the locus inside the unit circle. The gain K will be chosen so that the closed loop poles will be located at favorable positions.

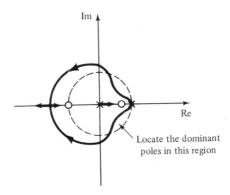

Fig. 3.12 The root locus of the stabilized plant

For the design of a system which consists of a pair of dominant complex poles the template 1 mentioned in Chapter 1 is useful. The root locus on the template yields immediately the parameters for the dynamic behavior of the system.

For more complicated cases a computer program is needed to solve the roots of the polynomial. Such programs are available in most software packages designed for control applications.

3.4   DESIGN ON THE w-PLANE AND THE w'-PLANE

Skilled control engineers acquire a great amount of experience by using frequency response methods. The w-plane method for the discrete design uses the same techniques of continuous design methods on the s-plane and in the frequency domain.

3.4.1   The w-Plane

Definition. The w-transformation is a bilinear transformation defined by eqn. (1.57) and repeated here for convenience.

$$z = \frac{1 + w}{1 - w} \qquad w = \frac{z - 1}{z + 1} \qquad \text{(1.57 repeated)}$$

The w-transformation transforms the unit circle back to the left hand side of the complex plane.

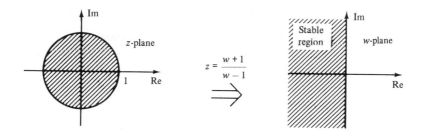

Fig. 1.19 (repeated)   The w-transformation

The bilinear transformation is a one-to-one map, but it distorts the frequency response. The distortion (frequency warping) is described in Chapter 2. It will be repeated here for the w-transformation

$$\left. w \right|_{w = j\nu} = \left. \frac{z - 1}{z + 1} \right|_{z = e^{j\omega T}} = j \tan\left(\frac{\omega T}{2}\right) \\ \nu = \tan\frac{\omega T}{2} \quad \Bigg\} \qquad (3.35)$$

Note:
The frequency response of $G(z)$ is $G(j\omega)$ and the frequency response of $G(w)$ is $G(j\nu)$. The design will be done on the w-plane using the Bode plot and the root locus. Proper matching between the fictitious frequency ν and the desired frequency ω should be implemented.

The *w*-plane design procedure consists of five steps which are described below.

Step 1: Given the continuous plant $G(s)$ and the hold, transform the model to the *z*-plane.

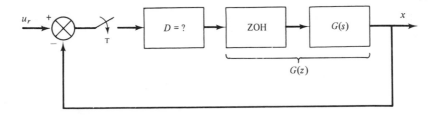

Fig. 3.13   First step in the *w*-plane design, obtain $G(z)$

Step 2:   Transform $G(z)$ to the *w*-plane,

$$\text{i.e. } G(w) = G(z)\Big|_{z = \frac{1+w}{1-w}} \tag{3.36}$$

Then select *T*.

Step 3:   Design $D(w)$ on the Bode plot or by using the root locus method on the *w*-plane. If the frequency response design method (Bode) is used, trace simultaneously the root locus (on the *w*-plane). There may be some ambiguity with the phase on the Bode plot for non-minimum phase systems, therefore it is recommended to make sure that the phase compensation is not mistakenly in the wrong direction.
     Remember that the frequency axis is distorted, i.e. if a bandwidth, ω_c, is required, you have to design for

$$\nu_c = \tan \frac{\omega_c T}{2} \tag{3.35 repeated}$$

Step 4:   Transform back to the *z*-plane

$$D(z) = D(w)\Big|_{w = \frac{z-1}{z+1}} \tag{3.37}$$

It is advisable to trace the root locus on the *z*-plane and check if the dominant complex poles are satisfactory.

Step 5:   Transform $D(z)$ to a computational algorithm.

To transform $G(s)$ to $G(z)$, an extensive table of s- to z-transforms is required. For complicated transfer functions a partial fraction factorization is inevitable. Fortunately, computer programs which perform this task are available.

   To transform $G(z)$ into $G(w)$ algebra is required, to help with this manipulation a ready-to-use formula was developed,

$$G(z) = \frac{\displaystyle\prod_{j=1}^{m} (z + a_j)}{(z - 1)^k \displaystyle\prod_{l=1}^{n} (z + b_l)} \tag{3.38}$$

by substituting

$$z = \frac{1 + w}{1 - w} \quad \text{we obtain}$$

$$G(w) = \frac{\displaystyle\prod_{j=1}^{m} (1 + a_j)(1 - w)^{k-m+n} \prod_{j=1}^{m}\left(1 + \frac{w}{(1 + a_j)/(1 - a_j)}\right)}{\displaystyle\prod_{l=1}^{n} (1 + b_l)(2w)^k \prod_{l=1}^{n}\left(1 + \frac{w}{(1 + b_l)/(1 - b_l)}\right)} \tag{3.39}$$

For a backward transformation $w \rightarrow z$, a similar formula may be used with appropriate changes of signs, constants and subscripts. Again, computer programs are available.

3.4.2   The w'-transformation

The w-transformation is a well established design method. A slight, but highly practical modification of the w-transformation, was proposed by Whitbeck and Hofmann (WH-1).

   The w'-transformation is a bilinear transformation scaled with the factor $T/2$.

$$w' = \frac{2}{T} w \tag{3.40}$$

i.e.

$$w' = \frac{2}{T} \frac{z - 1}{z + 1}$$

and hence,

$$z = \frac{1 + T/2 \, w'}{1 - T/2 \, w'}$$

Consequently the relationship given in eqn. (3.35) between ω and the fictitious frequency v' is

$$v' = \frac{2}{T} \, \tan \frac{\omega T}{2} \tag{3.41}$$

It is immediately evident that for high sampling rates and low frequencies $v' \sim \omega$. The major benefit is that the w'-plane has not only a geometrical resemblance to the s-plane, but the actual quantities (numbers) are also similar. This useful property helps to reduce the numerical errors through the design process and increases insight into the system.

Example:

$$G(s) = \frac{5}{s + 5}$$

The incoming sampled signal will be reconstructed using a ZOH.

$$G(z) = \mathbf{Z}\left\{ \frac{1 - e^{-sT}}{s} \cdot \frac{5}{s + 5} \right\} \qquad T = 0.1\text{s}$$

$$G(z) = \frac{1 - e^{-0.5}}{z - e^{-0.5}} = \frac{0.3935}{z - 0.6065}$$

$$G(w) = \frac{0.2449(1 - w)}{w + 0.2449}$$

$$G(w') = \frac{4.899(1 - 0.05w')}{w' + 4.899}$$

For $T \to 0$ the location of the additional zero in the w' plane moves to infinity and

$$G(w') \underset{T \to 0}{\longrightarrow} G(s)$$

3.5 COMPENSATION DESIGN USING FREQUENCY RESPONSE ON THE w-PLANE

The design of analog compensation networks using the frequency response properties of the plant and of the compensation network is well-established and extensively documented in numerous books. Elaborate graphical methods have been developed and since a generation of designers are used to them, the methods are still widely used in practical design. Computer programs help the designer to calculate and to trace the various plots such as Bode, Nichols, Nyquist and others. The basic frequency related plots will be overviewed. We will use the nomenclature of the w-plane and of the fictitious frequency ν.

3.5.1 The Bode Plot

The Bode plot consists of two separate plots, the $\log_{10}$ of magnitude of $G(w)$ i.e. $|G(j\nu)|$ versus $\log \nu$ and the phase angle ϕ of $G(j\nu)$ vs. $\log \nu$.

The magnitude $|G(j\nu)|$ is usually expressed in decibels (dB), i.e., $20 \log_{10} |G(j\nu)|$. This unit says that, as the magnitude increases by a factor of 10, the decibel value increases by 20, and if $|G_1|$ is 100 times larger than $|G_0|$, its decibel value is 40 dB larger.

The decibel is a widely used unit but some recent articles express the increase of magnitude in a direct manner, i.e. if $|G_1/G_0| = 1$ the ratio is 1 and not 0 dB, similarly if $|G_1/G_0| = \frac{1}{2}$ the ratio is $\frac{1}{2}$ and not -6 dB.

On the Bode plot the frequency is also expressed using a logarithmic scale. Two units are used to express the increase of frequency, an octave, which is a frequency band from ν_1 to ν_2 where $\nu_2/\nu_1 = 2$, and a decade, which is a frequency band from ν_3 to ν_4 where $\nu_4/\nu_3 = 10$. These units are illustrated in the diagram of Fig. 3.14.

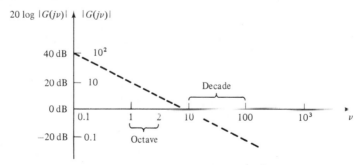

Fig. 3.14   The log plot of $|G|$ vs. ν

On this plot (Fig. 3.14), the slope of the straight line is -20 dB per decade or -6 dB per octave or simply -1.

The technique used to sketch the log magnitude plot is based on the factorization of $G(jv)$, so that we may use addition of various terms in $\log |G(jv)|$ instead of multiplication of terms in $|G(jv)|$ and on approximation by straight lines (asymptotes) of the various factors.

The general expression for $G(jv)$, the fictitious frequency transfer function is

$$G(jv) = \frac{K(1 + jvT_a) \ldots}{(jv)(1 + jvT_b)[1 + (2\,\xi/v_n)^{jv} + (1/jv_n^2)(jv)^2] \ldots} \tag{3.42}$$

Taking the logarithm of both sides of eqn. (3.42) we obtain

$$\log G(jv) = \log K + \log(1 + jvT_a) - \log jv \ldots \tag{3.43}$$

The plots of the individual factors are as follows:

(i)   Factor K (gain)

In dB form this is $20 \log_{10} K$ which is a straight line with a phase angle of zero degrees.

(ii) Factor $\dfrac{1}{jv}$

$$\log\left|\frac{1}{jv}\right| = -20 \log v \tag{3.44}$$

This is a straight line with a negative slope of -1 (20 dB per decade). The phase angle is constant at $-90°$.

(iii) Factor $\dfrac{1}{1 + jvT_b}$ and $1 + jvT_a$

$$\log\left|\frac{1}{1 + jvT_b}\right| = -20 \log\sqrt{1 + v^2 T_b^2}\ \ \text{dB} \tag{3.45}$$

$$\log|1 + jvT_a| = 20 \log\sqrt{1 + v^2 T_a^2}\ \ \text{dB} \tag{3.46}$$

These factors may be approximated by two straight lines (asymptotes).

For $vT \ll 1$;   0 dB line

and

for $vT \gg 1$ a line with slope of 20 dB per decade.

The slope is positive for a zero and negative for a pole. The frequency at which the asymptotes intersect is defined as the corner frequency, $v_c = 1/T$.

The phase angle goes from zero to $\pm 90°$ (positive for zero) with $\pm 45°$ at the corner frequency v_c.

Note:

v is a nondimensional fictitious frequency, therefore T_a, T_b or T are non-dimensional time constants.

(iv) The quadratic factor

$$\left[1 + \frac{2\zeta}{\nu_n} j\nu + \frac{1}{\nu_n^2} (j\nu)^2 \right]^{-1} \tag{3.47}$$

This element is complex for $\nu/\nu_n \ll 1$ the asymptote is 0 dB and for $\nu/\nu_n \gg 1$ the slope is -40 dB per decade. The behavior near to the corner frequency $\nu = \nu_n$, depends on the damping coefficient ζ for low values of ζ there is a resonance peak. For $\zeta < 0.707$ the behavior of the log magnitude plot is similar to a double time constant.

The phase angle varies from $0°$ to $-90°$ at the corner frequency and to $-180°$ at infinite frequency.

As an example of a Bode plot let us consider the lead network $G(j\nu)$, where

$$G(j\nu) = \frac{\alpha(1 + j\nu T)}{(1 + j\nu T\alpha)}$$

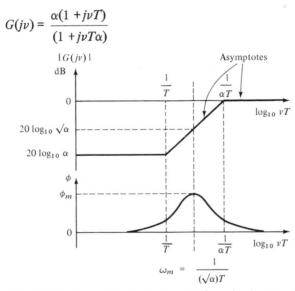

Fig. 3.15 Example of a Bode plot for a lead network.

Note:

There is a basic difference between the Bode plot of a continuous system and the Bode plot of the same system sampled and transformed from the s-plane to the z-plane to the w-plane. The w-plane transfer function has usually the same number of poles as zeros. This property is closely related to the sampling theorem and to repetition of the frequency spectra every sampling bandwidth $\omega_s/2$.

Consequently, the Bode plot of the magnitude as a function of the fictitious frequency ν, asymptotically converges to a constant, even if the magnitude of the frequency response of the continuous system diminishes to zero for $\omega \to \infty$.

Example:

$$G(s) = \frac{1}{s^2}$$

$$G(z) = \frac{Tz}{(z-1)^2}$$

$$G(w) = \frac{T(1+w)(1-w)}{4w^2}$$

The frequency response on the *s*-plane is obtained from

$$G(j\omega) = \frac{1}{(j\omega)^2}$$

i.e. $$|G(j\omega)| = 0$$
$$\omega \to \infty$$

The frequency response on the *w*-plane is obtained from

$$G(jv) = \frac{T(1+jv)(1-jv)}{4(jv)^2}$$

i.e. $$|G(jv)| = -\frac{T}{4}$$
$$v \to \infty$$

The inconsistency in the Bode plots on the *s*-plane and the *w*-plane is insignificant. The actual design is relevant only to the bandwidth $0 \leqslant \omega \leqslant \omega_s/2$. In this region the Bode plots are very similar.

3.5.2   The Polar Plot

The polar plot consists of plotting the magnitude vs. the phase shift of the function as polar coordinates for values of *v* as *v* varies from zero to infinity.

The open-loop frequency function is usually plotted after finding the magnitude and phase angle from the Bode plot. As an example let us consider the lead network of the previous section (Fig. 3.16).

The polar plot is often used in connection with the Nyquist stability criterion therefore it is often called the Nyquist plot. The ability to sketch the polar plot is an asset because it is very useful to be able to determine whether a

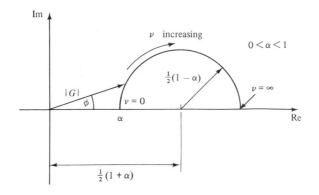

Fig. 3.16 Polar plot of a lead network $G(j\nu) = \alpha \dfrac{(1 + j\nu T)}{(1 + j\nu T\alpha)}$

closed loop system is stable using only the open loop frequency function. For the closed loop system (D in cascade with G),

$$\frac{x(w)}{u_r(w)} = \frac{D(w)\, G(w)}{1 + D(w)\, G(w)} \qquad \text{(eqn. (3.31) repeated)}$$

The Nyquist stability criterion relates the open-loop frequency response $D(j\nu)$ $G(j\nu)$ to the number of zeros and poles of the characteristic equation $F(w) = 1 + D(w)G(w)$ that lie in the right half w-plane. Rigorous treatment of the criterion is given in numerous books, only an outline will be given in this book.

The Nyquist stability criterion states:

The characteristic function $F(w)$ does not contain any roots (zeros) on the right half of the w-plane if the polar plot of $F(w)$ encircles the origin in the following pattern: the net number of rotations of $F(w)$ about the origin must be counterclockwise and equal to the number of unstable poles of $F(w)$. The poles of $F(w)$ are known; they are the poles of $D(w)\, G(w)$. The net number of rotations of $F(w)$ is the number of counterclockwise rotations less the clockwise rotations of $F(w)$ (around the origin).

Let us consider tracing the polar plot of $1 + D(w)\, G(w)$ using the polar plot of $D(w)\, G(w)$. The polar plot of the characteristic equation $1 + D(w)\, G(w)$ is the vector sum of the unit vector $-1 + 0j$ and the vector $D(j\nu)\, G(j\nu)$. This is shown in Fig. 3.17.

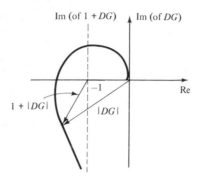

Fig. 3.17   Polar Plots of $D(jv)\, G(jv)$ and $1 + D(jv)\, G(jv)$

As seen from Fig. 3.17 the polar plot of $1 + D(jv)\, G(jv)$ and the polar plot of $D(jv)\, G(jv)$ are both contained on the same diagram. The Nyquist criterion of root location of $1 + DG$ may be applied by using the polar plot of DG and by replacing the encirclement rule around the origin by an encirclement rule around the point $-1 + 0j$.

There are various limitations to the criteria. If the plot crosses the point $-1 + 0j$, there are poles or zeros on the jv-axis and the criteria is invalid. The reader is advised to look for the proof and for a detailed description in various text books (e.g. DA − 1).

Using the polar plot, the frequency response of a stable closed-loop system can be easily obtained from that of the open-loop system.

The closed loop frequency response will be defined as

$$Me^{j\alpha} = \frac{x(jv)}{u_r(jv)} = \frac{D(jv)\, G(jv)}{1 + D(jv)\, G(jv)} \tag{3.48}$$

The loci of a constant magnitude M are circles and when plotted on the polar plot are called M-circles. Similarly, loci which represent a constant phase angle of the closed loop are also circles, called N-circles. Various non-dimensional charts with M and N circles are available. In dealing with design problems, it is convenient to construct the constant M circles and the constant N circles on a gain-phase plane.

3.5.3   The Gain-phase Plot and the Nichols Chart

The gain-phase plot displays the magnitude vs. the phase angle with v as a parameter varying from 0 to ∞. The abscissa is the phase angle. Like the polar plot, the gain-phase plot is usually derived from the Bode plot (see Fig. 3.18).

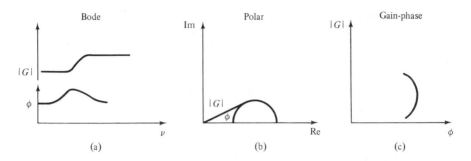

Fig. 3.18 The Bode plot (a) the polar plot (b), and the gain-phase plot (c) of $G = \dfrac{\alpha(1 + jvT)}{(1 + jvT\alpha)}$

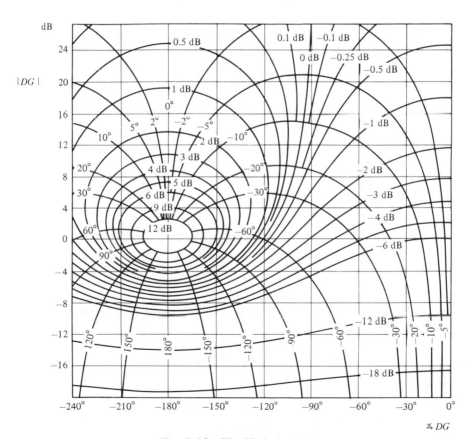

Fig. 3.19 The Nichols chart

The Nichols chart is a chart containing the constant M and N loci on the gain-phase plane. Recall, M is the log magnitude of the closed loop frequency response and N is the loci of the constant phase angle of the closed loop frequency response.

The M and N contours are not circles as on the polar plot, but appear somewhat 'squashed'. The Nichols charts with M and N loci are commercially available. The Nichols chart is illustrated in Fig. 3.19.

3.5.4   Compensation Design Using the Various Frequency Response Plots

(i)   Determine the gain of the open loop. Assume that the (yet undesigned) compensation gain is unity and use the final value theorem to satisfy the requirement of the error coefficients.

(ii)   Using the Bode diagram, determine the relative stability, i.e. the phase and gain margins of the uncompensated system.

(iii)   If the specifications of the phase and gain margins are not satisfied, choose a compensation network. Shift to the desired crossover frequency. Do not forget to use the relationship between ω and the fictitious frequency ν.

(iv)   Using the Nichols diagram, check the behavior of the closed loop system.

3.6   EXAMPLE OF w- AND w'-PLANE DESIGN METHOD*

An angular position servo is described in Fig. 3.20.

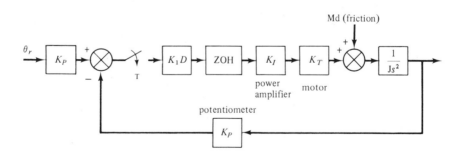

Fig. 3.20   An angular position servo

The physical properties of the system are

$$K_p = 1.9 \text{ (V/rad)} \qquad K_I = 1 \text{ (A/V)}$$
$$K_T = 0.385 \text{ Nm/A} \qquad J = 3.22 \times 10^{-3} \text{ Nm.sec}^2$$

*Design by A. Ben–Zwi

Design requirements

(i) $\Delta\theta_{max}$ = 10 mrad for M_d = 0.028 Nm
(ii) Maximum closed loop phase at 3 Hz should be φ_{max} = 13°
(iii) M_p = 5 dB

Method:

Step 1: $G_1(z) = (1 - z^{-1})\mathbf{Z}\left[K_I K_T \dfrac{1}{Js^3}\right]$

$$G_1(z) = K_2 T^2 \frac{z+1}{(z-1)^2}$$

$$K_2 = \frac{K_I K_T}{2J} = 59.8$$

Step 2: $G_1(w) = G_1(z)\Big|_{z=\frac{1+w}{1-w}} = \dfrac{K_2 T'^2}{2} \cdot \dfrac{1-w}{w^2}$

Step 3: Design on the w-plane and w'-plane.

(a) Calculation of the DC gain K_1. The DC gain depends on the balance between the static friction M_d and the required $\Delta\theta_{max}$. Using the final value theorem we obtain

$$M_d = 2w\left[\frac{\Delta\theta\,(1+w)}{2w}\ K_p K_1 D(w) K_I K_T\right]_{\lim w\to 0}$$

$$K_1 = \frac{M_d}{\Delta\theta_{max} K_p K_I K_T} = 3.83$$

$$G_1(w) = 0.003\,\frac{1-w}{w^2}\quad(T=0.01\mathrm{s})$$

(b) Calculation of the compensation network $D(w)$. The open loop transfer function is

$$G(w) = K_p K_1 G_1(w)$$

$$G(w) = 0.022\,\frac{1-w}{w^2}$$

and this is plotted on the Bode plot

$$G(jv) = 0.022\,\frac{1-jv}{(jv)^2}$$

All plots are traced on w-plane and w'-plane.

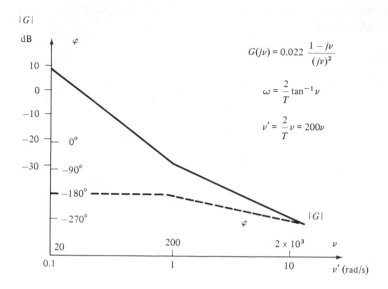

$$G(jv) = 0.022 \, \frac{1 - jv}{(jv)^2}$$

$$\omega = \frac{2}{T} \tan^{-1} v$$

$$v' = \frac{2}{T} v = 200v$$

Fig. 3.21   The Bode plot of the plant

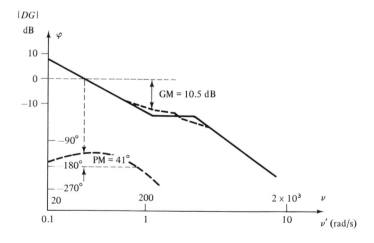

GM = 10.5 dB

PM = 41°

Fig. 3.22   The Bode plot of the compensated system

Using analog design techniques, the final compensation network is:

$$K_1 D(w) = 3.83 \; \frac{\left(\dfrac{w}{0.1} + 1 \right)}{\left(\dfrac{w}{2.15} + 1 \right)^2}$$

The root locus plot on the *w*-plane is shown in Fig. 3. 23.

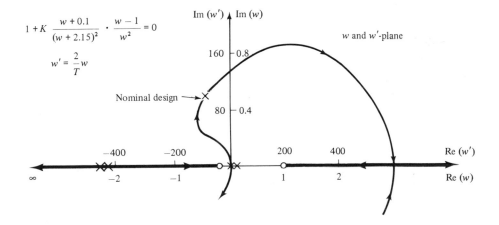

Fig. 3.23 The root locus on the *w*-plane

The frequency response of the compensated system (open loop) is traced on the Nichols diagram.

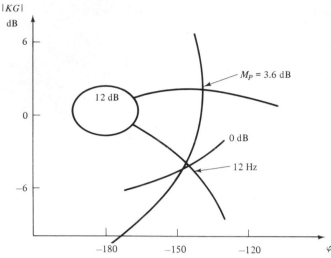

Fig. 3.24 The Nichols diagram

As can be seen from the Nichols diagram the designed controller satisfies the design requirements:

(1) $M_P < 3.6$ dB
(2) $\varphi_{max} \simeq 13°$ for $\omega = 3$ Hz

Step 4: $\quad D(z) = K_1 D(w) \Big|_{w = \frac{z-1}{z+1}}$

$$D(z) = 19.63 \, \frac{(z+1)(z-0.82)}{(z+0.365)^2}$$

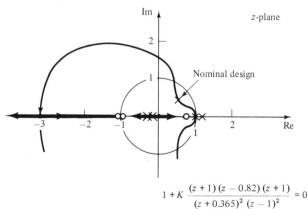

$$1 + K \, \frac{(z+1)(z-0.82)(z+1)}{(z+0.365)^2(z-1)^2} = 0$$

Fig. 3.25 The root locus on the z-plane

Step 5: The computational algorithm is:

$$\frac{u(z)}{e(z)} = D(z) = 19.63 \ \frac{(z + 1)(z - 0.82)}{(z + 0.365)^2}$$

As will be extensively described in Chapter 5, there are various methods for converting the transfer function $D(z)$ to a numerical algorithm. The easiest way (but not the recommended one) is the direct method. Using the direct method for the transfer function we obtain

$$\frac{u(z)}{e(z)} = 19.63 \ \frac{z^2 - 0.82z + z - 0.82}{z^2 + 2 \times 0.365z + (0.365)^2}$$

which is formulated as a computational algorithm as

$$u_i = 19.63 \ (e_i + 0.18e_{i-1} - 0.82e_{i-2}) - 0.73u_{i-1} - 0.13u_{i-2}$$

In order to achieve maximum numerical accuracy for a given computer word length, another method should be chosen. See Chapters 5 and 6.

EXERCISES

3.1 Obtain a suitable compensator D that will stabilize the plant shown.

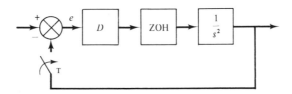

Check the influence of the sampling interval T.

3.2 Design a digital controller for a plant which has values of $H(s)$, ω_n and ζ as given.

$$H(s) = \frac{1}{s(s + 2)} \qquad \begin{aligned} \omega_n &= 5 \text{ rad/s} \\ \zeta &\geqslant 0.7 \end{aligned}$$

(a) Using the continuous time domain and the bilinear transformation where $T = 100$ ms.
(b) Using design on the z-plane (root locus) where $T = 100$ ms.

3.3   A proportional process controller with a measurement error (diameter of a round part) is given in the diagram below where:

μ_i – the measured diameter

m_i – the actual diameter

D – the desired diameter

μ_i $= m_i + \epsilon_i$ ϵ_i – measurement error

ρ_i $= \Delta D - u_i$

a_i – adjustment

u_i $= K\rho_i$

P_i $\triangleq$ perturbation (wear).

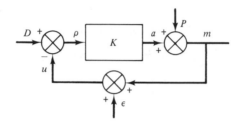

(i)   Find the difference equations of the system.

(ii)   Choose K for a stable region of operation.

(iii)   Solve $m_i = f(K, P_i, \epsilon_i)$

(iv)   If $P \perp \epsilon$ and $E\{\epsilon_i\} = \epsilon$ $V(\epsilon_i) = \sigma_\epsilon^2$ prove that $E\{m_i\} = \epsilon[1 - (1 - k)^2]$.

$$V(m_i) = \frac{K\sigma_\epsilon^2}{2 - K} [1 - (1 - K)^{2i}]$$

(v)   What are the steady state values of $E\{m_i\}$ and $V(m_i)$?

3.4   For the system shown,

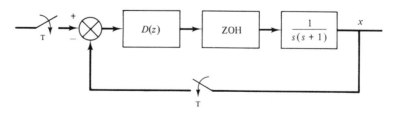

design $D(z)$ such that x will respond to a step input in a minimum settling time with a zero steady-state error response.

3.5   Use the w-plane approach to stabilize a system with

$$G(s) = \frac{K_1}{s(1+s)(1+0.25)}$$

for a required M_P of 1.26.

Design a lead compensator such that the bandwidth will be $\omega = 1.5$ rad/s.

3.6   Let $D(z)$ be the transformation of $D_2(w)$, i.e.,

$$D_1(z) = D_2(w)\Big|_{w = \frac{z-1}{z+1}}$$

Show that $D_1(z)$ has the same number of poles as zeros except for the case when $D_2(w)$ has poles or zeros at $w = 1$.

3.7   Let $D_2(w)$ be the transformation of $D_1(z)$,

i.e. $$D_2(w) = D_1(z)\Big|_{z = \frac{1+w}{1-w}}$$

Show that $D_2(w)$ has the same number of poles as zeros except for the case when $D_1(z)$ has poles or zeros at $z = -1$.

3.8 n — is the number of poles of $D_1(z)$
m — is the number of zeros of $D_1(z)$
Show that if $n > m$ then $D_2(w)$ has $n - m$ positive zeros.

4

Multivariable Digital Control, State Space Approach

4.1 INTRODUCTION

The main advantage of the state space approach to control is its ability to handle multi-input/multi-output systems. However it is more difficult to fulfill the traditional criteria of performance such as the maximum overshoot, and the phase margin.

Design using state space methods does not have the established criteria of performance as the classical approach. The various cost functions and quadratic criteria do not adequately represent the desired behavior of realistic controlled plants. However, the increasing use of computers in control systems is influencing the design philosophy adopted by practising engineers and state space techniques are receiving more attention.

The state space representation is traditionally linked to optimal control and to an optimal estimation of the states. These are three different aspects, with different advantages, which should be treated accordingly. The enthusiasm for optimal linear control theory reached its zenith during the last decade but practical industrial applications remain few in number. On the other hand, smoothing, filtering or prediction of data based optimal estimators such as Kalman-Bucy algorithm are well used but not in real time controllers. The optimal estimators are more often used for measurements, navigation and data collection of physical observations. The availability of a low-cost microcontroller, together with the extensive education of engineers in optimal control, may increase the practical implementation of optimal linear controllers based on quadratic criteria.

This book deals with linear systems only, but it should be stressed that non-linear optimal control techniques have been successfully applied for a long time.
In this chapter the following methods will be described:

(i) Closed loop poles placement based on state variable feedback. For the case when all states cannot be measured an observer is incorporated in the control loop.

(ii) Controllers and observers design based on the minimization of a quadratic cost function. Optimal filters and optimal regulators in steady state applications and model following methods for improving the transient behavior.

4.2 STATE SPACE APPROACH; POLE PLACEMENT, OBSERVER DESIGN

4.2.1 Pole Placement

In Sec. 1.3 a state space representation of a linear non-time varying system was formulated. It is here repeated for a discretized system

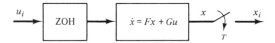

Fig. 4.1   The discrete state space formulation

$$x_{i+1} = \Phi(T) x_i + \Gamma(T) u_i \qquad (4.1)$$

where

$$\Phi(T) = I + FT + \frac{FT^2}{2!} + \ldots$$

$$\Gamma(T) = \int_0^I \Phi(\tau) G d\tau$$

We will also repeat the z-transform of the state space representation, i.e.

$$x(z) = [I - \Phi z^{-1}]^{-1} \Gamma z^{-1} u(z) + IC \qquad (4.2)$$

How do we control the system? If all the states are measured a state variable feedback may be applied.

$$u = Cx \qquad (4.3)$$

We obtain the closed loop system depicted in Fig. 4.2.

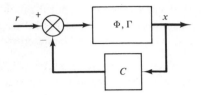

Fig. 4.2 The state space representation of a system with a state variable feedback

$$x_{i+1} = \Phi x_i + \Gamma(u_i + r_i) \left. \right\}$$
$$u_i \;\;= C x_i$$

$$(4.4)$$

The closed loop system is represented by a combination of eqns. (4.4)

$$x_{i+1} = [\Phi + \Gamma C] x_i + \Gamma r_i \tag{4.5}$$

The z-transform of eqn. (4.5) is:

$$x(z) = [\Phi + \Gamma C - zI]^{-1} [zx(0) + r(z)] \tag{4.6}$$

From matrix theory * the characteristic function of the closed loop system is

$$|\Phi + \Gamma C - zI| = 0 \tag{4.7}$$

By a proper selection of C we may relocate the poles of the controlled system to a more favorable position. Or, if the desired poles are given, we may solve eqn. (4.7) for C.

Example

Control of a second order plant shown in Fig. 4.3 must meet the requirements stated.

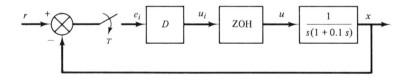

Fig. 4.3 A block diagram of the system

$*M^{-1} = \dfrac{C_M}{|M|}$ where C_M is a co-factor matrix of the matrix M.

Requirements

(i) $\omega_n = 1.5$ rad/s
(ii) $\zeta = 0.5$
(iii) 6 rad/s input bandwidth

(a) Selection of sampling rate:

$$\omega_s \geqslant \max (5 \text{ to } 10) \times (\omega_n \text{ or BW})$$

$$\frac{2\pi}{T} \geqslant (10)\,(6 \text{ rad/s})$$

$$\therefore T = 0.1 \text{ s}$$

(b) Pole placement:
Using the template 1 from Chapter 1 we find that for $\zeta = 0.5$, $\omega_n = 1.5$ rad/s, the closed loop complex poles are located at:

$$z_{1,2} = 0.8 \pm j0.25$$

State space representation of the plant is given by:

$$\frac{x(s)}{u(s)} = \frac{10}{s^2 + 10s} \qquad \Rightarrow \ddot{x} = -10\dot{x} + 10u$$

Defining the states as

$$x_1 = x$$

$$x_2 = \dot{x}$$

gives

$$\begin{bmatrix} \dot{x}_1 \\ \dot{x}_2 \end{bmatrix} = \begin{bmatrix} 0 & 1 \\ 0 & -10 \end{bmatrix} \begin{bmatrix} x_1 \\ x_2 \end{bmatrix} + \begin{bmatrix} 0 \\ 10 \end{bmatrix} u$$

On discretization we obtain

$$\begin{bmatrix} x_1 \\ x_2 \end{bmatrix}_{i+1} = \begin{bmatrix} 1 & \frac{1}{10}(1 - e^{-10T}) \\ 0 & e^{-10T} \end{bmatrix} \begin{bmatrix} x_1 \\ x_2 \end{bmatrix}_i + \begin{bmatrix} T + \frac{1}{10} e^{-10T} - 1 \\ 1 - e^{-10T} \end{bmatrix} u_i$$

and for $T = 0.1$ s this gives

$$\begin{bmatrix} x_1 \\ x_2 \end{bmatrix}_{i+1} = \begin{bmatrix} 1 & 0.06 \\ 0 & 0.36 \end{bmatrix} \begin{bmatrix} x_1 \\ x_2 \end{bmatrix}_i + \begin{bmatrix} -0.864 \\ 0.63 \end{bmatrix} u_i$$

Closing the loop we obtain

$$x_{i+1} = \Phi x_i + \Gamma u_i$$

$$u_i = C x_i$$

$$x_{i+1} = [\Phi + \Gamma C] x_i$$

We are looking for C, i.e. the solution of

$$\det [\Phi + \Gamma C - zI] = 0$$

Explicitly

$$\det \left[\begin{vmatrix} \phi_1 & \phi_2 \\ 0 & \phi_4 \end{vmatrix} + \begin{vmatrix} \Gamma_1 C_1 & \Gamma_1 C_2 \\ \Gamma_2 C_1 & \Gamma_2 C_2 \end{vmatrix} - \begin{vmatrix} z_1 & 0 \\ 0 & z_2 \end{vmatrix} \right] = 0$$

where

$$z_1 = 0.8 + j0.25 \quad \phi_1 = 1 \qquad \phi_2 = 0.06$$

$$z_2 = 0.8 - j0.25 \quad \phi_4 = 0.36$$

$$\Gamma_1 = -0.864 \quad \Gamma_2 = 0.63$$

the solution gives

$$C_1 = 0.377$$

$$C_2 = -1.079$$

The controlled plant is depicted in Fig. 4.4.

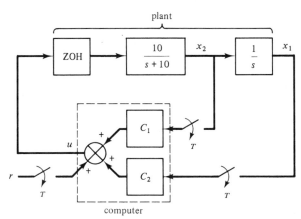

Fig. 4.4 The discretely controlled plant, using state variable
feedback

We have assumed that the state x_2 is measured; if it is not measured it has to be reconstructed. Reconstruction of missing states will be covered in Sec. 4.2.2.

There are several problems related to the pole placement design method. These are:

(i)   The application of this method if integral control is necessary.
(ii) Assuming that all the states are known, will it always be possible to relocate the roots to any position?
(iii) The application of the method if the states are not directly measured.

The answer to problem (iii) will be given in Sec. 4.3. Answers to the first two problems are given in the next section.

4.2.2   Integral Control

Integral control is achieved by adding an artificial state to the system.

The basic system (n-states) is given by

$$\dot{x} = Fx + Gu \tag{4.8}$$

If we let

$$x_{n+1} = \int x_1 dt \tag{4.9}$$

we may write

$$\begin{bmatrix} \dot{x}_1 \\ \cdot \\ \cdot \\ \cdot \\ \dot{x}_n \\ \hline \dot{x}_{n+1} \end{bmatrix} = \begin{bmatrix} F & \vdots & 0 \\ \hline 1 & \vdots & 0 & \vdots & 0 \end{bmatrix} \begin{bmatrix} x_1 \\ \cdot \\ \cdot \\ \cdot \\ x_n \\ \hline x_{n+1} \end{bmatrix} + \begin{bmatrix} G \\ \hline 0 \end{bmatrix} u \tag{4.10}$$

and the control, including the integral control, is given by

$$u = [C_1' \ \ldots \ C_n' \ C_{n+1}'] \begin{bmatrix} x_1 \\ \cdot \\ \cdot \\ \cdot \\ x_n \\ x_{n+1} \end{bmatrix} \tag{4.11}$$

The space dimension has been artificially increased in order to include integral control.

Example

Consider a first order system $G(s) = 1/(s + a)$ in the closed loop control system shown in Fig. 4.5.

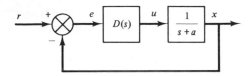

Fig. 4.5 Example of integral control

The control objective is a zero error to a step input function. In the continuous time domain the transfer function is given by

$$\frac{x(s)}{r(s)} = \frac{D(s)}{s + a + D(s)}$$

For $r(s) = 1/s$ and $D(s) = K$ (gain) the steady state output, x, is given by

$$\lim_{t \to \infty} x(t) = \frac{K}{a + K}$$

The error e is constant at the value $(1 - K/(a + K))$ and does not diminish. Control incorporating the integral of the error e will help to achieve the design objective. For $D(s) = K/s$ we obtain

$$\frac{x(s)}{r(s)} = \frac{K}{s(s + a) + K}$$

and hence steady-state response to a unit step function is

$$\lim_{t \to \infty} x(t) = \lim_{s \to 0} \frac{K}{s(s + a) + K} = 1$$

The value of K should be chosen to give the required time response. The state space formulation gives

$$\begin{bmatrix} \dot{x}_1 \\ \dot{x}_2 \end{bmatrix} = \begin{bmatrix} -a & 0 \\ 1 & 0 \end{bmatrix} \begin{bmatrix} x_1 \\ x_2 \end{bmatrix} + \begin{bmatrix} 1 \\ 0 \end{bmatrix} u$$

$$\begin{bmatrix} x_1 \\ x_2 \end{bmatrix}_{i+1} = \begin{bmatrix} e^{-aT} & 0 \\ T & 1 \end{bmatrix} \begin{bmatrix} x_1 \\ x_2 \end{bmatrix}_i + \begin{bmatrix} \dfrac{1 - e^{-aT}}{a} \\ 0 \end{bmatrix} u_i$$

where x_2 is the integral of x.

The required control is

$$u_i = [C_1 C_2] \begin{bmatrix} x_1 \\ x_2 \end{bmatrix} + C_3 (\int r dt)$$

The last term is a numerical integration of the input r.

4.2.3 Controllability

If a state variable or a combination of states is not influenced by the input, u, then the system $(\phi,\ \Gamma)$ is not controllable. In other words, system $(\phi,\ \Gamma)$ is controllable if the state vector x_i may be relocated to any arbitrary state in a finite number of steps.

Let the initial state be x_0 while a sequence of controls $u_0,\ u_1. \ . \ . \ u_{n-1}$ transforms the vector x_0 to x_n. The procedure is as follows.

First step $x_1 = \Phi x_0 + \Gamma u_0$ (4.12)

next steps give

$$x_2 = \Phi x_1 + \Gamma u_1$$

$$x_2 = \Phi^2 x_0 + \Phi \Gamma u_0 + \Gamma u_1$$
$$\vdots$$

and the final step gives

$$x_n = \Phi^n x_0 + \Phi^{n-1} \Gamma u_0 + \ldots + \Phi \Gamma u_{n-2} + \Gamma u_{n-1} \qquad (4.13)$$

Adding left-hand sides and right-hand sides of eqn. (4.12) to eqn. (4.13) yields eqn. (4.14)

$$x_n - \Phi^n x_0 = [\Phi^{n-1}\Gamma \ \ \Phi^{n-2}\Gamma \ldots \Phi\Gamma \ \ \Gamma] \begin{bmatrix} u_0 \\ u_1 \\ \cdot \\ \cdot \\ \cdot \\ u_{n-1} \end{bmatrix} \qquad (4.14)$$

We are looking for the control sequence $u_0,\ u_1 \ldots u_{n-1}$, its solution is given by

$$[\Phi^{n-1}\Gamma \ldots \Gamma]^{-1} [x_n - \Phi^n x_0] = \begin{bmatrix} u_0 \\ u_1 \\ \cdot \\ \cdot \\ \cdot \\ u_{n-1} \end{bmatrix} \qquad (4.15)$$

We may solve for $u_0 \ldots u_{n-1}$, for any arbitrary x_n and x_0 only if

$$|\Phi^{n-1}\Gamma \ \Phi^{n-2}\Gamma \ldots \Gamma| \neq 0 \tag{4.16}$$

otherwise the matrix $[\Phi^{n-1}\Gamma \ldots \Gamma]$ is singular and the inverse does not exist. Equation (4.16) is the condition of controllability.

Example 1

Consider the following pulse transfer function

$$\frac{y(z)}{u(z)} = \frac{(z+a)}{(z+a)(z+b)}$$

Clearly, cancellation of the factor $z+a$ occurs in the numerator and denominator of this pulse transfer function and one degree of freedom is lost. Because of this cancellation the system is not controllable. The same conclusion can be obtained by writing this transfer function in the form of state equations.

The state space representation may be obtained as follows,

if we let $\quad x_i = y$

$$x_2 = zx_i - u$$

then

$$z\begin{bmatrix} x_1 \\ x_2 \end{bmatrix} = \begin{bmatrix} 0 & 1 \\ -ab & -(a+b) \end{bmatrix} \begin{bmatrix} x_1 \\ x_2 \end{bmatrix} + \begin{bmatrix} 1 \\ -b \end{bmatrix} u$$

The matrix

$$[\Gamma^T\Phi\Gamma] = \begin{bmatrix} 1 & -b \\ -b & b^2 \end{bmatrix}$$

is singular and therefore the system is not controllable.

Example 2

The controllability test helps to give an insight into the system. Sometimes, by inspection only, it is not immediately obvious if a system is controllable, even for simple cases.

We will investigate an elementary mechanical system which consists of two masses connected by a friction rod as shown in Fig. 4.6.

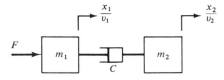

Fig. 4.6 Mechanical system of example 2

By applying a force only to one mass, is it possible to control the velocities and positions of both masses?

We will use a controllability test for continuous systems, which is the same as eqn. (4.16).

The equations of motions are given by

$$\ddot{x}_1 + C(\dot{x}_1 - \dot{x}_2) = F/m$$

$$\ddot{x}_2 + C(\dot{x}_2 - \dot{x}_1) = 0$$

Testing the controllability of the velocities gives

$$\begin{bmatrix} \dot{v}_1 \\ \dot{v}_2 \end{bmatrix} = \begin{bmatrix} C & -C \\ -C & C \end{bmatrix} \begin{bmatrix} v_1 \\ v_2 \end{bmatrix} + \begin{bmatrix} 1 \\ 0 \end{bmatrix} F/m = A + Bu$$

The matrix

$$[AB \ B] = \begin{bmatrix} C & 1 \\ -C & 0 \end{bmatrix}$$

has rank 2, therefore the system is controllable and using only F we may reach any combination of velocities v_1 and v_2.

The controllability of position.

The state space system is

$$\begin{bmatrix} \dot{v}_1 \\ \dot{v}_2 \\ \dot{x}_1 \\ \dot{x}_2 \end{bmatrix} = \begin{bmatrix} C & -C & 0 & 0 \\ -C & C & 0 & 0 \\ 1 & 0 & 0 & 0 \\ 0 & 1 & 0 & 0 \end{bmatrix} \begin{bmatrix} v_1 \\ v_2 \\ x_1 \\ x_2 \end{bmatrix} + \begin{bmatrix} 1 \\ 0 \\ 0 \\ 0 \end{bmatrix} F/m$$

the matrix $[AB \ B]$

$$[AB \ B] = \begin{bmatrix} 1 & C & 2C^2 & 4C^3 \\ 0 & -C & -2C^2 & -4C^3 \\ 0 & 1 & C & 2C^2 \\ 0 & 0 & -C & -2C^2 \end{bmatrix}$$

Using elementary operations on matrices it is easy to show that the matrix $[AB \ B]$ is singular. Consequently this mechanical system is uncontrollable. By applying force on one mass only we cannot reach every combination of the states.

4.3 OBSERVER DESIGN

Observer, or reconstruction of the necessary states, is required for state variable feedback. Usually, only a part of the states, or a combination of them, are measured. We are assuming that a linear combination of the states is measured.

$$y_i = Hx_i \tag{4.17}$$

where y — measurements
          x — states

An example of this is a vertical accelerometer mounted on an aircraft body to measure the combination of the following states: vertical acceleration, pitch angular acceleration and an elastic deflection of the body.

4.3.1   Observer Reconstructs the States

Basically an observer reconstructs the states by simulating (in real time) the behavior of the system and compares the results to the measurements.

The model of the system given in state space form is

$$\dot{x} = Fx + Gu \tag{4.18}$$

and its discretized version is

$$x_{i+1} = \Phi x_i + \Gamma u_i \tag{4.19}$$

The simulated model never behaves exactly as the actual system, so we have to correct the simulation, using the measurements. It will now be demonstrated for the continuous case.

Let us consider the system of Fig. 4.7 where the model and correction is given by

$$\left. \begin{array}{c} \hat{x} = F\hat{x} + Gu + K(y - \hat{y}) \\ \text{reconstructed measurements are} \\ \hat{y} = H\hat{x} \end{array} \right\} \tag{4.20}$$

$\hat{x}$ are the reconstructed states,
K is a correcting factor (explained later),
y are the actual measurements.

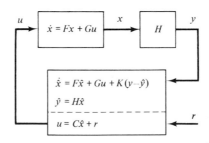

Fig. 4.7 Continuously controlled plant including an observer

The controller does not necessarily have to be a state variable feedback type. For the discrete observer we have two choices, i.e.

(i)
$$\bar{x}_{i+1} = \Phi \hat{x}_i + \Gamma u_i$$
$$\hat{x}_{i+1} = \bar{x}_{i+1} + K(y_i - \hat{y}_i)$$
$$\hat{y}_{i+1} = H\hat{x}_{i+1}$$

(4.21)

(ii)
$$\bar{x}_{i+1} = \Phi \hat{x}_i + \Gamma u_i$$
$$\hat{x}_{i+1} = \bar{x}_{i+1} + K(y_{i+1} - \bar{y}_{i+1})$$
$$\bar{y}_{i+1} = H\bar{x}_{i+1}$$

(4.22)

Observer (i) uses 'obsolete' measurements of y_i for generating $\hat{x}_{i+1}$.
Observer (ii) uses up-to-date information y_{i+1}, but requires zero time for computing $\hat{x}_{i+1}$ and $u_{i+1} = C\hat{x}_{i+1}$.

The difference between these two observers is summarized on a time axis in Fig. 4.8.

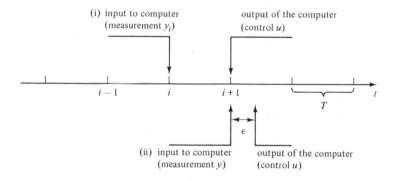

Fig. 4.8   Time axis description of delays in observers

ϵ, the time needed for computing, depends on the properties of the computer and on the efficiency of the program, most of the computing may be done before the y_{i+1} arrives.

For a complete control system using state variable feedback and observer (i) the scheme depicted in Fig. 4.9 is necessary.

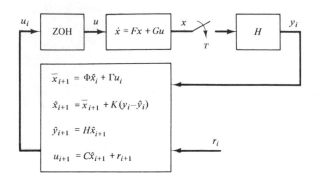

Fig. 4.9 Observer of type (i) in a control loop

4.3.2 How to Choose K

We will define $\tilde{x}$, the error made by the observer during the reconstruction of the states, as

$$\tilde{x} = x - \hat{x} \tag{4.23}$$

By subtracting the model of the plant given by eqn. (4.19) from the model of the observer given by eqn. (4.22) we obtain (for observer (i)) the error equation

$$\tilde{x}_{i+1} = (\Phi - KH)\tilde{x}_i \tag{4.24}$$

This equation represents the dynamics of the error and as we have seen K modifies the dynamics. By appropriate choice of K we may relocate the poles of the observer errors to desirable positions.

Usually, the observer has to be faster than the plant in order to supply quickly the states needed for control, especially if there are external disturbances, or the initial conditions are not known. In these cases the observer has to catch up with the plant. In another situation, when the measurements are coming to the system contaminated by noise, the observer should smooth the measurements. The Kalman filter described in Sec. 4.5 tries to compromise between these effects. Until we reach this section, we will handle the observer error dynamics as a pole placement problem.

4.3.3 The Separation Theorem

There is a simple and useful theorem which shows that the dynamics of the plant is independent of the dynamics of the observer and vice versa. Consequently the controller and the observer may be designed separately.

Proof:

Combining the equations of the controlled plant and of the observer, we get

$$x_{i+1} = \Phi x_i + \Gamma C(x_i - \tilde{x}_i)$$
$$\tilde{x}_{i+1} = (\Phi - KH)\tilde{x}_i \tag{4.25}$$

The characteristic equation of the system is given by eqn. (4.26).

$$\begin{vmatrix} \Phi + \Gamma C - Iz & \Gamma C \\ \hline 0 & \Phi - KH - Iz \end{vmatrix} = 0 \tag{4.26}$$

The closed loop poles are the poles of the closed loop plant and of the observer error system

$$|\Phi + \Gamma C - Iz| \ |\Phi - KH - Iz| = 0 \tag{4.27}$$

Relocation of the observer error poles does not influence the location of the poles of the controlled plant.

Example:

Design an observer for the controlled system from Sec. 4.2. The observer error dynamics should be ten times faster than the dynamics of the controlled plant. The system is depicted in Fig. 4.10.

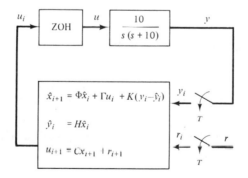

Fig. 4.10 Computer control of the plant $G(s) = \dfrac{10}{s(s + 10)}$

The plant has dynamics

$$G(s) = \frac{10}{s(s + 10)}$$

The state space formulation gives

$$\begin{bmatrix} \dot{x}_1 \\ \dot{x}_2 \end{bmatrix} = \begin{bmatrix} 0 & 1 \\ 0 & -10 \end{bmatrix} \begin{bmatrix} x_1 \\ x_2 \end{bmatrix} + \begin{bmatrix} 0 \\ 10 \end{bmatrix} u$$

The measurements may be written as

$$y = [1 \quad 0] x = Hx$$

The discrete versions of these equations are

$$x_{i+1} = \Phi x_i + \Gamma u_i$$

$$y_i = H x_i$$

The matrixes Φ and Γ were calculated in Sec. 4.2.1 and are repeated here for convenience

$$\Phi = \begin{bmatrix} \Phi_1 & \Phi_2 \\ 0 & \Phi_4 \end{bmatrix} = \begin{bmatrix} 1 & 0.06 \\ 0 & 0.36 \end{bmatrix}$$

$$\Gamma = \begin{bmatrix} \Gamma_1 \\ \Gamma_2 \end{bmatrix} = \begin{bmatrix} -0.864 \\ 0.63 \end{bmatrix}$$

$$H = [1 \quad 0]$$

The closed loop dynamics are given by

$$x_{i+1} = (\Phi + \Gamma C) x_i$$

The desired poles on the z-plane were calculated in Sec. 4.2, they are:

$$z_{1,2} = 0.8 \pm j0.25$$

These poles correspond to continuous dynamics, represented by the following damping and frequency:

$$\zeta = 0.5$$

$$\omega_n = 1.5 \text{ rad/s}$$

For a ten times faster observer we have to modify the observer's error dynamics to the following values:

$$\zeta = 0.5$$

$$\omega_n = 15 \text{ rad/s}$$

Using again the template 1 and assuming the same sampling rate ($T = 0.1$ s), the z-plane pole locations are:

$$z_{1,2} = 0.3 \pm j0.5$$

Using the values of the poles we may solve for the proper K, i.e.

$$\tilde{x}_{i+1} = (\Phi - KH)x_i$$

$$\det (zI - \Phi + KH) = 0$$

$$\left| \begin{bmatrix} z & 0 \\ 0 & z \end{bmatrix} - \begin{bmatrix} \Phi_1 & \Phi_2 \\ 0 & \Phi_4 \end{bmatrix} + \begin{bmatrix} K_1 \\ K_2 \end{bmatrix} \begin{bmatrix} 1 & 0 \end{bmatrix} \right| = 0$$

$$\left| \begin{matrix} z - \Phi_1 + K_1 & -\Phi_2 \\ K_2 & z - \Phi_4 \end{matrix} \right| = 0$$

Solution of the last determinant for the previously mentioned values of ϕ and $z_{1,2}$ yields

$$K = \begin{bmatrix} 0.76 \\ 3.83 \end{bmatrix}$$

The complete block diagram of the controlled plant (example from 4.2.1) is depicted in Fig. 4.11.

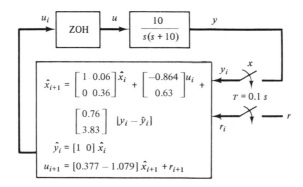

Fig. 4.11 Discrete control of the plant $\dfrac{10}{s(s + 10)}$

4.3.4 Observability

As explained in Sec. 4.2, the pole placement method requires all the state variables as feedback. Is it always possible to measure or to reconstruct all the states? A relatively simple test checks the observability of a system, i.e. the test analyzes the possibility of reconstructing all the states in a finite number of steps independently of the initial conditions. The observability depends on the dynamics of the system (Φ) and on the kind of information we measure (H).

Example:

The system is a rotating body, its dynamics is that of a simple angular second order system.

$$I\ddot{\theta} = M$$

There are two states, θ and $\dot{\theta}$.

If θ is measured, $\dot{\theta}$ may be obtained in a finite number of steps (depending on the accuracy required). However if only $\dot{\theta}$ is measured, the initial conditions and all the history of $\dot{\theta}$ are needed in order to integrate $\dot{\theta}$ to obtain θ. In this case the state θ is not observable.

Definition of the observability test.

For a system

$$x_{i+1} = \Phi x_i \tag{4.28}$$

and the measurements y, where

$$y_i = Hx_i \tag{4.29}$$

assuming we start the n-measurements at i, i.e.

$$x_{i+1} = \Phi x_i \Rightarrow \left. \begin{cases} y_i \quad = Hx_i \\ y_{i+1} = Hx_{i+1} \\ y_{i+1} = H\Phi x_i \\ y_{i+2} = H\Phi^2 x_i \\ \quad \cdot \\ \quad \cdot \\ \quad \cdot \\ y_{i+n-1} = H\Phi^{n-1} x_i \end{cases} \right\} n\text{-measurements} \tag{4.30}$$

in a matrix formulation we may write

$$Y = [A]\, x_i \tag{4.31}$$

where

$$Y = \begin{bmatrix} y_i \\ \cdot \\ \cdot \\ \cdot \\ y_{i+n-1} \end{bmatrix}, \text{ and } A = \begin{bmatrix} H \\ H\Phi \\ \cdot \\ \cdot \\ H\Phi^{n-1} \end{bmatrix}$$

We are looking for x_i.

x_i is obtained by solving eqn. (4.31) i.e.

$$x_i = [A]^{-1} Y \tag{4.32}$$

A^{-1} exists only if A is a non-singular matrix. The system is observable if $|A| \neq 0$.

Example:

Consider the system given by:

$$\ddot{\theta} = \frac{M}{I}$$

The states are,

$$\theta_1 = \theta$$

$$\theta_2 = \dot{\theta}$$

State space formulation gives

$$\begin{bmatrix} \dot{\theta}_1 \\ \dot{\theta}_2 \end{bmatrix} = \begin{bmatrix} 0 & 1 \\ 0 & 0 \end{bmatrix} \begin{bmatrix} \theta_1 \\ \theta_2 \end{bmatrix} + \begin{bmatrix} 0 \\ 1 \end{bmatrix} M/I$$

$$\begin{bmatrix} \theta_1 \\ \theta_2 \end{bmatrix}_{i+1} = \Phi \begin{bmatrix} \theta_1 \\ \theta_2 \end{bmatrix}_i + \Gamma u_i$$

$$\Phi = \begin{bmatrix} 1 & T \\ 0 & 1 \end{bmatrix}$$

See Sec. 1.4.5.

Case 1: Only θ is measured

$$H = \begin{bmatrix} 1 & 0 \end{bmatrix}$$

$$H\Phi = \begin{bmatrix} 1 & 0 \end{bmatrix} \begin{bmatrix} 1 & T \\ 0 & 1 \end{bmatrix} = \begin{bmatrix} 1 & T \end{bmatrix}$$

$$A = \begin{bmatrix} H \\ H\Phi \end{bmatrix} = \begin{bmatrix} 1 & 0 \\ 1 & T \end{bmatrix}$$

$$|A| \neq 0$$

The system is observable.

Case 2: Only $\dot{\theta}$ is measured

$$H = \begin{bmatrix} 0 & 1 \end{bmatrix}$$

$$H\Phi = \begin{bmatrix} 0 & 1 \end{bmatrix} \begin{bmatrix} 1 & T \\ 0 & 1 \end{bmatrix} = \begin{bmatrix} 1 & T \end{bmatrix}$$

$$A = \begin{bmatrix} H \\ H\Phi \end{bmatrix} = \begin{bmatrix} 0 & 1 \\ 0 & 1 \end{bmatrix}$$

$$|A| = 0$$

The system is not observable.

4.4   OPTIMAL CONTROL BASED ON QUADRATIC SYNTHESIS

There is considerable literature on this topic. Every reader will be familiar, to some extent, with expressions such as cost function, Riccati equations, etc. The purpose of this section is to simplify and to explain the basic theory. The familiarity with optimal control will help the designer to use various computer programs for control synthesis. Theorems and some computational tools are given in Appendix A.

Consider the system

$$x_{i+1} = \Phi x_i + \Gamma u_i \tag{4.33}$$

The cost function is given by eqn. (4.34),

$$J = \tfrac{1}{2} \sum_{i=0}^{N-1} x_i^T A x_i + u_i^T B u_i \tag{4.34}$$

where N is the number of steps.

The optimal linear controller follows a control law

$$u_i = C(i)\, x_i \tag{4.35}$$

which minimizes the cost function J, for any initial conditions.

If N increases to infinity and a steady state is reached, then $C(i) = C =$ constant, and the controller is called a regulator.

The major problem for a designer is to determine the weighting matrices A and B. Intuitively, it is clear that if our objective is to spare control (e.g. electric supply for a servosystem using a limited source of energy), we have to emphasize the matrix B. On the other hand, if our objective is to stay in the linear range and to keep a quiet and smooth behavior of the system, we have to decrease the variation on x, i.e. increase A. The final design will be a compromise between A and B. Some hints on how to choose the matrices will be given later.

The solution of the optimal linear controller was given by Kalman (KA-1) who used the dynamic programming approach. In our solution, we will use Bryson's approach (BR-1) which solves the optimal control via the calculus of variation. Here we review only the basic concepts.

Let us consider the outline of the optimal controller. In the minimization procedure used in the calculus of variation, the cost function J is augmented by the constraints multiplied by a Lagrange undetermined multiplier λ_i^T (vector). The constraints are the equations of motion.

The minimization procedure of the calculus of variation leads to equations called the 'Euler-Lagrange difference equations' formulated in state space notation as:

$$\begin{bmatrix} x \\ \lambda \end{bmatrix}_{i+1} = \begin{bmatrix} \Phi + \Gamma B^{-1} \Gamma^T \Phi^{-T} A & -\Gamma B^{-1} \Gamma^T \Phi^{-T} \\ -\Phi^{-T} A & \Phi^{-T} \end{bmatrix} \begin{bmatrix} x \\ \lambda \end{bmatrix}_i, \quad (4.36)$$

The initial conditions are given at $i = 0$ and $i = N$. This is a two-point boundary problem, a solution by sweep methods assumes $\lambda_i = Sx_i$. This solution leads to a matrix Riccati difference equation, which in the steady state form is given by:

$$S_{ss} = \Phi^T (S_{ss}^{-1} + \Gamma B^{-1} \Gamma^T)^{-1} \Phi + A \qquad (4.37)$$

Solving for S_{ss}, the optimal regulator is given as:

$$u_i = -B^{-1} \Gamma \Phi^{-T} (S_{ss}^{-1} - A) x_i = Cx_i \qquad (4.38)$$

Solution of the optimal linear controller and of the matrix Riccati difference equation using eigenvector decomposition are given in Appendix A.

Example

The short period dynamics of an aircraft is modelled as a second order system. This is given by

$$\dot{q} = (M_q) q + (M_\alpha) \alpha_T + (M_{\delta e}) \delta e$$

$$\dot{\alpha}_T - q + \frac{z_\alpha}{u_0} \alpha_T + \frac{z_{\delta e}}{u_0} \delta e$$

where q is the pitch rate, α_T the total angle of attack and δ_e the elevator angle. The open loop pole locations vary according to the flight conditions which are summarized in the coefficients ($M_q, M_\alpha, z_\alpha, z_{\delta e}, M_{\delta e}, u_0$). The objective is to improve the dynamics in different flight conditions.

A simple weighting matrix will be chosen

$$A = \begin{bmatrix} A_q & 0 \\ 0 & A_{\alpha T} \end{bmatrix}$$

B is a scalar (i.e. only one control input).

The first approximations of A and B may be done by Bryson's method. Let the weights be proportional to the inverse of the squared maximum value of the state or of the control, i.e.

$$A_q = \frac{1}{q^2_{max}} \qquad A_{\alpha T} = \frac{1}{\alpha^2_{T max}} \qquad B = \frac{1}{\delta^2_{e max}}$$

Using this choice of weights the optimal controller will keep the dynamics and control inside the linear range. Another approach is to use some trial-and-error method. By varying the weights A and B, the optimal control actually turns out to be a pole placement method.

Numerical example

This example is concerned with high altitude supersonic flight.

In the following diagrams note how the fast undamped open loop poles are relocated to more favorable positions. This is accomplished by solving the optimal controller several times and calculating the closed loop poles for different weights A and B.

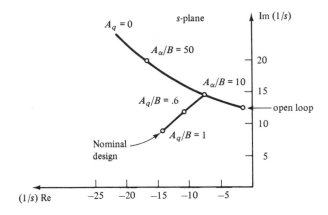

Fig. 4.12 Pole locations vs weight of the short period mode, s-plane

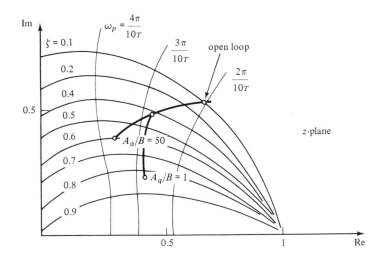

Fig. 4.13 Pole locations vs weight of the short period mode, z-plane

4.5 OPTIMAL FILTERING IN THE PRESENCE OF NOISE

There is some ambiguity with names like filter, observer, estimator, Kalman filter, maximum likelihood estimator, and so on. We will use the names observer and estimator for any reconstruction scheme and the Kalman (Kalman–Bucy) filter for a maximum likelihood estimator. In this section we are dealing with a steady state discrete Kalman filter. The purpose of this filter (observer, estimator, etc.) is:

(i)   to reconstruct unmeasured states,
(ii)   to minimize the influence of white noise.

There are two principal sources of noise:

(i)   the process noise, which directly influences the plant, e.g., turbulence,
(ii)   the measurement noise, e.g., instrument noise.

There is a vast amount of literature on these subjects and our purpose here is to review the basic theory and to point out how it may help us to design a digital controller.

4.5.1   Discretization of a Continuous System Driven by White Noise

The disturbed system is given by

$$\dot{x} = Fx + G_w w \qquad w \rightarrow N(0, Q) \tag{4.39}$$

where w is white noise.

$w \rightarrow N(0, Q)$ means that w is a random disturbance, normally distributed, with a zero mean and a power spectral density matrix Q.

The disturbed system is represented at sampling points by

$$x_{i+1} = \Phi x_i + w_{d_i} \qquad w_{d_i} - N(0, Q_d) \tag{4.40}$$

where,

Q_d is the covariance matrix, sometimes called the variance matrix.

$$Q_d = \int_0^T \Phi(\tau)\, G_w\, Q G_w^T\, \Phi(\tau)^T\, d\tau \tag{4.41}$$

For a proof see the work by Bryson and Ho (BR-1).

4.5.2   Discretization of the Measurement Noise

White noise by definition is a disturbance equally distributed along the frequency axis. This definition has a weak mathematical basis, because the total energy is infinite. Furthermore, by sampling white noise $v \to N(Q, R)$, its covariance matrix R_d is meaningless. Therefore to stay on a physical basis, it will be assumed (physically correct) that the measurement noise is slightly colored. Bucy and Joseph (BU-1) suggested that the discrete covariance r_d is

$$r_d = \sigma^2 \; \frac{1 + e^{-T/\tau}}{1 - e^{-T/\tau}} \tag{4.42}$$

where σ^2 is the power spectral density of the measurement noise and τ is its correlation time.

4.5.3   The Optimal Filter

The steady state optimal (Kalman) filter is an observer which minimizes the error $(\tilde{x})$ covariance matrix at the steady state.

For the physical system,

$$x_{i+1} = \Phi x_i + \Gamma_1 u_1 + \Gamma_2 w_i \qquad w_i \to N(0, Q_d) \tag{4.43}$$

$$y_i \; = H x_i + v_i \qquad\qquad\qquad v_i \to N(0, R_d) \tag{4.44}$$

The optimal steady state filter is given by

$$\left. \begin{aligned}
\overline{x}_{i+1} &= \Phi \hat{x}_i + \Gamma_1 u_i \\
\hat{x}_{i+1} &= \overline{x}_{i+1} + K\,(y_{i+1} - H\overline{x}_{i+1}) \\
K &= PH^T R_d \\
P &= \Phi^{-1}\,(M - \Gamma_2 Q_d \Gamma_2^T)\,\Phi^{-T}
\end{aligned} \right\} \tag{4.45}$$

where M is the error covariance matrix before measurements are taken, and P is the error covariance matrix after the measurements y_{i+1} were done. This formulation is correct for the observer (ii) (Sec. 4.2), which assumes a zero computation time between the measurements y_{i+1} and the output of the filter $\hat{x}_{i+1}$.

Let us now consider how we may calculate M. By using a similar approach to the one used in calculating the optimal controller a recursive equation for M is obtained. This recursive equation has the same structure as that for S in the optimal control problem.

The equations are identical if we consider the following equivalence, first recognized by Kalman (KA-1).

$$
\begin{array}{ccc}
\text{Control} & & \text{Filter} \\
\Phi & \longleftrightarrow & \Phi^T \\
H & \longleftrightarrow & \Gamma_2^T \\
\Gamma_1 & \longleftrightarrow & H^T \\
A & \longleftrightarrow & Q_d \\
B & \longleftrightarrow & R_d
\end{array}
$$

Replacing the matrices of the control in the Euler–Lagrange equation by matrices of the filter, the recursive equations for M are obtained (see Appendix A).

4.5.4 Steady State Response to an External Noise

A stable discrete system Φ, disturbed by an external noise with a covariance matrix Q_d, reaches a steady state. The average behavior of its states is characterized by a covariance matrix X, which is the solution of eqn. (4.46)

$$
X = \Phi X \Phi^T + Q_d \tag{4.46}
$$

Following (BR-1) the average behavior of an optimally controlled discrete system, with an external noise disturbance and measurement noise, is characterized by the state covariance matrix X. This is the solution of eqn. (4.47).

$$
X - M = (\Phi + \Gamma_1 C)(X - P)(\Phi + \Gamma_1 C)^T \tag{4.47}
$$

4.5.5 Example

We shall consider observing a first order system, disturbed by white noise w_i, in which the measurements are contaminated by white noise v_i.

The system may be written in the form:

$$
\begin{aligned}
x_{i+1} &= \Phi x_i + w_i & w_i &= N(0, q) \\
y_i &= x_i + v_i & v_i &= N(0, r)
\end{aligned}
$$

The optimal observer is

$$
\hat{x}_{i+1} = \Phi \hat{x}_i + K(y_{i+1} - \Phi \hat{x}_i)
$$

The proportional constant K is derived from solving eqn. (4.45) (see also Appendix A).

$$
K = \frac{P}{r} = \frac{1}{2\Phi^2}\left[\sqrt{\left(\frac{q}{r} + 1 - \Phi\right)^2 + 4\frac{q}{r}\Phi^2} - \left(\frac{q}{r} + 1 - \Phi\right) \right]
$$

Let us consider the behavior of the optimal filter for various ratios q/r.

(i) $\dfrac{q}{r} \ll 1$

In this case the process noise is negligible compared to the measurement noise.

$$\lim_{q/r \to 0} K = \lim \frac{1}{2\Phi^2}\left[\sqrt{(1-\Phi^2)^2} - (1-\Phi^2)\right] \to 0$$

The constant K is very small and in the steady state the optimal estimation $\hat{x}$ of the state x is highly influenced from previous values of $\hat{x}$.

(ii) $\dfrac{q}{r} \gg 1$

The process noise is much larger than the measurement noise. In this case

$$\lim_{q/r \to 0} K = \lim \frac{1}{2\Phi^2}\left[\sqrt{\left(\frac{q}{r}+1-\Phi^2\right)^2 + \frac{4q}{r}\Phi^2} - \left(\frac{q}{r}+1-\Phi^2\right)\right] = 1$$

which yields

$$y_{i+1} = \hat{x}_{i+1}$$

In this case of precise measurements and a noisy process the optimal estimation of the state is based on the last measurement.

4.6   MODEL FOLLOWING METHODS

Besides relocation of poles to more favorable positions, the purpose of control is to obtain a proper response to input commands. In the model following method of design, the desired transient response is translated to a transfer function which is the model. Input commands, u_{in}, are applied to the system and model, and the control law is determined so that the system's output is similar to the model output.

Explicitly:

For the system given by

$$\left. \begin{aligned} \dot{x} &= Fx + G(u' + u_{in}) \\ y &= Hx \end{aligned} \right\} \tag{4.48}$$

and the model given by

$$\left. \begin{aligned} \dot{x}_m &= F_m x_m + G_m u_{in} \\ y_m &= H_m x_m \end{aligned} \right\} \tag{4.49}$$

The objective is to synthesize a control u' which will minimize the difference between y and y_m.

4.6.1   The Explicit Model Following Method

The control law is a control u',

$$\left. \begin{aligned} u' &= Cx + C_m x_m \\ u &= u' + u_{\text{in}} \end{aligned} \right\}$$

(4.50)

which minimizes the cost function J,

$$J = \int_0^\infty [(y - y_m)^T A (y - y_m) + u^T Bu] \, dt$$

(4.51)

C and C_m are the feedback and feedforward gain matrices. Various minimization procedures are used for calculating these gains. (See PE-1).

It is not necessary that the model be of the same order as the plant, simpler models are usually preferred.

Note: The model is continuously calculated in the controller in real time, its output arc the x_m's.

4.6.2   The Implicit Model Following Method

In the implicit model following method, the objective is the same as in the explicit model following method, i.e. to synthesize such control that the controlled plant will follow a predetermined model of behavior.

However in the implicit model following method, this objective is achieved without incorporating the desired model in the real time controller. The fitting of the controlled plant to the model is achieved by optimizing the state variable feedback gains only, i.e. the control law is

$$u' = Cx$$

(4.52)

which minimizes the cost function J, where

$$J = \int_0^\infty [(\dot{y} - \dot{y}_m)^T A (\dot{y} - \dot{y}_m) + u^T Bu] \, dt$$

(4.53)

It is quite clear that in the implicit model following method we have less degrees of freedom to select the gains in order to achieve the same objective as in the explicit method because the states x_m are not available.

Sometimes it is extremely difficult to design a controller, and the closed loop behavior is improved by incorporating in the controller some kind of simple compensation network.

In this case the number of states is increased and the optimization procedure also calculates the gains proportional to the states of the compensator,

$$u = Cx + C_c x_c \tag{4.54}$$

where x_c are the compensator states.

4.6.3 Solution Quality Criterion

The quality ratio given by eqn. (4.55)

$$r = \frac{\displaystyle\sum_{i=0}^{\infty} (y - y_m)_i^2}{\displaystyle\sum_{i=0}^{\infty} (y_m)_i^2} \tag{4.55}$$

measures how well our solution fits the model.

U. Peled (PE-1) proposed a quantitative scale for grading the match between the output of the plant and the output of the model. His proposals are:

$r < 0.01$: excellent match
$0.01 \leqslant r < 0.1$: very good match
$0.1 \leqslant r < 1$: good match for continuous systems, moderate for discrete
$r \geqslant 1$: no distinct grade; specific cases should be checked.

4.6.4 Example

An illustrative example of the implicit method of design and of the grading of quality match is given in the dissertation of U. Peled (PE-1). The outline of his example is now presented.

The system considered is shown in Fig. 4.14.

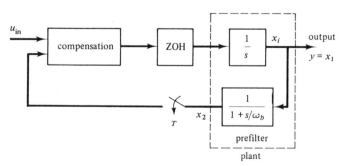

Fig. 4.14 Implicit model following control

The model of the plant is

$$\begin{bmatrix} x_1 \\ x_2 \end{bmatrix}_{i+1} = \begin{bmatrix} 1 & 0 \\ 1 - e^{-\omega_b T} & e^{-\omega_b T} \end{bmatrix} \begin{bmatrix} x_1 \\ x_2 \end{bmatrix}_i + \begin{bmatrix} T \\ 1 - \dfrac{1 - e^{-\omega_b T}}{\omega_b} \end{bmatrix} u_i$$

The model of the desired behavior is given by

$$x_{m_{i+1}} = e^{-T} x_{m_i}$$

The basic cost function is

$$J = \sum_{i=0}^{\infty} (x_1 - x_m)_i^2$$

The control law is

$$u_i = Cx_{2_i} + u_{in_i}$$

The quality ratio given by

$$r = \frac{\displaystyle\sum_{i=0}^{\infty} (x_1 - x_m)_i^2}{\displaystyle\sum_{i=0}^{\infty} x^2_{m_i}} = (1 - e^{-2T}) \sum_{i=0}^{\infty} (x_1 - x_m)_i^2$$

The results are:

For prefilter breakpoints ω_b larger than 1 rad/s the match is satisfactory (see Fig. 4.15).

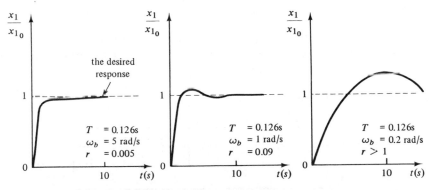

Fig. 4.15 Time response of the implicit model following controlled plant

For prefilter breakpoint frequencies less than 1 rad/s the response is not satisfactory, additional compensation is necessary.

The compensation added is a lead-lag network.

$$x_{3_{i+1}} = P_1 x_{3_i} + (1 - P_1) x_{2_i}$$

and the control law becomes:

$$u_i = C_2 x_{2_i} + C_3 x_{3_i} + u_{in_i}$$

This compensation improves the quality ratio for $\omega_0 = 0.2$ rad/s and $T = 0.126$ s to $r = 0.002$.

EXERCISES

4.1 Given a system represented by

$$x_{i+1} = \Phi x_i + \Gamma u_i$$

$$u_i = C x_i$$

Prove that the finite time response (deadbeat) requires that the closed loop eigenvalues should be relocated to $z = 0$.

4.2 For the system shown

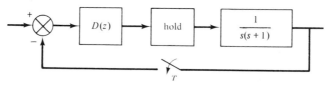

the designed $\begin{cases} u_i = 2e_i + 0.2e_i' \\ e_i' = e_{i-1}' + e_i \end{cases}$
controller is

(i)   Investigate the steady state error to a step function.
(ii) Reformulate the system to a state space representation with state proportional feedback.

4.3 Given the system shown

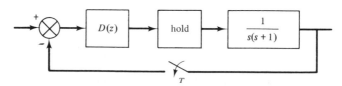

(i)   Show that this system is controllable.

(ii) What initial states may be forced to the origin in one iteration time? *Hint:* $\Phi^{-2}\Gamma$, $\Phi^{-1}\Gamma$ should be linearly dependent.

4.4 Determine the controllability characteristics of the following systems:

(i) $$G(z) = \frac{z + 2}{(z + 1)(z + 3)}$$

(ii) $$G(z) = \frac{z}{(z + 1)^2}$$

4.5 For a system defined by

$$x_{i+1} = \begin{bmatrix} 0 & 1.0 \\ -0.72 & 1.7 \end{bmatrix} x_i + \begin{bmatrix} 0 \\ 1 \end{bmatrix} u_i$$

$$y = \begin{bmatrix} -0.72 & 1.7 \end{bmatrix} x_i + u_i$$

(i)   Show that the eigenvalues are $z_{1,2} = 0.8, 0.9$

(ii) Find x_i and y_i for $u_i = 0$ and initial conditions $x_0 = \begin{bmatrix} 1.0 \\ 0.8 \end{bmatrix}$

(iii) Find x_i and y_i for $u_i = 0$ and initial conditions $x_0 = \begin{bmatrix} 1.0 \\ 0.9 \end{bmatrix}$

4.6 Show that the system represented by

$$x_{i+1} = \begin{bmatrix} 0.2 & -0.1 \\ -0.1 & 0.2 \end{bmatrix} x_i + \begin{bmatrix} 0.5 \\ 0.5 \end{bmatrix} u_i$$

$$y_i = \begin{bmatrix} 2 & 0 \end{bmatrix} x_i$$

is uncontrollable.
Define the new state vector by the transformation

$$x_i' = \begin{bmatrix} 1 & -1 \\ 1 & 1 \end{bmatrix} x_i$$

Find the new state equation.

4.7 Show that the system

$$x_{i+1} = \begin{bmatrix} 0.4 & -0.3 \\ -0.3 & 0.4 \end{bmatrix} x_i + \begin{bmatrix} 1 \\ 0 \end{bmatrix} u_i$$

$$y_i = \begin{bmatrix} 1 & 1 \end{bmatrix} x_i$$

is unobservable.

5

Mechanization of Control Algorithms on Microcontrollers

5.1 INTRODUCTION

It is well known to designers of digital control systems that major difficulties are found in the mechanization of the control algorithm. By mechanization we mean the selection of the digital equipment, the A/D and D/A converters, the word length of the computer, speed of computation, the actual programming of the algorithm, the numerical errors and their influence on the dynamics of the controller, etc. Chapters 5, 6 and 7 deal with many of these problems.

In this chapter, we will present a rather general approach for the conversion of an algorithm to a program for the implementation in the computer of the control system. In the following chapters, a thoroughly detailed analysis of the influence of finite word length and limited sampling rate will be carried out.

5.2 ITERATIVE COMPUTATION VIA PARALLEL, DIRECT, CANONICAL AND CASCADE MECHANIZATION

Digital algorithms may be formulated in two different forms, namely,

(i)   State space representation of the difference equations.
(ii) Transfer functions in z^{-1}.

In the first case, the state space formulation of the digital compensation may be directly programmed on the control microcomputer. If the algorithm is given as a transfer function, this transfer function (filter) may be basically realized in two different ways:

(a)   Using digital hardware (adders, summers, delay elements),
(b)   Programming on a computer.

In both cases there are different ways to realize the discrete transfer function. Four basic realization will be presented here: Direct form 1, Direct form 2, Cascade and Parallel form. There is often confusion in the use of the names. The name Canonical is sometimes related to a realization in which the number of delay elements is equal to n (order of the system), and at other times to any realization with a minimum number of adders, multipliers and delay elements. Direct form 1 is sometimes called Series realization, and Direct form 2 is sometimes called Canonical realization.

Practical selection of any particular realization depends on programming and on the numerical accuracy required (see Chapter 6 for details).

5.2.1   Direct Form 1 (Series)

The transfer function is expressed as a ratio of two polynomials, i.e.

$$\frac{u(z)}{e(z)} = D(z) = \frac{\sum\limits_{j=0}^{n} a_j z^{-j}}{1 + \sum\limits_{j=1}^{n} b_j z^{-j}} \tag{5.1}$$

Hardware realization may be of the form shown in Fig. 5.1.

For software realization we consider the difference equation based on transfer function given by eqn. (5.1), i.e.

$$u_i = \sum_{j=0}^{n} a_j e_{i-j} - \sum_{j=1}^{n} b_j u_{i-j} \tag{5.2}$$

Matrix formulation of direct form 1 gives

$$\begin{bmatrix} x_1 \\ x_2 \\ \cdot \\ \cdot \\ \cdot \\ x_n \end{bmatrix}_{i+1} = \begin{bmatrix} -b_1 & 1 & 0 & \cdot & \cdot & \cdot \\ -b_2 & 0 & 1 & \cdot & \cdot & \cdot \\ \cdot & & & & & \\ \cdot & & & & & \\ \cdot & & & & & \\ b_n & \cdot & \cdot & \cdot & 0 & 1 \end{bmatrix} \begin{bmatrix} x_1 \\ x_2 \\ \cdot \\ \cdot \\ \cdot \\ x_n \end{bmatrix}_i + \begin{bmatrix} a_1 - a_0 b_1 \\ a_2 - a_0 b_2 \\ \cdot \\ \cdot \\ \cdot \\ a_n - a_0 b_n \end{bmatrix} e_i \tag{5.3}$$

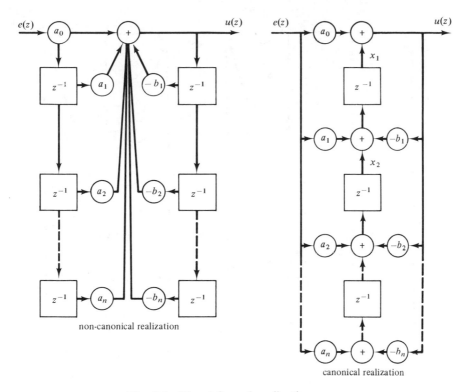

Fig. 5.1　Direct form 1 realization

$$u_i = [1 \quad 0 \cdot \quad \cdot \quad \cdot \quad 0] \begin{bmatrix} x_1 \\ x_2 \\ \cdot \\ \cdot \\ \cdot \\ x_n \end{bmatrix} + a_0 e_i \qquad (5.4)$$

5.2.2　Direct Form 2 (canonical)

$$\frac{u(z)}{e(z)} = D(z) = \frac{\displaystyle\sum_{j=0}^{n} a_j z^{-j}}{1 + \displaystyle\sum_{j=1}^{n} b_j z^{-j}} \qquad \text{(5.1 repeated)}$$

Hardware realization is shown in Fig. 5.2.

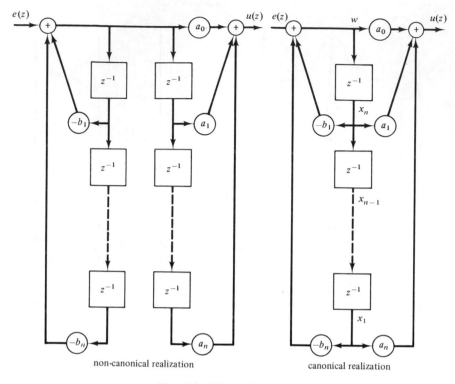

Fig. 5.2   Direct form 2 realization

Software realization comes from the difference equation of direct form 2

$$
\left.
\begin{aligned}
w_i &= e_i - \sum_{j=1}^{n} b_j w_{i-j} \\[2em]
u_i &= \sum_{j=0}^{n} a_j w_{i-j}
\end{aligned}
\right\}
\tag{5.5}
$$

The matrix formulation of direct form 2 is

$$
\begin{bmatrix} x_1 \\ x_2 \\ \cdot \\ \cdot \\ \cdot \\ x_n \end{bmatrix}_{i+1}
=
\begin{bmatrix}
0 & 1 & 0 & \cdot & \cdot & \cdot & 0 \\
\cdot & & 1 & & & & \cdot \\
\cdot & & & & & & \cdot \\
\cdot & & & & & & \cdot \\
\cdot & & & & & & \cdot \\
-b_n & \cdot & \cdot & \cdot & \cdot & \cdot & -b_1
\end{bmatrix}
\begin{bmatrix} x_1 \\ x_2 \\ \cdot \\ \cdot \\ \cdot \\ x_n \end{bmatrix}_i
+
\begin{bmatrix} 0 \\ \cdot \\ \cdot \\ \cdot \\ \cdot \\ 1 \end{bmatrix} e_i
\tag{5.6}
$$

$$u_i = [a_n - a_{n-1}b_n \ \cdots \ a_1 - a_0 b_1] \begin{bmatrix} x_1 \\ \cdot \\ \cdot \\ \cdot \\ x_n \end{bmatrix} + a_0 e_i \tag{5.7}$$

5.2.3 Cascade Realization

The transfer function is expressed as a product of simple block elements (transfer functions).

$$\frac{u(z)}{e(z)} = D(z) = \alpha_0 D_1(z) \ldots D_l(z) \qquad 1 \leqslant l < n \tag{5.8}$$

The factorization of the transfer function yields two types of elements (i) first order elements, (ii) second order elements with real coefficients. It is not recommended to represent second order elements by two first order elements with complex coefficients.

(i)   First order elements are of the form

$$D_l(z) = \frac{1 + \alpha_l z^{-1}}{1 + \beta_l z^{-1}} \tag{5.9}$$

(ii)   Second order elements are of the form

$$D_l(z) = \frac{1 + \alpha_l z^{-1} + \alpha_{l+1} z^{-2}}{1 + \beta_l z^{-1} + \beta_{l+1} z^{-2}} \tag{5.10}$$

(a) Hardware realization. For graphic description only, we will assume that there is only one second order element.

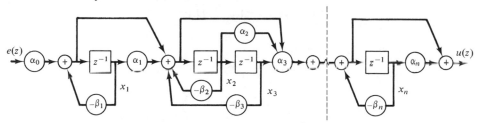

Fig. 5.3   Cascade form realization

(b) Software realization, for non-complex coefficients, is achieved using the following difference equations.

$$x_{i+1}^1 = -\beta_1 x_i + \alpha_0 e_i$$

$$x_{i+1}^2 = (\alpha_1 - \beta_1)x_i^1 - \beta_2 x_i^2 - \beta_3 x_i^3 + \alpha_0 e_i$$

$$x_{i+1}^3 = x_i^2$$

$$x_{i+1}^4 = (\alpha_1 - \beta_1)x_i^1 + (\alpha_2 - \beta_2)x_i^2 + (\alpha_3 - \beta_3)x_i^3 - \beta_4 x_i^4 + \alpha_0 e_i$$

$$\vdots$$

(5.11)

The matrix formulation of the realization is:

$$
\begin{bmatrix} x_1 \\ x_2 \\ x_3 \\ x_4 \\ \cdot \\ \cdot \\ \cdot \\ x_n \end{bmatrix}_{i+1}
=
\begin{bmatrix}
-\beta_1 & 0 & \cdot & \cdot\cdot\cdot & 0 \\
\alpha_1 - \beta_1 & -\beta_2 & -\beta_3 & \cdot\cdot\cdot & \cdot \\
0 & 1 & 0 & \cdot\cdot\cdot & \cdot \\
\alpha_1 - \beta_1 & \alpha_2 - \beta_2 & \alpha_3 - \beta_3 & \cdot\cdot\cdot & \cdot \\
\cdot & \cdot & \cdot & \cdot\cdot\cdot & \cdot \\
\cdot & \cdot & \cdot & \cdot\cdot\cdot & \cdot \\
\cdot & \cdot & \cdot & \cdot\cdot\cdot & \cdot \\
\alpha_1 - \beta_1 & \alpha_2 - \beta_2 & \alpha_3 - \beta_3 & \cdot\cdot & -\beta_n
\end{bmatrix}
\begin{bmatrix} x_1 \\ x_2 \\ x_3 \\ x_4 \\ \cdot \\ \cdot \\ \cdot \\ x_n \end{bmatrix}_i
+
\begin{bmatrix} \alpha_0 \\ \alpha_0 \\ 0 \\ \alpha_0 \\ \cdot \\ \cdot \\ \cdot \\ \alpha_0 \end{bmatrix} e_i
$$

(5.12)

$$u_i = [\alpha_1 - \beta_1 \quad \alpha_2 - \beta_2 \quad \cdot\cdot\cdot \quad \alpha_n - \beta_n] \begin{bmatrix} x_1 \\ \cdot \\ \cdot \\ \cdot \\ x_n \end{bmatrix} + \alpha_0 e_i$$

(5.13)

5.2.4   Parallel Realization

The transfer function is given in the factored form of eqn. (5.14)

$$\frac{u(z)}{e(z)} = \gamma_0 + D_1(z) + D_2(z) + \ldots D_l(z) \quad 1 < l < n$$

(5.14)

There are two principal factors,

(i)   First order elements of the form,

$$D_l(z) = \frac{\gamma_l}{1 + \beta_l z^{-1}}$$

(5.15)

(ii)   Second order elements of the form

$$D_l(z) = \frac{\gamma_{l_0} + \gamma_{l_1} z^{-1}}{1 + \beta_{l_1} z^{-1} + \beta_{l_2} z^{-2}}$$

(5.16)

(a) Hardware realization is shown in Fig. 5.4

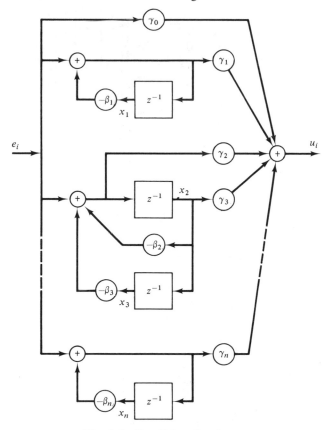

Fig. 5.4 Parallel realization

(b) Software realization, considering only one second order element is achieved using the difference equations of eqn. (5.17).

$$x_{i+1}^1 = -\beta_1 x_i^1 + e_i$$

$$x_{i+1}^2 = -\beta_2 x_i^2 - \beta_3 x_i^3 + e_i$$

$$x_{i+1}^3 = x_i^2$$

$$\cdot$$
$$\cdot$$
$$\cdot$$

$$x_{i+1}^n = -\beta_n x_i^n + e_i$$

$$u_i = \sum_k^n -\beta \, \gamma_k x_k + \sum_{k=1}^n \gamma_k e_i$$

(5.17)

The matrix formulation of this parallel realization is:

$$
\begin{bmatrix} x_1 \\ x_2 \\ x_3 \\ x_4 \\ \cdot \\ \cdot \\ \cdot \\ x_n \end{bmatrix}_{i+1}
=
\begin{bmatrix}
-\beta_1 & 0 & 0 & \cdot & \cdot & \cdot \\
0 & -\beta_2 & -\beta_3 & 0 & \cdot & \cdot \\
0 & 1 & 0 & 0 & \cdot & \cdot \\
0 & 0 & 0 & -\beta_4 & \cdot & \cdot \\
\cdot & \cdot & \cdot & \cdot & \cdot & \cdot \\
\cdot & \cdot & \cdot & \cdot & \cdot & \cdot \\
\cdot & \cdot & \cdot & \cdot & \cdot & 0 \\
0 & \cdot & \cdot & \cdot & 0 & -\beta_n
\end{bmatrix}
\begin{bmatrix} x_1 \\ x_2 \\ x_3 \\ x_4 \\ \cdot \\ \cdot \\ \cdot \\ x_n \end{bmatrix}_{i}
+
\begin{bmatrix} 1 \\ 1 \\ 0 \\ 1 \\ \cdot \\ \cdot \\ \cdot \\ 1 \end{bmatrix} e_i
\tag{5.18}
$$

$$
u_i = [-\beta_1 \gamma_1 \ -\beta_2 \gamma_2 + \gamma_3 \ -\beta_3 \gamma_2 \ -\beta_4 \gamma_4 \ \ldots -\beta_n \gamma_n]
\begin{bmatrix} x_1 \\ \cdot \\ \cdot \\ \cdot \\ x_n \end{bmatrix}
\tag{5.19}
$$

$$
+ (\gamma_0 + \gamma_1 \ldots \gamma_n) e_i
$$

5.2.5 Numerical Example

$$
\frac{u(z)}{e(z)} = D(z) = \frac{3 + 3.6 z^{-1} + 0.6 z^{-2}}{1 + 0.1 z^{-1} - 0.2 z^{-2}}
$$

(i) Direct 1,

$$
u_i = 3e_i + 3.6 e_{i-1} + 0.6 e_{i-2} - 0.1 u_{i-1} + 0.2 u_{i-2}
$$

or

$$
\begin{bmatrix} x_1 \\ x_2 \end{bmatrix}_{i+1}
=
\begin{bmatrix} -0.1 & 1 \\ 0.2 & 0 \end{bmatrix}
\begin{bmatrix} x_1 \\ x_2 \end{bmatrix}_i
+
\begin{bmatrix} 3.6 - 0.3 \\ 6.6 + 0.6 \end{bmatrix} e_i
$$

$$
u_i = [1 \quad 0] \begin{bmatrix} x_1 \\ x_2 \end{bmatrix}_i + 3 u_i
$$

(ii) Direct 2,

$$
w_i = e_i - 0.1 w_{i-1} + 0.2 w_{i-2}
$$

$$
u_i = 3 w_i + 3.6 w_{i-1} + 0.6 w_{i-2}
$$

or

$$
\begin{bmatrix} x_1 \\ x_2 \end{bmatrix}_{i+1}
=
\begin{bmatrix} 0 & 1 \\ 0.2 & -0.1 \end{bmatrix}
\begin{bmatrix} x_1 \\ x_2 \end{bmatrix}_i
+
\begin{bmatrix} 0 \\ 1 \end{bmatrix} e_i
$$

$$
u_i = [0.6 + 1.8 \quad 3.6 - 0.3] \begin{bmatrix} x_1 \\ x_2 \end{bmatrix}_i + 3 e_i
$$

(iii) Cascade,

$$\frac{u(z)}{e(z)} = D(z) = \frac{3(z + 1)(z + 0.2)}{(z + 0.5)(z - 0.4)} = \frac{3(1 + z^{-1})(1 - 0.2z^{-1})}{(1 + 0.5z^{-1})(1 - 0.4z^{-1})}$$

$$\begin{bmatrix} x_1 \\ x_2 \end{bmatrix}_{i+1} = \begin{bmatrix} -0.5 & 0 \\ 1 - 0.5 & 0.4 \end{bmatrix}_i \begin{bmatrix} x_1 \\ x_2 \end{bmatrix}_i + \begin{bmatrix} 3 \\ 3 \end{bmatrix} e_i$$

$$u_i = \begin{bmatrix} 1 - 0.5 & 0.2 + 0.4 \end{bmatrix} \begin{bmatrix} x_1 \\ x_2 \end{bmatrix}_i + 3e_i$$

(iv) Parallel,

$$\frac{u(z)}{e(z)} = \frac{3(z + 1)(z + 0.2)}{(z + 0.5)(z - 0.4)} = -3 - \frac{1}{1 + 0.5z^{-1}} + \frac{7}{1 - 0.4z^{-1}}$$

$$\begin{bmatrix} x_1 \\ x_2 \end{bmatrix}_{i+1} = \begin{bmatrix} -0.5 & 0 \\ 0 & 0.4 \end{bmatrix} \begin{bmatrix} x_1 \\ x_2 \end{bmatrix}_i + \begin{bmatrix} 1 \\ 1 \end{bmatrix} e_i$$

$$u_i = \begin{bmatrix} 0.5 & 7 \times 0.4 \end{bmatrix} \begin{bmatrix} x_1 \\ x_2 \end{bmatrix}_i + (-3 - 1 + 7)e_i$$

It will be shown in Chapter 6 that the direct method is the easiest to implement but the method generates the largest numerical errors. Methods which generate smaller errors (for the same word length) are the cascade and the parallel realization. Therefore, it should be advised: never use the direct realization except for a very low order controller.

5.3 PROPERTIES OF MICROCOMPUTERS

5.3.1 Background

Many excellent books on microprocessors are available, for example (ZI-1, BIB-1). The purpose of this section is to review recent developments in this area.

For most control engineers a microcontroller should be an input–output device, easily programmed by using a high level language. Certainly ADC and DAC should be included. The essential features of a desired controller are described in Fig. 5.5. Here we see that some of the channels are digital, for displays, interrupts, stepper motors, and others are analog.

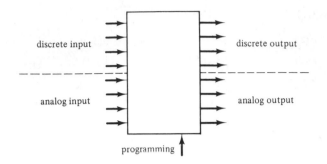

Fig. 5.5   The desired digital controller

A control engineer could ask for other features. There is a digital compensation network which looks and behaves like an analog network, see Fig. 5.6.

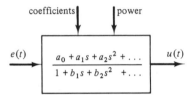

Fig. 5.6   The basic building block for an ideal digital
compensation network

In this ideal compensation building block the algorithm, the word length, the ADC and the DAC resolution will satisfy most control applications. The coefficients will be varied by the designer or on line by a master controller. Everything will be built-in, only the coefficients need to be inserted. The ideal compensation element is not available at present, but with advances in semiconductor technology it may become available in the future.

5.3.2   The System Design

Until the ideal (one chip) microcontroller is commercially available, the control engineer has to design his own system. The major component, the microprocessor, is available, but there is still a lot to be done.

(i)   Definition. A *microcontroller* is an assembly of microprocessor, clock, memories, ADC, DAC and other LSI components which are usually con-

nected together via a time-sharing channel called a bus. The function of
the microcontroller is to accept analog signals and logic interventions, to
process this information in real time and to deliver analog signals and logic
commands as an output. All this assembly is usually mounted on one
board and supplied with ±15 V and +5 V. Sometimes the memories require
±12 V. The ADC and DAC process and supply signals in some definite
range, e.g. max. ±10 V.

Sometimes it is necessary to reinforce the computing capacity with
special arithmetic devices such as fast multipliers or fast dividers.

In addition to the capability to process analog and digital signals in real
time, the microcontroller has to process digital information not in real
time, e.g. periodic checking, reprogramming capability, modification of
the software.

(ii)   The architecture of the microcontroller.
        The design of the microcontroller is based on building blocks. The basic
        building blocks are:
— *The clock*. The clock synchronizes the whole assembly.
— *The microprocessor*. The microprocessor is a program driven sequential
  circuit whose main functions are:
  (a) to execute programs,
  (b) to control the activities of a bus-organized system.
— *Memories*. Data and program are stored in memories, as ROM (read only
  memory), RAM (random access memory), PROM (programmable read
  only memory).
— *Fast multipliers and dividers*.
— *Buffers*. Tristates, Latches, Multiplexers, Decoders.
— *Interfaces*. A/D, D/A converters, Differential voltage buffers, I/O ports for
  digital information.

The elements described above are available as LSI chips. The actual assembly
of microcontrollers using building blocks is covered in numerous books (OS-1,
ZI-1). An actual working example is described in Sec. 5.4.

5.3.3 Development Systems for Microprocessors

Programming of microprocessors.
    In the digital controller design process, the next step after the design of the
algorithm and after the selection of an appropriate microcomputer is to program
the computer and to debug the program. The verification and final tuning of the
controller program should be done by using an analog or digital simulation
which represents the plant.

The programming can be done only with appropriate microprocessor support. The microcomputer alone is helpless. Extensive software, equipment and I/O peripherals are necessary in order to communicate with the computer.

(i)   The programming.

   The actual methods of programming are extensively explained in various books (ZI-1, BIB-1, etc.). Here, we will review and evaluate the different languages.

   (a) Machine language.

      The investment in peripheral equipment is minimal if the programming is done in a machine language, but this is the only benefit. The drawbacks are numerous, i.e.;

      — Considerable difficulties in writing and debugging the program.
      — Difficulties in modifications to the program.
      — Extensive difficulties for the software designer to provide the user with comprehensive documentation.

   (b) Assembly language.

      This is a mnemonic language which is translated to the machine language and requires organization of the registers and memory addresses by the programmer.

   (c) High level languages: PLM, Fortran, Basic, Pascal, etc. High level languages release the programmer from the tedious organization of the registers and the memory, but usually the efficiency of the object code is low when compared to programming in assembly language. It can be used, however, for a long program or if the time for programming and debugging is limited.

(ii) Description of the development system components (equipment and software).

   (a) Hardware.

      Essentially this is an I/O capability for communicating with the microcomputer and memory for the storage of the various programs and data. It may include some of the following:

         Keyboard — Display,
         Keyboard — Printer,
         Keyboard — CRT,
         Reader punch (paper tape),
         Magnetic tape,

Diskettes,
Microcomputers.
(b) The required software.
Monitor.
This program supervises the whole system including I/O. The monitor organizes the memory and transfers commands to various programs.

Examples of Monitor commands.
I (address)
aabbcc 001122. .
D (address, address)
M (address, address, address)
G (address)
Editor.
Organizes any text which consists of ASCII characters into lines and blocks.
Examples of Editor commands.

Text processing:
$$C(n) = \text{change}$$
$$-S\ \text{'expression'} = \text{search}$$
$$D(n, n) = \text{delete}$$
I/O:

R Read File
A Append File
L List File
P Punch File

Debugger (Simulator).
This program analyzes the object code (our control program). Debugger stops the object code in various control points (break points), advances the program in single steps and checks the contents of the registers and the memory.
Compiler, Assembler.
These programs translate programs from high level languages to a machine language.
Cross assembler.
This translates programs in an assembly language to the machine language of a different computer.
ICE (In Circuit Emulator).
This is a mix of software and hardware, which enables the user to debug, in real time, the written (and perhaps previously debugged) software, together with some parts or whole parts of the hardware.

5.4   STABILIZATION OF AN ANTENNA DISH. EXAMPLE OF MICROCONTROLLER DESIGN*

5.4.1   Introduction

The servomechanism of the antenna dish is basically a position servo controlled by an 8085 microprocessor. The power amplifier uses pulse width modulation (PWM). The main advantage of PWM lies in its high efficiency in the power stage.

5.4.2   Description of the System

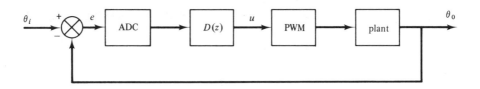

Fig. 5.7   The control system of the antenna dish

The ADC consists of two elements:

(i)   An analog switch, which selects the reference signal or the feedback from the potentiometer.

(ii)   A bipolar analog to digital converter. It is an eight bit converter including the sign bit.

The reference voltage is V_{ref} = 5 V.

Hence the ADC resolution is:

$$\text{Res} = \frac{5 \text{ V}}{128} \simeq 40 \text{ mV} \tag{5.20}$$

This resolution is determined according to the quantization noise level of the analog switch and the ADC.

The digital control element $D(z)$, implements the control algorithm which is the simple pole-zero configuration given by eqn. (5.21)

$$u_i = e_i + Be_{i-1} + Au_{i-1} \tag{5.21}$$

*Design by Nachum Nechemia

All numbers are represented in 2-complement form, and in all cases the multiplication product is truncated. During the design two word lengths were considered, eight bit arithmetic and sixteen bit arithmetic.

The design consideration for $D(z)$ and the influence of the word length on the performance will be described later.

The PWM Network

The pulse width modulator is actually a down counter controlled by the computer. The working procedure is as follows: after the control algorithm iteration is accomplished, the computer sends the absolute value of the command to the counter; it then starts to count down using the computer clock and during the count down the counter generates a pulse. Using appropriate logic the output is a pulse, its sign and width determined by the output of $D(z)$.

The Drivers and the Transistor Bridge

The output of the PWM is amplified by two drivers and a full transistor bridge (four transistors) activates the motor, see Fig. 5.8

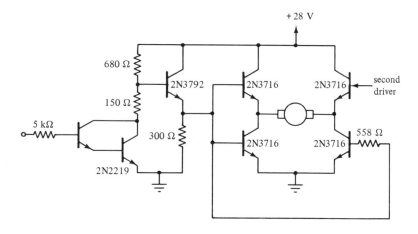

Fig. 5.8   The drivers and the transistor bridge

5.4.3   Design of the Digital Compensation

(i)   Model of the plant.

The controlled plant consists of the DC motor and the inertia load (antenna dish). Their physical properties are as follows:

K_T = 1.088 N m/A   moment amplification

K_e = 1.1 V/rad/s   electrical amplification

L_a = 10 mH $\Big\}$

R_a = 3.5 Ω   armature properties

J = 0.0945 kg m²   inertia moment of the load and the motor

Using these constants the transfer function of the plant is given by:

$$G(s) = \frac{1/1.1}{s(1 + s/3.6)(1 + s/350)} \qquad (5.22)$$

The two poles are given by:

$$\left.\begin{array}{l}\dfrac{1}{\tau_m} = \dfrac{K_e K_T}{R_a J} = 3.6 \text{ rad/s} \\[2em] \dfrac{1}{\tau_e} = \dfrac{R_a}{L_a} = 350 \text{ rad/s}\end{array}\right\} \qquad (5.23)$$

(ii)   The control requirements are:

(a) ζ ≡ 0.7

BW ≡ 10 Hz

(b) for 0.3 Nm moment disturbance, maximum pointing error of $0.5°$.

(iii)   The linear model of the PWM.

The linear model of the modulator is based on the area equivalence assumption, i.e., the integral of the voltage in time equals the area of the pulse.

$$V_M \times T_p = V_{\text{eq}} \times T_s \qquad (5.24)$$

where,

V_M — the amplitude of the pulse,

T_p — width of the pulse,

V_{eq} — equivalent voltage,

T_s — sampling time.

This model does not take into account the variation of the output impedance of the power amplifier due to the switching. This nonlinear effect is immediately visible in a digital simulation of the system, but it has an insignificant influence on the performance.

(iv)   Selection of sampling rate.

Two major constraints determine the sampling rate:

(a) the bandwidth of the closed loop, and

(b) heat dissipation of the power transistors.

From experience the sampling rate should be at least ten times faster than the bandwidth. Excessive heat generation is caused by transient effects of power transistor saturation. The rate of the transients depends on the sampling rate. Therefore this effect suggests lowering the sampling rate. The sampling rate selected was f_s = 100 Hz.

(v) The design of $D'(s)$, the analog compensation network. The closed loop system is described in Fig. 5.9

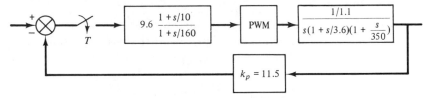

Fig. 5.9 The analog closed loop system

Using the Bode plot techniques the compensation network is:

$$D'(s) = 9.6 \; \frac{1 + s/10}{1 + s/160} \qquad (5.25)$$

(vi) The digital control algorithm.

The method used was bilinear transformation and frequency prewarping of the s-plane transfer function.

The pulse transfer function obtained is

$$D(z) = 101.8 \times \frac{1 - 0.904686z^{-1}}{1 + 0.014603z^{-1}}$$

The control algorithm mechanized in the computer is

$$u_i = e_i + B \times u_{i-1} + A \times e_{i-1},$$

where A and B are the coefficients of the compensation algorithm represented in 2-complement arithmetic.

Using 8 bit word length including the sign bit, the coefficients had the values,

$$\left.\begin{array}{l} B = -0.90625 = 8C \text{ (Hex)} \\ A = -0.015625 = FE \text{ (Hex)} \end{array}\right\} \qquad (5.26)$$

5.4.4 Simulation and Verification of the Design

Fig. 5.10 gives for comparison the closed loop frequency response of the discrete controller and analog compensation network.

Figs. 5.11 and 5.12 give the time response of the closed loop for 16 bit word length and 8 bit word length respectively. It is evident that in the case of 16 bit word length the dynamics are a little bit better damped, and in the case of 8 bit word length we may see a small deadband zone. The 16 bit word length was chosen for the implementation.

Power Transistors Simulation

Power transistor heat dissipation shows improved behavior when using PWM control. For an average correction of $10°$ per minute the heat dissipation (P_{PWM}) of the power transistors in the PWM mode compared to analog mode is as follows:

$$\left.\begin{aligned} P_{\text{PWM}} &= 0.014 \text{ W} \\ P_{\text{analog}} &= 0.11 \text{ W} \end{aligned}\right\} \tag{5.27}$$

The PWM mode of power transistor supply which alternates between cut-off and saturation is more efficient than the analog mode power supply.

5.4.5 Analysis of the Quantization Effects

The digital noise is generated by two sources, the ADC networks and the multiplication noise.

The quantization noise is generated by the quantization of the incoming signal to the ADC and by truncation of all multiplication products. These sources of noise may be modelled as white noise with an amplitude of 1 LSB (least significant bit) and a constant distribution function (see Chapter 6).

For the controller $D(z)$ where

$$D(z) = \frac{1 + Az^{-1}}{1 + Bz^{-1}} \tag{5.28}$$

the noise is given by

$$\sigma_q = \frac{2 + A + B}{1 + B} \times \text{LSB} \tag{5.29}$$

For an eight bit computer $\sigma_q \cong 11$ LSB and for a sixteen bit computer the amplification of the noise is negligible, $\sigma_q \cong 1$ LSB.

The dead band is caused by quantization. For a zero error control signal the quantization noise cannot be represented as white noise. In this case the quantization generates a numerical deadband (see Chapter 6).

The DC gain of the digital compensation element is given by

$$D(z) \Big|_{z=1} = \frac{1+A}{1+B} \cong 0.1 \qquad (5.30)$$

This compensation network decreases the information level of the incoming signal from the ADC. The significance of this is that the network will not detect signals lower than 10 LSB of the ADC. In other words, the actual deadband is ten times larger than the deadband of the ADC.

For sixteen bit arithmetic the quantization is decreased by a factor of 1/256 and the deadband is determined by the deadband of the ADC.

5.4.6 Hardware Mechanization

The implementation of the digital control loop based on an 8085 microprocessor has proved to be successful. The block diagram is described in Fig. 5.13. The assembler listing is also given.

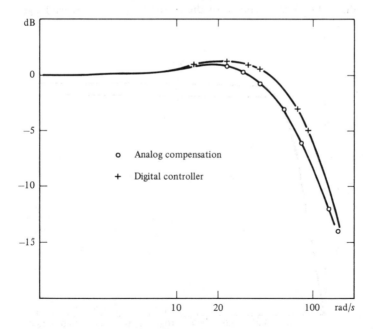

Fig. 5.10 Frequency response of the closed loop

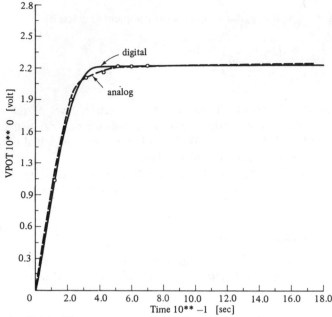

Fig. 5.11 Time response of the closed loop, 16 bit word length

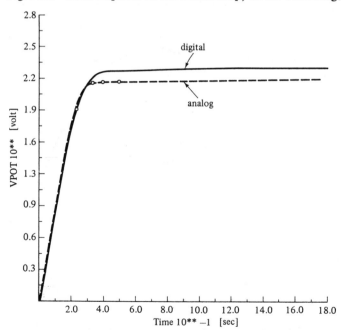

Fig. 5.12 Time response of the closed loop, 8 bit word length

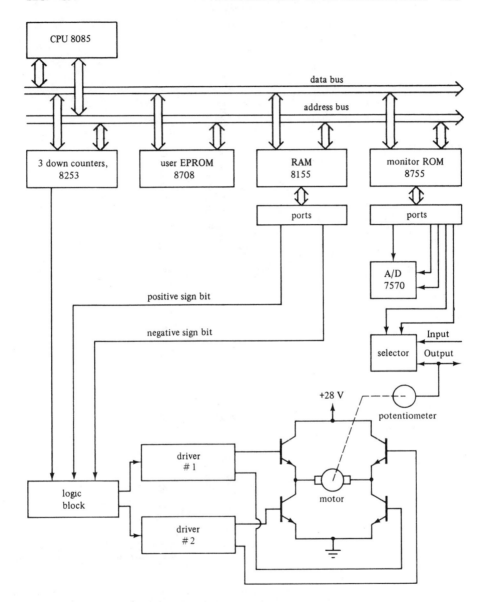

Fig. 5.13 Control of the antenna dish. The block diagram

```
;***********************************************************
;*  *  *  *  *  *  *  *                                    *
;*    ASSEMBLER PROGRAM FOR DIGITAL CONTROLLER OF          *
;*    POSITION LOOP WITH P.W.M. POWER AMPLIFIER.           *
;*    DESIGNED AND PROGRAMMED BY: NECHEMIA NACHUM.         *
;*  *  *  *  *  *  *  *                                    *
;***********************************************************
;--

2010            CONY    EQU     2010H       ;Y(N-1) COEFFICIENT
2011            CONU    EQU     2011H       ;U(N-1) COEFFICIENT
2013            UØL     EQU     2013H       ;LSBY OF U(N)
2014            UØM     EQU     2014H       ;MSBY OF U(N)
2015            UIL     EQU     2015H       ;LSBY OF U(N-1)
2016            UIM     EQU     2016H       ;MSBY OF U(N-1)
2017            YIL     EQU     2017H       ;LSBY OF Y(N-1)
2018            YIM     EQU     2018H       ;MSBY OF Y(N-1)
2019            ZIL     EQU     2019H       ;TEMPORARY RESULT
201A            ZIM     EQU     201AH
2021            DSP     EQU     2021H       ;DEAD SPACE FOR PWM OUTPUT
2022            PWMC    EQU     2022H       ;CLOCK FREQUENCY OF PWM

1000                    ORG     1000H
1000 31C220             LXI     SP,20C2H    ;SET STACK POINTER
1003 3EFF               MVI     A,0FFH      ;SET SAMPLING PERIOD
1005 D32C               OUT     2CH
1007 3E7F               MVI     A,7FH
1009 D32D               OUT     2DH
100B 3EC1               MVI     A,0C1H      ;SET PORTS MODE
100D D328               OUT     28H
100F 3E07               MVI     A,07H
1011 D302               OUT     02H
1013 AF                 XRA     A           ;CLEAR ACC
1014 321520             STA     UIL         ;CLEAR MEMORY
1017 321620             STA     UIM
101A 3E32               MVI     A,32H
101C D333               OUT     33H         ;PREPARE PWM
101E 3E54               MVI     A,54H
```

```
1020  D333          OUT   33H         ;LOAD PWM CLOCK
1022  3A2220        LDA   PWMC
1025  D331          OUT   31H
              START:
1027  3E01          MVI   A,01H       ;SELECT INPUT SIGNAL AND
1029  D300          OUT   00H         ;SEND START PULSE TO A/D
102B  00            NOP
102C  3E00          MVI   A,00H
102E  D300          OUT   00H,
1030  060F          MVI   B,0FH

              INCK:
1032  3E02          MVI   A,02H       ;SEND CLOCK PULSES TO A/D
1034  D300          OUT   00H
1036  00            NOP
1037  3E00          MVI   A,00H
1039  D300          OUT   00H
103B  05            DCR   B
103C  C23210        JNZ   INCK        ;IF B=0 STOP CONVERSION
103F  DB2A          IN    2AH         ;READ DIGITAL INPUT
1041  67            MOV   H,A
1042  2E00          MVI   L,0
1044  3E05          MVI   A,05H       ;SELECT FEEDBACK SIGNAL
1046  D300          OUT   00H         ;AND SEND START PULSE
1048  3E04          MVI   A,04H
104A  D300          OUT   00H
104C  060F          MVI   B,0FH

              FBCK:
104E  3E06          MVI   A,06H       ;SEND CLOCK PULSES TO A/D
1050  D300          OUT   00H
1052  00            NOP
1053  3E04          MVI   A,04H
1055  D300          OUT   00H
1057  05            DCR   B           ;SEND 15 PULSES
1058  C24E10        JNZ   FBCK        ;IF B=0 STOP CONVERSION
105B  DE2A          IN    2AH         ;READ DIGITAL FEEDBACK
105D  57            MOV   D,A
```

```
105E  1E00              MVI   E,0

              ;; THE FOLLOWING INTRUCTIONS CALCULATE
              ;; THE DIFFERENCE EQUATION.

1060  CD2D11           CALL   MINUS    ;CHANGE SIGN OF FEEDBACK DATA
1063  CDCA10           CALL   ADDS     ;ADD TO INPUT DATA
1066  221320           SHLD   U0L      ;KEEP IN MEMORY
1069  2A1520           LHLD   U1L      ;GET LAST CYCLE ERROR
106C  3A1120           LDA    CONU     ;CONU*U1
106F  CDE710           CALL   MULT
1072  221920           SHLD   Z1L      ;STORE PRODUCT IN MEMORY
1075  2A1720           LHLD   Y1L      ;GET LAST CYCLE CONTROLLER OUTPUT
1078  3A1020           LDA    CONY     ;CONY*Y1
107B  CDE710           CALL   MULT
107E  EB               XCHG
107F  2A1320           LHLD   U0L      ;UPDATE U0
1082  221520           SHLD   U1L      ;ADD U0 TO TEMPORARY RESULT
1085  CDCA10           CALL   ADDS
1088  221720           SHLD   Y1L      ;STORE RESULT FOR NEXT CYCLE

              ;; THE NEXT SECTION OF THE
              ;; LOADS PWM COUNTER AND SIGN.

108B  7C               MOV    A,H      ;MOVE MSBY TO ACC
108C  B7               ORA    A        ;SET FLAGS
108D  FAAA10           JM     REV      ;JUMP IF NEGATIVE
1090  3E02             MVI    A,02H
1092  D329             OUT    29H      ;SET POSITIVE SIGN BIT
1094  CAA010           JZ     DSPC     ;IF MSBY IS ZERO CHECK LSBY
1097  7D        LOAD:  MOV    A,L      ;LOAD LSBY OF PWM
1098  D330             OUT    30H
109A  7C               MOV    A,H
109B  D330             OUT    30H      ;LOAD MSBY OF PWM
109D  C3BB10           JMP    WAIT0    ;JUMP TO WAITING STATE
10A0  3A2120    DSPC:  LDA    DSP
10A3  BD               CMP    L        ;DSP>LSBY?
10A4  D29710           JNC    LOAD     ;NO,JUMP TO LOAD PWM
```

```
10A7  C3BB10            JMP    WAIT0      ;NO TRIGGER FOR PWM THIS CYCLE
10AA  EB       REV:     XCHG
10AB  CD2D11            CALL   MINUS      ;LOADING NEGATIVE PULSE
10AE  EB                XCHG              ;GET 2'C OF CONTROLLER OUTPUT
10AF  3E01              MVI    A,01H      ;SET NEGATIVE SIGN BIT
10B1  D329              OUT    29H
10B3  4F                XRA    A          ;CLEAR ACC
10B4  B4                ORA    H          ;CHECK IF MSBY IS ZERO
10B5  CAA010            JZ     DSPC       ;IF YES JUMP TO CHECK LSBY
10B8  C39710            JMP    LOAD       ;OTHERWISE JUMP TO LOAD PWM
10BB  DB2B              IN     2BH        ;GET TIMER OUTPUT
10BD  7F                RRC
10BE  DABB10   WAIT0:   JC     WAIT0      ;WAIT FOR '0'
10C1  DB2B              IN     2BH        ;GET TIMER OUTPUT
10C3  0F                RRC
10C4  D2C110   WAIT1:   JNC    WAIT1      ;WAIT FOR '1'
10C7  C32710            JMP    START      ;START NEW CYCLE

                        ; ADDS FUNCTION
                        ; ADD DE TO HL WITH OVERFLOW CHECKING
                        ; RESULT IN HL
                        ; ALL REGISTERS AND FLAGS ARE AFFECTED
                        ;

10CA  7C       ADDS:    MOV    A,H
10CB  E67F              ANI    7FH        ;RESET SIGN BIT
10CD  47                MOV    B,A
10CE  4D                MOV    C,L
10CF  19                DAD    D
10D0  F5                PUSH   PSW        ;STORE FLAGS
10D1  EB                XCHG
10D2  7C                MOV    A,H
10D3  F580              ORI    80H        ;SET SIGN BIT
10D5  E7                MOV    H,A
10D6  09                DAD    B
10D7  EB                XCHG
10D8  DAE110            JC     CPOF       ;POSITIVE OVERFLOW?
10DB  F1                POP    PSW        ;RECOVER FLAGS
```

```
10DC  D0              RNC                  ;NO CARRY, NO OVERFLOW
10DD  210080          LXI     H,8000H      ;NEGATIVE OVERFLOW
10E0  C9              RET
10E1  F1      CPOF:   POP     PSW          ;RECOVER FLAGS
10E2  D8              RC                   ;CARRY, NO OVERFLOW
10E3  21FF7F          LXI     H,7FFFH      ;POSITIVE OVERFLOW
10E6  C9              RET
                      ;
                      ; MULT FUNCTION
                      ; MULTIPLY CONTAIN OF HL AND ACC
                      ; RESULT IN HL
                      ; ALL REGISTERS AND FLAGS ARE AFFECTED
                      ;
10E7  EB      MULT:   XCHG                 ;MOVE MULTIPLICAND TO DE
10E8  210000          LXI     H,0          ;CLEAR HL
10EB  B7              ORA     A            ;SET FLAGS
10EC  C8              RZ                   ;PRODUCT IS ZERO
10ED  47              MOV     B,A
10EE  7A              MOV     A,D
10EF  B7              ORA     A            ;SET FLAGS
10F0  F5              PUSH    PSW          ;SAVE THEM
10F1  F2F710          JP      PHL          ;POSITIVE MULTIPLICAND
10F4  CD2D11          CALL    MINUS        ;IF NEGATIVE CHANGE SIGN
10F7  78      PHL:    MOV     A,B          ;SHIFT MULTIPLIER LEFT
10F8  87              ADD     A
10F9  D20511          JNC     PN           ;SIGN BIT ZERO
10FC  47              MOV     B,A
10FD  CD2D11          CALL    MINUS        ;CHANGE SIGN
1100  19              DAD     D            ;SAVE IN HL
1101  CD2D11          CALL    MINUS        ;ORIGINAL SIGN OF. MULTIPLICAND
1104  78      PN:     MOV     A,B          ;MULTIPLIER IN ACC
1105  010009          LXI     B,0900H      ;LOAD B TO COUNT AND CLEAR C
1108  05      MLOOP:  DCR     B            ;KEEP LOOPING UNTIL B IS ZERO
1109  CA1B11          JZ      EOM          ;END OF MULT
110C  CD2611          CALL    SHIFT        ;SHIFT TEMPORARY RESULT LEFT
110F  87              ADD     A
```

```
1110  D20811           JNC   MLOOP    ;BIT WAS ZERO
1113  19               DAD   D        ;BIT WAS ONE
1114  D20811           JNC   MLOOP    ;NO CARRY FROM ADDITION
1117  0C               INR   C
1118  C30811           JMP   MLOOP    ;DO IT AGAIN
111B  51       EOM:    MOV   D,C      ;ARRANGE RESULT
111C  5C               MOV   E,H
111D  F1               POP   PSW
111E  F22411           JP    ENM      ;GET SIGN OF MULTIPLICAND
1121  CD2D11           CALL  MINUS    ;SIGN IS OK
1124  EB       ENM:    XCHG           ;CHANGE SIGN
1125  C9               RET            ;END OF FUNCTION
1126  29       SHIFT:  DAD   H        ;SHIFT HL AND C LEFT
1127  F5               PUSH  PSW
1128  79               MOV   A,C
1129  17               RAL
112A  4F               MOV   C,A
112B  F1               POP   PSW
112C  C9               RET            ;END OF SHIFT

                       ;
                       ; MINUS FUNCTION
                       ; PRODUCE 2'C OF DE
                       ; ONLY ACC IS AFFECTED
                       ; --

112D  7B       MINUS:  MOV   A,E
112D  2F               CMA
112E  5F               MOV   E,A
112F  7A               MOV   A,D
1130  2F               CMA
1131  57               MOV   D,A
1132  13               INX   D
1133  C9               RET            ;END OF FUNCTION
                       ;******************************************
                       END

NO PROGRAM ERRORS
NO PROGRAM ERRORS
```

SYMBOL TABLE

```
  * Ø1
  A        ØØØ7      ADDS    1ØCA      B       ØØØØ      C       ØØØ1
  CONU     2Ø11      CONY    2Ø1Ø      CPOF    1ØE1      D       ØØØ2
  DSP      2Ø21      DSPC    1ØAØ      E       ØØØ3      ENM     1124
  EOM      111B      FBCK    1Ø4E      H       ØØØ4      INCK    1Ø32
  L        ØØØ5      LOAD    1Ø97      M       ØØØ6      MINUS   112D
  MLOOP    11Ø8      MULT    1ØE7      PHL     1ØF7      PN      11Ø5
  PSW      ØØØ6      PWMC    2Ø22      REV     1ØAA      SHIFT   1126
  SP       ØØØ6      START   1Ø27      UØL     2Ø13      UØM     2Ø14  *
  U1L      2Ø15      U1M     2Ø16      WAITØ   1ØBB      WAIT1   1ØC1
  Y1L      2Ø17      Y1M     2Ø18  *   Z1L     2Ø19      Z1M     2Ø1A  *
```

EXERCISES

5.1   A recursive filter is given by its pulse transfer function

$$D(z) = \frac{u(z)}{e(z)} = \frac{1 + 0.9z^{-1}}{1 + 0.6z^{-1}} \times \frac{1 + 0.8z^{-1}}{1 + 0.95z^{-1}}$$

Describe two methods of realization using,
(i)   direct form 1,
(ii) parallel form.
Include charts using delay elements and computer programs using an assembly language.

5.2   For the pulse transfer function $D(z)$

$$D(z) = \frac{3 + \frac{5}{4}z^{-1} + \frac{5}{8}z^{-2}}{1 + \frac{1}{4}z^{-1} - \frac{1}{4}z^{-2} - \frac{1}{16}z^{-3}}$$

determine,
(i)   a parallel programming state space representation, and draw the diagram. (*Hint*, one of the poles is $z = \frac{1}{2}$).
(ii) the same for cascade programming.

5.3   A filter with a pulse transfer function of the form

$$D(z) = a_0 + a_1 z^{-1} + \ldots + a_n z^{-n}$$

is called a transversal filter.
    Sketch the block diagrams and find the state space representation for direct form 1 and direct form 2.

5.4   Determine the state space representation of the discrete filter $D(z)$

$$D(z) = \frac{1}{(z + 1)^2 (z + 0.1)}$$

Use parallel programming and draw the block diagram.

6

Analysis of the Implementation
of the Numerical Algorithm

6.1 INTRODUCTION

The errors caused by finite word length and their influence on the behavior of the digital controller will be investigated in this chapter.

The major effort of a digital control designer is concentrated on achieving appropriate numerical implementation of the algorithm. After overcoming the difficulty of using sampled signals, every designer quickly decides on his own preferred design method. Using his method, the designer obtains in reasonable time a fairly good control algorithm, but this stage is only the first step towards a final implementation. Using an eight bit or even sixteen bit computer, the designer enters the fields of finite word length arithmetic and sampled signals. During the implementation he will encounter various arithmetic phenomena, such as numerical limit cycle, which is unknown in conventional continuous control methods.

In contrast to the sophisticated methods used in digital signal filtering, where floating point and round-off of numbers are used, in microcontrollers the methods are relatively simple. We use fixed point representation of numbers and truncation of finite word length.

A useful and extensive piece of work was undertaken by I. Shenberg (SH-1 and SH-2). His pioneer work in implementation of a digital controller on a microprocessor is discussed in this chapter.

6.2   BINARY ARITHMETIC WITH A FINITE WORD LENGTH, TYPES OF NUMERICAL ERRORS AND THEIR GENERATION IN VARIOUS FORMS OF REPRESENTATION

6.2.1   The Binary Arithmetic of Quantized Numbers

The arithmetic of binary numbers is well documented (OS-1, CA-1). We will concentrate our discussion on methods most used in microprocessor digital control. These are, two's-complement arithmetic, the truncation of numbers in A/D converters and in arithmetic operations, and the fixed point representation of numbers.

The Binary Representation of Numbers

We will assume that a word length of $C + 1$ bits is chosen to represent a number, C bits for the numerical value and one bit for the sign. Therefore 2^C different numbers may be represented with a C-bit word for the positive axis and the same for the negative axis. 2^{-C} is the least significant bit of the binary number and represents the limit of the resolution.

In fixed point representation, the binary point is fixed, e.g. for $C = 4$ we have

$$11.01 = 1 \times 2^1 + 1 \times 2^0 + 0 \times 2^{-1} + 1 \times 2^{-2}$$

$$= 2 + 1 + 0 + 0.25$$

$$= 3.25$$

Depending on the way negative numbers are represented, there are three different forms of fixed point arithmetic. They are:

(i)   The sign-magnitude representation in which the leading bit represents the sign, 0 for positive values and 1 for negative values, e.g.

$$-3.25 \simeq 011.01$$

$$+3.25 \simeq 111.01$$

In sign-magnitude form the number 0 has two representations, 000.00 and 100.000.

(ii)   The 2's-complement representation in which the positive numbers are identical to the sign-magnitude representation. The negative of a positive number is obtained by complementing all bits, and adding 1 in the least significant bit e.g.

$$-(111.01) = (000.10) + (000.01)$$

$$= 000.11$$

Using positive numbers we obtain

$$-(000.11) = (111.00) + (000.01)$$

$$= 111.01$$

(iii)   The 1's-complement representation where positive numbers are represented as in sign magnitude and 2's-complement, and the negative of a positive number is obtained by complementing all the bits of the positive number e.g.

$$-(111.01) = 000.10$$

The position of the binary point in fixed point arithmetic in microprocessors is just to the right of the first bit. Proper scaling is needed to represent all quantities in the range -1.0 to $+1.0 - 2^{-C}$.

6.2.2   Truncation and Rounding of Binary Numbers

We will assume a proper scaling, i.e. there is no overflow during A/D conversion and during arithmetic operations. However, there is a limit on the resolution because the width of the resolution is the value of the least significant bit (2^{-C}).

Truncation

In truncation all bits less than the least significant bit are discarded.

The relationship between the untruncated value x and the truncated number $Q(x)$ is depicted in Fig. 6.1.

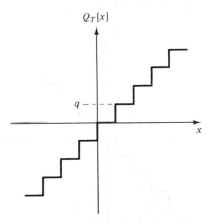

Fig. 6.1   Truncation, 2's-complement, $q = 2^{-C}$

For 2's-complement representation (fixed point) the truncation error ϵ_T, defined as,

$$\epsilon_T = Q_T[x] - x \tag{6.1}$$

is

$$0 \geqslant \epsilon_T > -2^{-C} \tag{6.2}$$

For 1's complement and sign-magnitude the truncation error is

$$0 \leqslant \epsilon_T < 2^{-C} \quad \text{for} \quad x < 0 \tag{6.3}$$
$$0 \geqslant \epsilon_T > -2^{-C} \quad \text{for} \quad x > 0 \tag{6.4}$$

Rounding

Rounding of a binary number to C-bits is accomplished by choosing the number in the C-bit closest to the unrounded quantity, e.g. 0.01101 rounded to a 4 bit number is 0.011.

A choice has to be made for rounding of numbers, e.g. 0.01010 rounded to a 4 bit number is either 0.010 or 0.011.

For fixed point arithmetic, the error made by rounding is the same for all three types of number representations (sign-magnitude, 1's-complement and 2's-complement).

The error is

$$\epsilon_R = Q_R[x] - x \tag{6.5}$$

$$\frac{-2^{-C}}{2} \leqslant \epsilon_R \leqslant \frac{2^{-C}}{2} \tag{6.6}$$

Behavior of $Q_R[x]$ compared to x is depicted in Fig. 6.2.

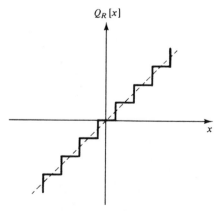

Fig. 6.2   Rounding, $q = 2^{-C}$

6.2.3   Sources of Numerical Errors

There are three main sources of errors.

Source 1.

Errors in A/D converters.

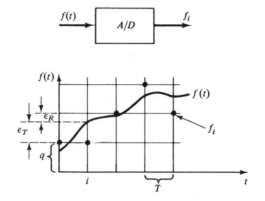

Fig. 6.3   Errors in A/D converter

T — sampling interval
q — quantization level (resolution)
ϵ — error due to quantization
ϵ_T — truncation error
ϵ_R — roundoff error (in this example $\epsilon_R < \epsilon_T$)

Source 2.

Truncation or roundoff errors in arithmetic operations (multiplication).

Multiplication of two numbers represented in floating point arithmetic or in binary fractions in fixed point arithmetic, generates these errors.

Example

Multiplication using decimal arithmetic and four digit word length.

$$0.140 \times 0.140 = 0.0196 \begin{cases} 0.019 \text{ truncation } |\epsilon_T| = 0.0006 \\ 0.020 \text{ round off } |\epsilon_R| = 0.0004 \end{cases}$$

Source 3.

Parameters and coefficients storage errors.

Example

The proper time constants for an nth-order digital filter were computed using five decimal digit accuracy (e.g. $a = 0.24635$), but the algorithm is to be implemented on an 8-bit microcomputer ($2^{-7} = 1/128$, one bit for a sign) i.e. $a \simeq 0.246$.

6.2.4   Visualization of the Numerical Errors

These errors will be demonstrated on an example.

Let us consider the first order system represented by eqn. (6.7) and Fig. 6.4.

$$\frac{u(z)}{e(z)} = D(z) = \frac{a_0 + a_1 z^{-1}}{1 - b_1 z^{-1}} \tag{6.7}$$

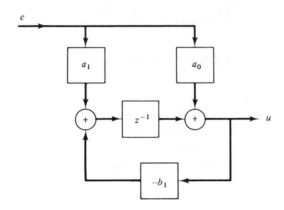

Fig. 6.4   Realization of a first order system

The errors may be included by modifying Fig. 6.4 as shown in Fig. 6.5.

Some conclusions which may be derived solely from inspection are:

(i) Fast varying roundoff errors (ϵ_a, ϵ_m) cause noisy outputs but do not influence stability;

(ii) Changes in coefficients influence dynamics and stability;

(iii) The influence of ϵ_a on the output does not depend on the systems structure, it depends on the transfer function only;

(iv) The generation of multiplication errors and their propagation depend on realization.

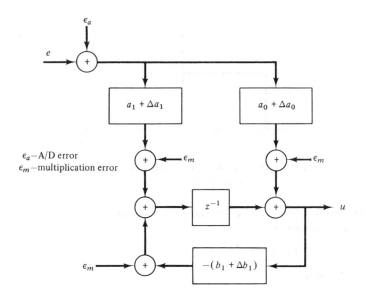

Fig. 6.5   Description of a first order system including the numerical errors

6.3   GENERATION AND PROPAGATION OF QUANTIZATION NOISE THROUGH THE SYSTEM

6.3.1   Model of Statistical Errors in Truncation and Roundoff

ϵ was defined as the difference between the exact number and the number represented in the ADC and in the processing unit by a finite word length. If $q = 2^{-C}$ is the least significant bit, statistically, ϵ may get any value in the interval $0 - q$.

In this section we will make an assumption about probability density function of c. We will assume that ϵ is generated by a fast varying signal and may be modelled as white noise, uniformly distributed along the interval $0 - q$. Furthermore, we will assume that there is no correlation between the various sources of errors.

Truncation Error Statistics

The probability density function for truncation errors in 2's-complement arithmetic (fixed point) is depicted in Fig. 6.6.

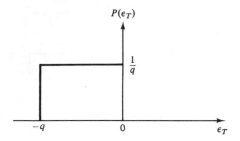

Fig. 6.6   Truncation error distribution, fixed point,
2's-complement

The mean and the variance of ϵ_T are easily calculated.
   The mean is given by:

$$\bar{\epsilon}_T = E\{\epsilon_T\} = -\frac{q}{2} \tag{6.8}$$

and the variance by:

$$\sigma^2_{\epsilon_T} = E\{\epsilon^2_T\} = \int_{-q}^{0} \frac{1}{q}(\epsilon - \bar{\epsilon})^2 \, d\epsilon = \frac{q^2}{12} \tag{6.9}$$

Roundoff Error Statistics

The probability density function for roundoff errors in fixed point representation
is depicted in Fig. 6.7.

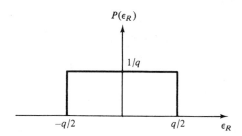

Fig. 6.7   Roundoff error distribution, fixed point arithmetic

The mean and the variance of the roundoff error noise are given by eqns. (6.10)
and (6.11) respectively.

$$\bar{\epsilon}_R = E\{\epsilon\} = 0 \tag{6.10}$$

$$\sigma^2_R = E\{\epsilon^2_R\} = \int_{-q/2}^{q/2} \frac{1}{q} \epsilon^2 d\epsilon = \frac{q^2}{12} \tag{6.11}$$

6.3.2 Propagation of the Quantization Noise Through the System

The propagation of the quantization noise, ϵ, depends on the transfer function between the source point of ϵ (ϵ_a or ϵ_m) and between the output. Given the statistics of the input noise ($\overline{\epsilon}$ and σ_ϵ) we are interested to know the statistics of the noise in the output, i.e. $\overline{u}$ and σ_u. In other words, we are interested to know whether the control algorithm amplifies or attenuates the quantization noise.

Since the central algorithm is a linear time invariant system and the various sources of the quantization noise are stationary and uncorrelated, we may use some results of the theory of random processes (OP-1).

Assuming we are given a stable, linear, time-invariant system, characterized by its impulse response, h_i, or by its transfer function $D(z)$ and we are given an input signal $\epsilon(i)$, characterized by its mean, $\overline{\epsilon}$, and its variance σ_ϵ, then, the mean of the output signal u is given by:

$$\overline{u} = E\{u_i\} = \sum_{k=0}^{\infty} h_k E\{\epsilon_{i-k}\} \tag{6.12}$$

$$\overline{u} = \overline{\epsilon} \sum_{k=0}^{\infty} h_k \tag{6.13}$$

Alternatively by using the transfer function representation

$$u(z) = D(a)\,\overline{\epsilon}(z) \tag{6.14}$$

and since $\overline{\epsilon}$ = constant, we may use the final value theorem

$$\overline{u} = \overline{\epsilon} \lim_{z \to 1} z\ D(z) \tag{6.15}$$

Example

If we are given

$$u_i = \beta\,u_{i-1} + \epsilon_i$$

and the impulse response $h_i = \beta^i$ then, using the convolution summation approach we obtain

$$\overline{u} = \overline{\epsilon} \sum_{i=0}^{\infty} \beta^i = \frac{\overline{\epsilon}}{1 - \beta}$$

Using the final value theorem based on the transfer function we obtain

$$D(z) = \frac{z}{z - \beta}$$

$$\bar{u} = \bar{\epsilon} \lim_{z \to 1} z \frac{z}{z - \beta} = \frac{\bar{\epsilon}}{1 - \beta}$$

The variance of the output signal u is calculated in a similar manner.
The variance σ_u is derived from the output autocorrelation sequence, i.e.

$$\sigma_u^2 = E\left\{u_i^2\right\} \tag{6.16}$$

where

$$u_i = \sum_{k=0}^{i} h_k \, \epsilon_{i-k} \tag{6.17}$$

which yields

$$\sigma_u^2 = \sigma_\epsilon^2 \sum_{k=0}^{1} |h_k|^2 \tag{6.18}$$

The same result may be obtained using the Parseval theorem, i.e.

given $\dfrac{u(z)}{e(z)} = D(z),$

$$\sigma_u^2 = \sigma_\epsilon^2 \frac{1}{2\pi j} \oint_{\substack{\text{around} \\ |z| = 1}} D(z) D(z^{-1}) z^{-1} \, dz \tag{6.19}$$

Example

If we are given,

$$u_i = \beta u_{i-1} + \epsilon_i$$

and the impulse response is $h_i = \beta^i$, and the transfer function is

$$D(z) = \frac{1}{1 - \beta z^{-1}}$$

then using convolution we obtain

$$\sigma_u^2 = \frac{q^2}{12} \sum_{k=0}^{\infty} \beta^{2k}$$

$$\sigma_u^2 = \frac{q^2}{12} \frac{1}{1 - \beta^2}$$

Parseval theorem gives

$$\sigma_u^2 = \frac{q^2}{12} \frac{1}{2\pi j} \oint \frac{1}{1 - \beta z^{-1}} \times \frac{1}{1 - \beta z} z^{-1} dz,$$

hence integrating around $|z| = 1$ and assuming $|\beta| < 1$, (otherwise $D(z)$ is unstable) we obtain

$$\frac{1}{2\pi j} \oint \frac{1}{z - \beta} \times \frac{1}{1 - \beta z} dz = \text{residue } (\beta = z)$$

$$= \frac{1}{1 - \beta z} \bigg|_{z = \beta}$$

consequently

$$\sigma_u^2 = \sigma_\epsilon^2 \frac{1}{1 - \beta^2}$$

The quantization noise may be amplified by fast sampling.

Example

Consider $\dfrac{u(s)}{\epsilon(s)} = \dfrac{1}{s + b}$

Discretizing gives

$$\frac{u(z)}{\epsilon(z)} = \frac{1}{1 - \beta z^{-1}} \qquad \text{where } \beta = e^{-bT}$$

and noise propagation is

$$\sigma_u^2 = \sigma_\epsilon^2 \frac{1}{1 - \beta^2}$$

Assuming $b = 1$ and $T \ll 1$, then, $\beta \simeq 1 - bT$, i.e.

T	β	$\dfrac{1}{1 - \beta^2}$
0.100	0.900	5.
0.010	0.990	50.
0.001	0.999	500.

The obvious explanation is that due to the fast sampling rate the difference between two successive numbers is small and only the least significant bits are changing.

6.3.3 Propagation of A/D Errors and Multiplication Errors Through the Controller

The propagation and amplification of the quantization noise depends on the structure of the algorithm. Various realizations (structures) were described in Chapter 5. There is no simple theory to help the designer estimate the noise which will be generated for a particular transfer function as realized in a particular structure. The only practical way is to demonstrate the phenomenon using an example and set some basic rules.

Example

Consider $\dfrac{u(z)}{e(z)} = D(z) = \dfrac{\gamma_1}{1 - \beta_1 z^{-1}} + \dfrac{\gamma_2}{1 - \beta_2 z^{-1}}$ (6.20)

We will investigate the parallel realization and see how the scaling influences the error propagation. We will also compare the error propagation between parallel realization and direct realization.

(i)   Parallel realization, case (a).

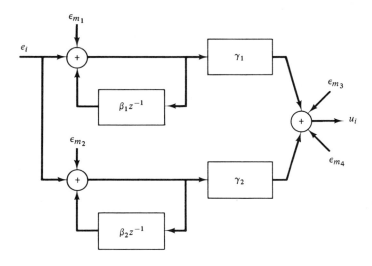

Fig. 6.8 Parallel realization case (a), including multiplication errors

We will investigate the multiplication noise generated through truncation of numbers in finite word length registers. Remember that the quantization noise in 2's-complement arithmetic has a mean $\overline{\epsilon}_T = q/2$ and a variance $\sigma_{\epsilon T}^2 = q^2 / 12$.

In the case of rounding instead of truncation the mean is zero and $\sigma_R^2 = q^2/12$. The propagation of $\overline{\epsilon}_m$, $\overline{u}$ is given by

$$\overline{u} = \overline{\epsilon} \lim_{z \to 1} z \, D(z) \qquad\qquad \text{(6.15 repeated)}$$

The mean is an additive function, i.e.

$$\overline{u} = \overline{\epsilon}_m z \left[\sum_{k=1}^{4} D_k(z) \right] \qquad\qquad (6.21)$$

where,

$$\left. \begin{array}{ll} D_1 = \dfrac{\gamma_1}{1 - \beta_1 z^{-1}} & D_2 = \dfrac{\gamma_2}{1 - \beta_2 z^{-1}} \\[2mm] D_3 = D_4 = 1 & \end{array} \right\} \qquad (6.22)$$

Eqn. (6.21) yields

$$\overline{u} = \overline{\epsilon}_m \left[\frac{\gamma_1}{1 - \beta_1} + \frac{\gamma_2}{1 - \beta_2} + 2 \right] \qquad\qquad (6.23)$$

When considering the propagation of $\sigma_{\epsilon m}$, we will need to recall eqn. (6.19) which is repeated here for convenience

$$\sigma_u^2 = \sigma_\epsilon^2 \; \frac{1}{2\pi j} \oint D(z) D(z^{-1}) z^{-1} \, dz \qquad\qquad \text{(6.19 repeated)}$$

The variance σ_ϵ^2 is additive so we may sum up the various terms, i.e.

$$\sigma_u^2 = \sigma_\epsilon^2 \; \frac{1}{2\pi j} \sum_{k=1}^{4} \oint D_k(z) D_k(z^{-1}) z^{-1} dz \qquad\qquad (6.24)$$

Consequently

$$\sigma_u^2 = \frac{q^2}{12} \left\{ \frac{\gamma_1^2}{1 - \beta_1^2} + \frac{\gamma_2^2}{1 - \beta_2^2} + 2 \right\} \qquad\qquad (6.25)$$

(ii) Parallel realization, case (b). The difference between cases (a) and (b) is in the allocation of the gain (scaling) γ.

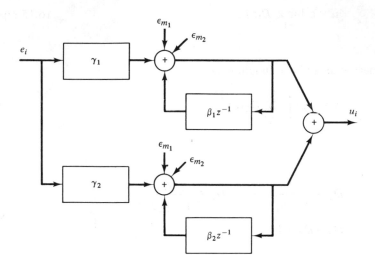

Fig. 6.9 Parallel realization, case (b)

The mean is given by eqn. (6.26),

$$\bar{u} = \bar{\epsilon} \, z \underbrace{\sum_{k=1}^{2} 2D_k(z)}_{z \to 1} \tag{6.26}$$

where

$$D_1 = \frac{1}{1 - \beta_1 z^{-1}} \qquad D_2 = \frac{1}{1 - \beta_2 z^{-1}}$$

This yields

$$\bar{u} = 2\bar{\epsilon}_m \left\{ \frac{1}{1 - \beta_1} + \frac{1}{1 - \beta_2} \right\} \tag{6.27}$$

The variance is given by:

$$\sigma_u^2 = \sigma_\epsilon^2 \, \frac{1}{2\pi j} \sum_{k=1}^{2} 2 \oint D_k(z) D_k(z^{-1}) z^{-1} dz \tag{6.28}$$

consequently

$$\sigma_u^2 = 2\sigma_\epsilon^2 \left\{ \frac{1}{1 - \beta_1^2} + \frac{1}{1 - \beta_2^2} \right\} \tag{6.29}$$

If we compare eqns. (6.25) and (6.29) we can see that for larger γ's the second realization case (b) generates a lower quantization noise.

(iii) Multiplication errors in direct realization. For the same example we obtain

$$D(z) = \frac{\gamma_1}{1 - \beta_1 z^{-1}} + \frac{\gamma_2}{1 - \beta_2 z^{-2}} = \frac{(\gamma_1 + \gamma_2) - (\gamma_1 \beta_2 + \gamma_2 \beta_1) z^{-1}}{1 - (\beta_1 + \beta_2) z^{-1} + \beta_1 \beta_2 z^{-2}} \quad (6.30)$$

which on simplifying gives

$$D(z) = \frac{a_0 + a_1 z^{-1}}{1 + b_1 z^{-1} + b_2 z^{-2}} \quad (6.31)$$

where,

$$\left. \begin{array}{ll} a_0 = \gamma_1 + \gamma_2 & a_1 = -(\gamma_1 \beta_1 + \gamma_2 \beta_1) \\ b_1 = -(\beta_1 + \beta_2) & b_2 = \beta_1 \beta_2 \end{array} \right\} \quad (6.32)$$

The multiplication white noise, ϵ_m, is generated in three different nodes, see Fig. 6.10.

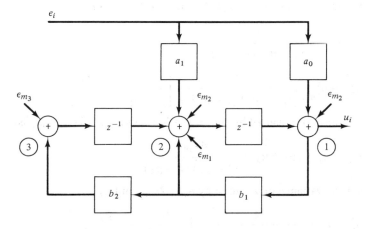

Fig. 6.10 Direct realization of the example

The corresponding transfer functions, the mean $\bar{u}$ and the noise variance are as follows.

Node 1.

$$\frac{u_1(z)}{\epsilon_{m_1}(z)} = \frac{1}{1 + b_1 z^{-1} + b_2 z^{-1}} = \frac{z^2}{(z - \beta_1)(z - \beta_2)} \quad (6.33)$$

$$\bar{u}_1 = \bar{\epsilon}_{m_1} \frac{1}{(1 - \beta_1)(1 - \beta_2)} \tag{6.34}$$

$$\sigma_{u_1}^2 = \sigma_{\epsilon_{m_1}}^2 \frac{1}{(\beta_1 - \beta_2)(1 - \beta_1\beta_2)} \left[\frac{\beta_1}{1 - \beta_1^2} - \frac{\beta_2}{1 - \beta_2^2} \right] \tag{6.35}$$

Node 2.

$$\frac{u_2(t)}{\epsilon_{m_2}(t)} = \frac{z^{-1}}{1 + b_1 z^{-1} + b_2 z^{-2}} = \frac{z}{(z - \beta_1)(z - \beta_2)} \tag{6.36}$$

$$\bar{u}_2 = \bar{\epsilon}_{m_2} \frac{1}{(1 - \beta_1)(1 - \beta_2)} \tag{6.37}$$

$$\sigma_{u_2}^2 = \sigma_{\epsilon_{m_2}}^2 \frac{1}{(\beta_1 - \beta_2)(1 - \beta_1\beta_2)} \left[\frac{\beta_1}{1 - \beta_1^2} - \frac{\beta_2}{1 - \beta_2^2} \right] \tag{6.38}$$

Node 3.

$$\frac{u_3(z)}{\epsilon_{m_3}(z)} = \frac{z^{-2}}{1 + b_1 z^{-1} + b_2 z^{-2}} = \frac{1}{(z - \beta_1)(z - \beta_2)} \tag{6.39}$$

$$\bar{u}_3 = \bar{\epsilon}_{m_3} \frac{1}{(1 - \beta_1)(1 - \beta_2)} \tag{6.40}$$

$$\sigma_{u_3}^2 = \sigma_{\epsilon_{m_3}}^2 \frac{1}{(\beta_1 - \beta_2)(1 - \beta_1\beta_2)} \left[\frac{\beta_1}{1 - \beta_1^2} - \frac{\beta_2}{1 - \beta_2^2} \right] \tag{6.41}$$

The total mean of u caused by the truncation noises ϵ_{m_1}, $2\epsilon_{m_2}$, ϵ_{m_3} is:

$$\bar{u}_m = \bar{u}_1 + 2\bar{u}_2 + \bar{u}_3 = \frac{4\bar{\epsilon}_m}{(1 - \beta_1)(1 - \beta_2)} \tag{6.42}$$

and the total variance of u caused by ϵ_{m_1}, $2\epsilon_{m_2}$ and ϵ_{m_3} is:

$$\sigma_u^2 = \sigma_\epsilon^2 \frac{4}{(\beta_1 - \beta_2)(1 - \beta_1\beta_2)} \left[\frac{\beta_1}{1 - \beta_1^2} - \frac{\beta_2}{1 - \beta_2^2} \right] \tag{6.43}$$

$$= 4\sigma_\epsilon^2 \frac{1 + \beta_1\beta_2}{(1 - \beta_1\beta_2)(1 - \beta_1^2)(1 - \beta_2^2)} \tag{6.44}$$

We may compare this noise amplification to the noise amplification in the parallel realization

$$\frac{\sigma_u^2 \text{ Parallel}}{\sigma_u^2 \text{ Direct}} \simeq \frac{(2 - \beta_1^2 - \beta_2^2)(1 - \beta_1\beta_2)}{1 + \beta_1\beta_2} \tag{6.45}$$

For high sample rates, the numerical values of β_1 and β_2 are very close to 1. Consequently, the ratio given by eqn. (6.45), shows that the parallel realization has a lower multiplication noise amplification.

The results for comparison of the mean, propagated through the parallel and the direct realization using eqns. (6.27) and (6.42) gives

$$\frac{\bar{u} \text{ Parallel}}{\bar{u} \text{ Direct}} = \frac{(1 - \beta_1)(1 - \beta_2)}{2} \tag{6.46}$$

6.4 COEFFICIENT ERRORS AND THEIR INFLUENCE ON THE DYNAMICS OF THE CONTROLLER

It is well known in analog design procedures that some particular implementation of a control network may be more sensitive to the variation of parameters than others.

The same form of sensitivity is encountered in the implementation of the digital controller. Because of the finite word length, the coefficients of the controller $D(z)$ are slightly different from their precalculated value. The difference causes variation of the pole and zero locations of the controller $D(z)$. This sensitivity depends on the numerical structure (implementation) of the controller $D(z)$. In Chapter 5, four different methods for implementation of digital algorithms were described. It may be shown that some are more sensitive than others.

6.4.1 Formulation of the Problem

Consider the transfer function $D(z)$ given by

$$D(z) = \frac{N(z)}{1 + \displaystyle\sum_{k=1}^{n} b_k z^{-k}} = \frac{N(z)}{\displaystyle\prod_{j=1}^{n}\left(1 - \frac{z^{-1}}{z_j}\right)} \tag{6.47}$$

where z_j are the poles of $D(z)$ and b_k are the filter coefficients which specify the poles. $N(z)$ defines the zeros.

Kaiser and Kuo (KAI-1) derived a formula which describes the relocation of the pole z_m as a function of the variation of b_k, i.e.

$$\Delta z_m = \frac{z_m^{k+1}}{\displaystyle\prod_{\substack{j=1 \\ j \neq m}}^{n}\left(1 - \frac{z_m}{z_j}\right)} \Delta b_k \tag{6.48}$$

Using this formula we may estimate the influence of Δb in the case of direct realization. For other realizations similar formulas should be developed. It is beyond the scope of this book to compare the sensitivity of realization of general filters. Instead, the second order filter will be worked out in detail in order to illustrate the approach.

6.4.2   Sensitivity to Variation of Coefficients of a Second Order Filter

Given a second order filter, represented in a parallel realization, i.e.,

$$D(z) = \frac{u(z)}{e(z)} = \frac{\gamma_1}{1 - \beta_1 z^{-1}} + \frac{\gamma_2}{1 - \beta_2 z^{-1}} = \frac{\gamma_1 + \gamma_2 - (\gamma_1 \beta_2 + \gamma_2 \beta_1) z^{-1}}{1 - (\beta_1 + \beta_2) z^{-1} + \beta_1 \beta_2 z^{-1}}$$

$$(6.49)$$

We will compare three different realizations.

(i)   Direct form 1.

$$u_i = (\beta_1 + \beta_2) u_{i-1} - \beta_1 \beta_2 u_{i-2} + (\gamma_1 + \gamma_2) e_i - (\gamma_1 \beta_2 + \gamma_2 \beta_2) e_{i-2} \quad (6.50)$$

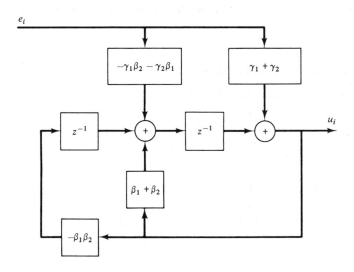

Fig. 6.11   Direct form 1 realization of the second order filter

(ii) Parallel realization.

$$x_{1(i)} = \beta_1 \, x_{1(i-1)} + e_i$$
$$x_{2(i)} = \beta_2 \, x_{2(i-1)} + e_i$$
$$u_i \quad = \gamma_1 \, x_{1(i)} + \gamma_{2(i)}$$

(6.51)

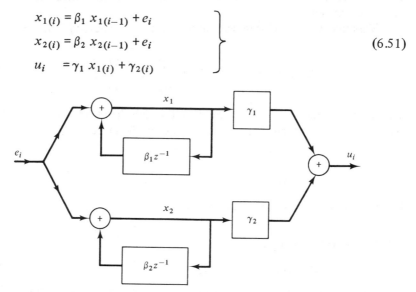

Fig. 6.12   Parallel realization of the second order filter

(iii) Cascade realization.

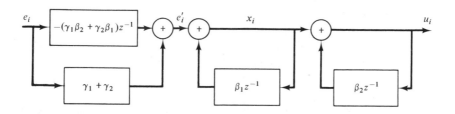

Fig. 6.13   Cascade realization of the second order filter

$$e_i' = (\gamma_1 + \gamma_2) e_i - (\gamma_1 \beta_2 + \gamma_2 \beta_1) e_{i-1}$$
$$x_i = \beta_1 x_{i-1} + e_i'$$
$$u_i = \beta_2 u_{i-1} + x_i$$

(6.52)

Note:

The coefficients of the poles in the cascade and in the parallel realization are based on β_1 and β_2. In the direct realization the coefficients are $\beta_1 \beta_2$ and $\beta_1 + \beta_2$. In order to consider the sensitivity of pole locations to a change in coefficients we shall let $P(z, \lambda)$ be the characteristic equation, where the values of λ are the coefficients.

Variation $\lambda + \delta\lambda$ yields relocation of poles to $z_1 + \delta z_1, z_2 + \delta z_2 \cdots$

$$P(z_j + \delta z_j, \lambda + \delta\lambda) = P(z_j, \lambda) + \frac{\partial P}{\partial z_j}\, \delta z + \frac{\partial P}{\partial\lambda}\, \delta\lambda \qquad (6.53)$$

The left-hand side and the first term in the right-hand side of eqn. (6.32) are zero by definition of the characteristic equation, therefore

$$\delta z_j = -\left.\frac{\partial P/\partial\lambda}{\partial P/\partial z}\,\delta\lambda\right|_{z=z_j} \qquad (6.54)$$

For sensitivity of the second order system:

(i)   Direct realization gives

$$P = z^2 - (\beta_1 + \beta_2)z + \beta_1\beta_2 \qquad (6.55)$$

We will define $\beta_1 + \beta_2 = \lambda_1$ and $\beta_1\beta_2 = \lambda_2$. Partial differentiation yields,

$$\frac{\partial P}{\partial\lambda_1} = -z, \quad \frac{\partial P}{\partial z} = 2z - \lambda_1, \quad \frac{\partial P}{\partial\lambda_2} = 1 \qquad (6.56)$$

Consequently

$$\frac{\delta z}{\delta\lambda_1} = -\left.\frac{-z}{2z - \lambda_1}\right|_{z=\beta_1} = \frac{\beta_1}{2\beta_1 - (\beta_1 + \beta_2)} = \frac{\beta_1}{\beta_1 - \beta_2} \qquad (6.57)$$

$$\frac{\delta z}{\delta\lambda_2} = \left.\frac{-1}{2z - \lambda_1}\right|_{z=\beta_1} = \frac{-1}{\beta_1 - \beta_2} \qquad (6.58)$$

For closely located poles ($\beta_1 \simeq \beta_2$) the direct realization, based on $\beta_1 + \beta_2$ and $\beta_1\beta_2$, is highly sensitive to variation in coefficients.

(ii)   Cascade and parallel realization.
In the cascade and parallel realization the coefficients mechanized in the algorithm are the poles themselves.

We have seen that in a second order filter the cascade and parallel realization are less sensitive than the direct realization. Therefore, as a general rule, we can see that it is best not to use the direct realization for limited length memory words.

6.5 NONLINEAR PROPERTIES OF THE CONTROLLER CAUSED BY QUANTIZATION, DEADBAND, LIMIT CYCLE

Another source of error is a slow varying quantization error. Essentially, a recursive filter with finite word length arithmetic, represents a nonlinear feedback system which generates nonlinear effects such as deadband and limit cycle. Furthermore, a finite word length ADC may generate a limit cycle of the whole closed loop system.

6.5.1   Illustration of the Phenomenon

Before a more indepth analysis will be done, we will demonstrate the deadband and the limit cycle on decimal arithmetic. We will use an equivalent 2's complement for truncation, e.g. 8.6 truncated to decimal point is 8 and −8.6 truncated is −9.

Example 1.

Consider a first order filter defined by

$$\frac{u(z)}{e(z)} = \frac{1}{1 - 0.9z^{-1}} \qquad (6.59)$$

Let the input be a step function, i.e.

$$e(z) = \frac{1}{1 - z^{-1}} \qquad (6.60)$$

and the initial condition

$$u_0 = 3$$

The output is given by the recursive equation

$$u_{i+1} = 0.9u_i + e_{i+1} \qquad (6.61)$$

We will calculate a table of u_i using decimal arithmetic.

i	e_i	roundoff u_i		truncation u_i	
0	0	3	3	3	3
1	1	3.7	4	3.7	3
2	1	4.6	5	3.7	3
3	1	5.5	5	.	.
4	1	5.5	5	.	.
5	1	.	.	.	.
6	1	.	.	.	.

For a large word length the asymptotic solution is $u_\infty = 10$.

It will be shown later that there is a deadband which cannot be crossed. For this example the deadband is between the numbers 5–15 for rounding and 0–10 for truncation. Any initial conditions within the ranges serve as a steady state solution.

Example 2.

Consider a first order filter defined by

$$\frac{u(z)}{e(z)} = \frac{1}{1 + 0.9z^{-1}} \tag{6.62}$$

Let the input be an impulse at $i = 1$, $e(z) = 10$, and initial condition $u_0 = 0$.
We will solve

$$u_{i+1} = -0.9u_i + e_{i+1} \tag{6.63}$$

The steady state value for an infinite word length is

$$u_\infty = \lim_{z \to 1} \frac{(1 - z)z}{z + 0.9} = 0 \tag{6.64}$$

We will describe the behavior of the output, u, for a finite word length.

i	e_i	u_i	rounded	u_i	truncated
0	0	0	0	0	0
1	10	10	10	10	10
2	0	−9	−9	−9	−9
3	0	8.1	8	8.1	8
4	0	−7.2	−7	−7.2	−8
5	0	6.3	6	7.2	7
6	0	−5.4	−5	−5.3	−7
7	0	4.5	5	6.3	6
8	0	−4.5	−5	−5.4	−6
				5.4	5

The rounded value of u_i is oscillating between the limit cycle ±5. On the other hand, for this case only, the truncated value of u_i asymptotically converges to the correct steady state.

Example 3.

To avoid the deadband and the limit cycle a numerical dither may be used.

$$u(z) = \frac{1}{1 - 0.9z^{-1}} [e(z) + d] \tag{6.65}$$

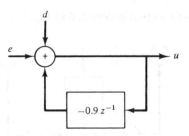

Fig. 6.14   The first order filter including dither

Let $d = \pm 0.5$ be a randomly distributed signal and

$$e(z) = \frac{1}{1 - z^{-1}} \qquad u_0 = 3$$

i	e_i	d	rounded u_i		truncated u_i	
0	0	0	3	3	3	3
1	1	0.5	4.2	4	4.2	4
2	1	0.5	5.1	5	5.1	5
3	1	−0.5	5.0	5	5.0	5
4	1	0.5	6.0	6	6.0	6
5	1	0.5	6.9	7	6.9	6
6	1	−0.5	6.8	7	5.9	5
7	1	0.5	7.8	8	6.0	6
.	.	.	.	.	.	.
.	.	.	.	.	.	.
.	.	.	.	.	.	.
				10		6

In the case of rounding, the dither helps to convert u_i to the steady state value.

This example is demonstrated for interest, it is impractical to use numerical dither in a real time digital controller.

6.5.2   Zero Input Limit Cycle in Open Loop, 2's-Complement Truncation

We will follow essentially the work of Shenberg (SH-1, SH-2).

The basic element of a parallel or cascade realization of a controller is a first order section defined by

$$D(z) = \frac{1 + a z^{-1}}{1 + b z^{-1}} \tag{6.66}$$

The block diagram of this section is depicted in Fig. 6.15.

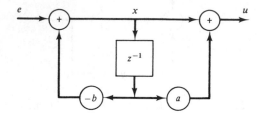

Fig. 6.15   The first order section

The recursive computation is given by:

$$x_i = -b\, x_{i-1} + e_i \tag{6.67}$$

$$u_i = x_i + a\, x_{i-1} \tag{6.68}$$

where x is the state variable of the section. In fixed point arithmetic, x is less than or equal to 1.

The 2's-complement truncation will be represented by a truncation operator $Q[\ ]$.

The 2's-complement truncated state variable x_i can be computed in one of two ways, i.e.

$$x_i = -Q\,[b\, x_{i-1}] + e_i \tag{6.69}$$

$$x_i = Q\,[(-b)\, x_{i-1}] + e_i \tag{6.70}$$

Usually $b < 0$, in real time controllers, therefore the form of eqn. (6.70) is preferred.

Two distinct cases will be considered.

(i) $b > 0$

There is no limit cycle. As demonstrated in example 2 (Sec. 6.5.1), the state variable alternates its sign, and whenever it is positive the truncation operator reduces its absolute value until it reaches the steady state.

(ii) $b < 0$

If $x_0 > 0$ and eqn. (6.70) is used we say that there is no limit cycle. For $x_0 < 0$ there is a limit cycle.

It can be shown that the conditions for a limit cycle are:

$$\frac{-q}{1 - |b|} \leqslant \text{limit cycle} \leqslant 0 \tag{6.71}$$

where $q = 2^{-C}$ the least significant bit and $|b| > 0.5$.

The limit cycle amplitude of u_i is

$$u_i = x_i + a \; x_{i-1} \tag{6.72}$$

For $a < 0$ eqn. (6.72) truncated yields

$$u_i = x_i - Q[(-a)x_{i-1}] \tag{6.73}$$

Using eqn. (6.71) the limit cycle amplitude of the output u is given by

$$|u_i| \leqslant \left\{ \frac{1 - |a|}{1 - |b|} + 1 \right\} \; q \tag{6.74}$$

Shenberg's result (SH-1) demonstrates that the open loop limit cycle of the filter is negligible compared to the closed loop limit cycle.

6.5.3   Zero Input Closed Loop Limit Cycle Caused by Truncation of the Word Length

The limit cycle of the plant is a significant phenomenon of the closed loop. This limit cycle, which is different from the limit cycle of the digital filter, is mainly caused by three factors; the ADC resolution, the digital algorithm scaling, and the scaling of the sensors and the servo actuators.

Again we will follow Shenberg (SH-1).

(i)   The deadband of the ADC depends on the range (ADRANGE) and on the resolution ($q = 2^{-C}$).

$$\text{ADC deadband} = \text{ADRANGE} \times q \tag{6.75}$$

The range is selected according to the requirements of the range of the incoming signal. Any increase of the ADC deadband causes a noticeable limit cycle behavior.

This phenomenon is demonstrated for a roll angle controller, see Fig. 6.16.

(ii)   The deadband of the algorithm depends on its word length, on the range of the ADC, and on the DC gain of the algorithm.

Let us consider the controller given by eqn. (6.66),

$$\text{deadband (D)} = \frac{\text{LSB}}{D(\omega = 0)} \text{ADRANGE} = \frac{1 + b}{1 + a} \; 2^{-C} \text{ ADRANGE} \tag{6.76}$$

For 2's complement artihmetic, whenever the absolute value of the output is lower than the LSB of the controller, it is truncated to zero and there is a constant deadband of the plant not corrected by the controller.

In 1's-complement arithmetic this arithmetic deadband disappears. This is shown in Fig. 6.17.

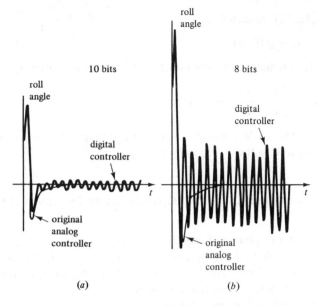

Fig. 6.16   Shenberg's results, limit cycle of a closed loop roll angle controller caused by the deadband of the ADC

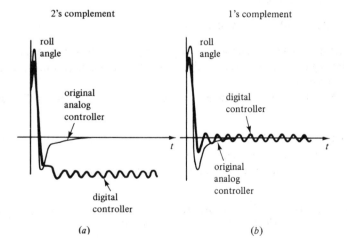

Fig. 6.17   Shenberg's results, closed loop constant error caused by deadband of the arithmetic

Since most microcontrollers use 2's-complement arithmetic, to implement 1's-complement truncation we must use Shenberg's rules which state:
(a) Multiply and truncate in 2's-complement arithmetic,
(b) If the product is negative, add 1 LSB to the result.

(iii) Filter gains, ordering of elements.
In the case of the cascade controller the overall gain should be distributed between all sections of the controller. If a high gain is given to the first section the arithmetic limit cycle decreases but overflow may occur.

6.5.4 Zero Input, Open Loop Deadband and Limit Cycle, Caused by Roundoff of the Word Length

We shall develop a general approach to the treatment of roundoff effects. Consider a digital filter represented in direct realization form

$$\frac{u(z)}{e(z)} = \frac{\sum\limits_{k=0}^{m} a_k z^{-k}}{1 + \sum\limits_{l=1}^{n} b_l z^{-l}} \tag{6.77}$$

The output u is given by the recursive equation

$$u_i = \sum_{k=0}^{m} a_k e_{i-k} - \sum_{l=1}^{n} b_l u_{i-l} \tag{6.78}$$

For a constant input e_0 and if the stored output u is rounded to the nearest multiple of q we will obtain the computed output as:

$$u_i = e_0 \sum_{k=0}^{m} a_k - \sum_{l=1}^{n} b_l Q[u_{i-l}] \tag{6.79}$$

where Q is the rounding operator.

Let us assume that the stored output $Q[u_i]$ reaches a steady state value $Q[u]$,

$$Q[u] = u - \epsilon \tag{6.80}$$

where u is the steady state value without rounding, i.e.

$$u = e_0 \sum_{k=0}^{m} a_k - u \sum_{l=1}^{n} b_l \tag{6.81}$$

and the error ϵ is a multiple of q.

Using eqns. (6.78) and (6.79) we find that computed output is

$$u_i = e_0 \sum_{k=0}^{m} a_k - u \sum_{l=1}^{n} b_l + \epsilon \sum_{l=1}^{n} b_l \tag{6.82}$$

Using the steady state value of u we obtain:

$$u_i = u \, \epsilon + \epsilon \, (1 + \sum_{l=1}^{n} b_l) \tag{6.83}$$

$$\triangleq Q[u] + \epsilon B$$

The computed output u_i will be rounded to $Q[u]$ if

$$- \frac{q}{2B} \leqslant \epsilon < \frac{q}{2B} \tag{6.84}$$

therefore the stored output $Q[u]$ will remain at the value $Q[u]$ if

$$u - \frac{q}{2B} < Q[u] \leqslant u + \frac{q}{2B} \tag{6.85}$$

This interval is the deadband of the open loop filter. The deadband can be many quantization steps wide and if the signs of the computed output are alternating, the deadband is a limit cycle.

6.6   WORD LENGTH IN A/D CONVERTERS, MEMORY, ARITHMETIC UNIT AND D/A CONVERTERS

The word length and the sampling rate are interdependent, and the selection of a maximum sampling interval and a minimum word length is an iterative process. The practical choice of the word length is determined by the decision to use an 8 bit or 16 bit microcomputer. However the designer has to estimate the required word length for the various components of the whole system. Usually his design goal is the minimum cost of the system. Obviously the cost is directly related to the word length and sampling rate. We shall analyze the word length requirements for the various components.

6.6.1   The Word Length of the A/D Converter (Open Loop)

The analog to digital converter quantizes the incoming analog signal. The digital word length $C + 1$ (numerical value + sign) of the ADC is determined by two factors.

(i)   Dynamic range of the incoming analog signal,
(ii) The quantization noise of the ADC.

Explicitly.

(i)   The dynamic range is determined by the ratio between the maximum value e_{max} of the analog signal to its minimum value e_{min}. Assuming that $e_{max} = 1$ the quantization level is $q = e_{min}/e_{max}$ where $q = 2^{-C}$ is the least significant bit. Solving for C we obtain

$$C = \log_2 \frac{e_{max}}{e_{min}} \tag{6.80}$$

(ii) The influence of the quantization noise of the ADC.

As explained in Sec. 6.3 the mean square of the quantization noise is given by:

Truncation: $\overline{\epsilon}_T^2 = \dfrac{q^2}{3} = \dfrac{2^{-2C_T}}{3}$

Roundoff: $\overline{\epsilon}_R^2 = \dfrac{q^2}{12} = \dfrac{2^{-2(C_R+1)}}{3}$

$$\left. \vphantom{\begin{array}{c} a \\ b \\ c \\ d \end{array}} \right\} \tag{6.87}$$

where q^{-C} is the least significant bit. We will consider the calculation for truncation and for roundoff replace $C_T = C_R + 1$.

Assuming that the analog signal is a random gaussian signal with a mean of 0.5 and maximum amplitude of 1 (corresponding to 3σ).

The variance of the analog signal is

$$\overline{e}^2 = 1/9$$

and the signal to noise ratio will be

$$\frac{\overline{e}^2}{\overline{\epsilon}_T^2} = \frac{1/9}{\frac{1}{3}(2^{-2C_T})} = \frac{2^{2C_T}}{3} \tag{6.88}$$

Using dB nomenclature we may write

$$F(\text{dB}) = 10 \log_{10} \frac{\overline{e}^2}{\overline{\epsilon}_T^2} = 10 \log_{10} \frac{2^{2C_T}}{3} \tag{6.89}$$

$$F(\text{dB}) = 20 C_T \log_{10} 2 - 10 \log_{10} 3 \tag{6.90}$$

Solving for C gives

$$C_T = \frac{F + 10 \log_{10} 3}{20 \log_{10} 2} = \frac{F}{6} + 0.8 \tag{6.91}$$

The ADC word length is determined by the largest value of e derived from the two requirements given by eqns. (6.86) and (6.91).

$$C_T \geq \max \left\{ \left[1 + \log_2 \frac{e_{max}}{e_{min}} \right], \left[\frac{F(\mathrm{dB})}{6} + 0.8 \right] \right\} \tag{6.92}$$

Example

The incoming signal has a saturation to threshold ratio 250 (corresponding to 0.4% resolution). The required signal to noise ratio is 40 dB. These values yield

$$C_T \geq \left\{ [1 + 8], [7.47] \right\}$$
$$C_T \geq 9 \text{ bits}$$

6.6.2   The Arithmetic Unit Word Length (Open Loop)

The quantization noise generated in the ADC is amplified through the computing process in the arithmetic unit.

The ratio between the input quantization noise $(\overline{e^2})$, to the output noise (σ_u^2), was calculated in Sec. 6.3 and will be repeated here.

$$K_m = \frac{\sigma_u^2}{\overline{e}^2} = \frac{1}{2\pi j} \oint_{|z|=1} D(z) D(z^{-1}) z^{-1} dz \tag{6.19 repeated}$$

$D(z)$ is the transfer function of the control algorithm and

$$\left. \begin{aligned} \overline{e}_R^2 &= \frac{2^{-2C_T}}{3} \\ \overline{e}_T^2 &= \frac{2^{-2(C_R+1)}}{3} \end{aligned} \right\} \tag{6.87 repeated}$$

and 2^{-C} is the least significant bit.

Assuming that the processed signal is gaussian with a maximum amplitude 1 corresponding to 3σ, the signal to noise ratio at the output will be given by

$$F(\mathrm{dB}) = 10 \log_{10} \frac{\overline{e}^2}{\sigma_u^2} \tag{6.93}$$

where $\sigma_u^2 = K_m \overline{e}^2$

$$F(\mathrm{dB}) = 10 \log \frac{1/9}{[2^{-2C_T}] K_m/3} \tag{6.94}$$

Solving for C gives

$$C_T \geqslant \frac{F(\text{dB})}{6} + 0.8 + \frac{10}{6} \log_{10} K_m \qquad (6.95)$$

Example:

Consider $D(z) = \dfrac{1}{1 - 0.9z^{-1}}$ for required $F = 40$ dB.

This gives

$$K_m = \frac{1}{1 - (0.9)^2} = 5.26$$

$$C_T \geqslant 6.7 + 0.8 + 1.2 = 8.7$$

$$C_T \geqslant 9$$

Recall, the word length is C_T + one bit for sign.

6.6.3 Memory Word Length

At the beginning of this chapter it was demonstrated that a truncation of stored coefficients may cause an instability. It was also demonstrated that the direct method of realization is not recommended.

We will estimate the influence of coefficient word length on pole relocations. The maximum permitted relocation of pole P on the s-plane is ΔP. The corresponding relocation on the z-plane is

$$\Delta z = e^{-(P+\Delta P)T} - e^{-(P-\Delta P)T} \qquad (6.96)$$

$$\Delta z = 2e^{-PT} \sinh(\Delta PT) \qquad (6.97)$$

where T is the sampling interval.

For Δz the least significant bit $(\Delta z = 2^{-C})$ we obtain,

$$2^{-C} = 2e^{-PT} \sinh(\Delta PT) \qquad (6.98)$$

$$C = -\log_2 PTe^{-PT} - \log_2 \frac{2\Delta P}{P} \qquad (6.99)$$

The coefficient word length depends on the absolute position of pole P and on the ratio $\Delta P/P$. In eqn. (6.99) we notice the close relationship between the word length and the sampling interval. Shorter sampling intervals increase the coefficient word length.

Example

For a pole location $P = 1.5$ rad/s, a sampling interval $T = 4$ ms and 1% maximal pole sensitivity, we obtain

$$C \geqslant 7.4 + 5.6$$

$$C \geqslant 13 \text{ bits}$$

$$C + 1 \geqslant 14 \text{ bits}$$

6.6.4   Digital to Analog Converter Word Length

The transfer function of a zero order hold is characterized by an amplitude relationship given by

$$\left| H_{\text{ZOH}}(f) \right| = \left| \frac{\sin f/f_s}{f/f_s} \right| \tag{6.100}$$

where $f_s = 1/T_s$, and a phase lag, $\phi_{\text{ZOH}}(f)$ given by

$$\phi_{\text{ZOH}}(f) = 180° \frac{f}{f_s} \tag{6.101}$$

For a low frequency signal the gain is almost unity but the phase lag may be significant. The DAC word length is determined by the dynamic range of the analog actuator,

$$C = \log_2 \frac{u_{\text{sat}}}{u_{\text{th}}} \tag{6.102}$$

where u_{sat} is the maximum value of the actuator output and u_{th} is its resolution limit.

6.6.5   Closed Loop Considerations of the Word Length

Shenberg's results show that the major numerical difficulties of a closed loop digital controller, using fixed point and truncated arithmetic, are caused by the deadband of the ADC and the controller.

Since the ADC is the most expensive component of the digital controller, his recommendation is that the ADC resolution shall be determined by the maximum allowable value of the closed loop limit cycle. He also found that the cost effective choice of word length is given by the following:

$(C+1)_{A/D}$ is determined by the allowable limit cycle;

$$\left.\begin{aligned}(C+1)_{\text{arithmetic}} &= 4 + (C+1)_{A/D} \\ (C+1)_{D/A} &= (C+1)_{A/D} - 2\end{aligned}\right\} \qquad (6.103)$$

6.7   DESIGN EXAMPLE. MICROPROCESSOR IMPLEMENTATION OF A DIGITAL AUTOPILOT*

6.7.1   Description of the Problem

An analog control system used for the stabilization of a small tactical missile is described in Fig. 6.18,

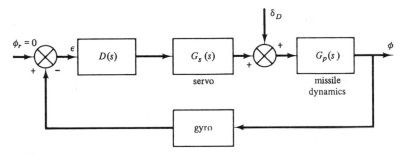

Fig. 6.18   Roll stabilization of a small tactical missile (analog compensation)

The analog compensation network has the following properties:

(i)   Transfer function

$$D(s) = 0.035 \; \frac{(0.33s + 1)\,(0.28s + 1)}{s(0.018s + 1)} \qquad (6.104)$$

(ii)   Phase margin, PM = 50°.
(iii) Gain margin, GM = 12 dB.
(iv) $f_{\text{cutoff}}, f_{\text{co}} = 2.5$ Hz.
(v)   Closed loop bandwidth BW = 5 Hz.

Disturbances:

(i)   Initial conditions $\dot{\phi}_0 = 1$ rad/s
(ii)   Disturbing moment $\delta_D = 1/10^{\delta\,\text{max}}$

*Design by Baruch Glick.

Digital autopilot requirements:

(i)   Design based on the analog compensation network.
(ii) $\Delta PM < 15°$.
(iii) Limit cycle $< 0.09°$.
(iv) Discrete step response similar to the analog network response.

6.7.2   The Digital Compensation Design, Open Loop

The design will be based on bilinear transformation and frequency prewarping.

(i)   Selection of sampling rate.
      (a) Sampling frequency will be chosen at least 6 times faster than the closed loop bandwidth.

$$f_s = 6 \times \text{BW} \cong 30 \text{ Hz} \tag{6.105}$$

      (b) The ZOH causes a phase lag of

$$\Delta PM = \frac{\omega T}{2} \tag{6.106}$$

therefore

$$f_s \geqslant \frac{\omega_{c_o}}{2\Delta PM_{\text{max}}} = \frac{2\pi \times 2.5}{15 \times (\pi/180) \times 2} = 30 \text{ Hz} \tag{6.107}$$

The sampling rate should be around f_s, i.e. 30 Hz to 40 Hz.

(ii) Discretization of $D(s)$. (Bilinear transformation and frequency prewarping).
      The discretization procedure was programmed, and the program was run for different coefficient word lengths and different sampling rates. The final discrete design of the compensation is as follows:

$$f_s = 30 \text{ Hz}$$

$$D(z) = -0.123 + \frac{0.275}{1 - 0.942z^{-1}} + \frac{0.00167}{1 - z^{-1}} \tag{6.108}$$

The frequency response of the compensation is traced in Fig. 6.20 and compared to the analog compensation.

We may draw the conclusions that:

(i)   For $0 \leqslant \omega \leqslant \omega_{\text{cutoff}} \, (\omega_{\text{co}})$

$$D(s)\big|_{s=j\omega} \cong D(z)\big|_{z=e^{j\omega T}}$$

(ii)   8 bit coefficient word length was used for poles representation.
(iii) At ω_{co} $\Delta PM < 15°$.
(iv)   In spite of the fact that the discretization program was based on cascade realization, we will prefer a parallel realization. This is chosen in order not to run into difficulties such as pole matching, organization of blocks and allocation of scaling gains.

6.7.3   Design of the Digital Compensation, Closed Loop

The discrete closed loop is depicted in Fig. 6.19.

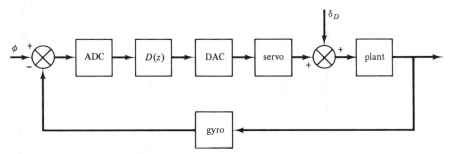

Fig. 6.19   The discrete roll stabilization system

The open loop transfer function $D(z)$ was investigated in the previous section. It was found that its frequency response was similar to the frequency response of the designed analog compensation element. We are now closing the loop with three essentially nonlinear elements, the ADC, the computer and the DAC. Various nonlinear numerical phenomena such as deadband or limit cycle may occur.

(i)   The ADC word length.
       The deadband magnitude, DB, is given by:

$$DB \leqslant \frac{\phi_{max}}{2^C} \qquad (6.109)$$

where ϕ_{max} = maximum range of the roll angle.

$C + 1$ > ADC number of bits.

Using eqn. (6.109) we obtain

$$C + 1 = \ 8 \Rightarrow DB \geqslant 0.35°$$

$$C + 1 = 12 \Rightarrow DB \geqslant 0.021°$$

The step responses for eight and twelve bit ADC are traced in Fig. 6.21. As can be seen a 12 bit ADC is required.

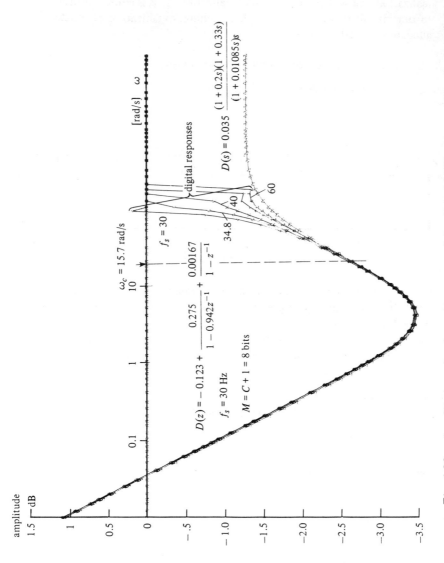

$$\omega_c = 15.7 \text{ rad/s}$$

$$f_s = 30$$

digital responses

$$D(s) = 0.035 \, \frac{(1 + 0.2s)(1 + 0.33s)}{(1 + 0.01085s)s}$$

60

40

34.8

$$D(z) = -0.123 + \frac{0.275}{1 - 0.942z^{-1}} + \frac{0.00167}{1 - z^{-1}}$$

$$f_s = 30 \text{ Hz}$$

$$M = C + 1 = 8 \text{ bits}$$

Fig. 6.20a   Amplitude vs frequency responses of the digital (different sampling frequencies) and analog compensation elements

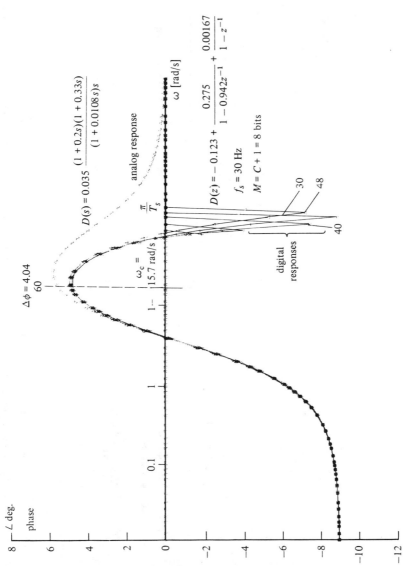

Fig. 6.20b Frequency response of the digital compensator compared to an analog compensation phase response f_s — parameter

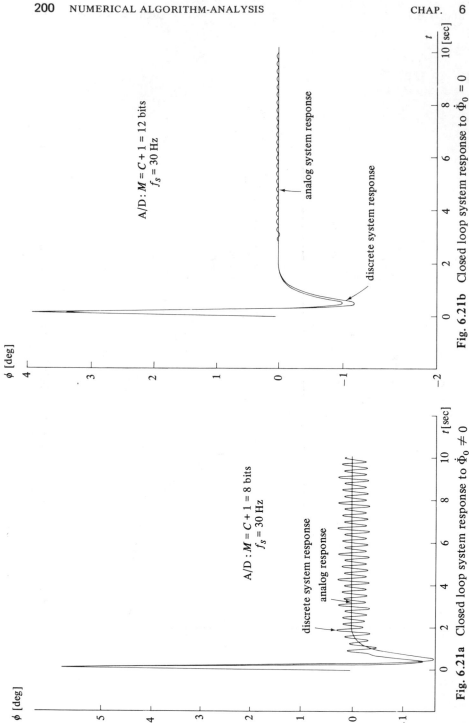

ϕ [deg]

A/D : $M = C + 1 = 12$ bits
$f_s = 30$ Hz

analog system response

discrete system response

Fig. 6.21b Closed loop system response to $\dot{\Phi}_0 = 0$

ϕ [deg]

A/D : $M = C + 1 = 8$ bits
$f_s = 30$ Hz

discrete system response
analog response

Fig. 6.21a Closed loop system response to $\dot{\Phi}_0 \neq 0$

(ii)   The CPU word length.

The CPU must have a sixteen bit word length for the following reasons:

(a) It must have at least the same number of bits as the ADC, i.e. 12 bits.

(b) Scaling factor IFAC (explained below in (iv)) requires 3-bit shifting of the ADC output. This three-bit right-hand side shift adds to the ADC twelve bits i.e. 15 bits altogether.

(c) The amplification of the roundoff error propagated through the algorithm demands $C + 1 = 12$ bits.

(iii) DAC word length.

Using a simulation scheme it was found that 8 bits for the DAC will provide for a smooth behavior of the closed loop.

(iv) Scaling factor IFAC.

Scaling IFAC = -3 was empirically determined. The scaling factor has the following functions:

(a) Minimizes the saturation limit of the state variable v_2 (see Fig. 6.22).

(b) Permits eight bit coefficient representation, e.g. coefficient A1(2) is stored as $A1(2) \times 2^{-IFAC}$.

(c) In case of $v_2(i)$ saturation, the integrator output increases by a factor 2^3.

The state variable representation of the discrete controller is given by:

$$\left.\begin{array}{l} v_1(i) = e_i - 0.942 \times v_1(i-1) \\[4pt] v_2(i) = 2^{-3} \times e_i + v_2(i-1) \\[4pt] \text{OUT1} = -0.123 \times e_i + 0.275 v_1(i) + 0.00167 \times 2^3 v_2(i) \\[4pt] \text{OUT} = 2^6 \times \text{OUT1} \end{array}\right\} \qquad (6.110)$$

The complete realization of the roll compensator is depicted in Fig. 6.22.

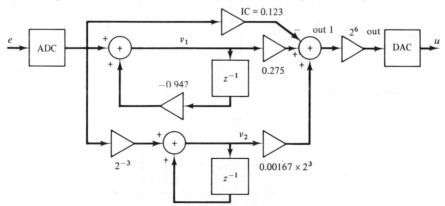

Fig. 6.22   The digital compensator for roll stabilization

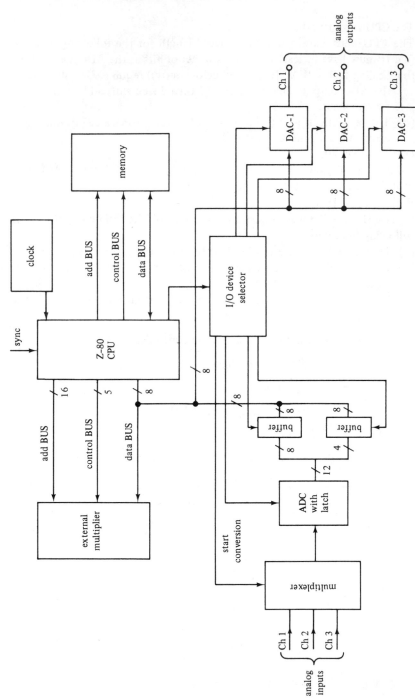

Fig. 6.23   Hardware configuration for a digital autopilot

```
MOSTEK XFOR-80 CROSS ASSEMBLER                              PAGE   1
ADDR OBJECT  STMT LABEL OPCD OPERAND       COMMENT

F               1       ;**************************************************
F               2       ;**************************************************
F               3       ;-------------------------------------------------
F               4       ;************* DESIGNER AND PROGRAMMER-
F               5       ;                 BARUCH GLICK
F               6       ;              -----------------
F               7       ;DIGITAL AUTOPILOT PROGRAM WRITTEN WITH
F               8       ;Z80 ASSEMBLY LANGUAGE.
F               9       ;THIS PROGRAM UTILIZE DIGITAL CONTROL TECHNIQUES
F              10       ;FOR IMPLEMENTING ROLL COMPENSATING NETWORK:
F              11       ;ROLL:H(Z)=(C1+2E-1*A1/(1+B1*ZE-1)+2E-3*A2/(1-ZE-1)
F              12       ;EXISTENCE OF OVF IS VIEW ON CONT OUTPUT (DAC)
F              13       ;**************************************************
F              14       ;DECLARATIONS**
F                       ;*************
                        ;
>1000          15  VR1  EQU  1000H         ;STATE VARIABLES(S.POLE)
>1002          16  VR2  EQU  1002H         ;STATE VARIABLES(INTEG)
>1004          17  VSPF EQU  1004H         ;VSPF--SINGLE POLE FEEDBACK
>1006          18  C1   EQU  1006H
>1007          19  A1   EQU  1007H
>1008          20  A2   EQU  1008H
>1009          21  B1   EQU  1009H
               22       ;
               23       ;
>101E          24  VY1  EQU  101EH         ;YAW STATE VARIABLES...
>101C          25  VY2  EQU  101CH         ;...
>1020          26  VP1  EQU  1020H         ;PITCH STATE VARIABLE
>1022          27  VP2  EQU  1022H         ;...
>1024          28  P1   EQU  1024H         ;****
>1025          29  P3   EQU  1025H         ;PITCH,YAW CONSTANTS
>1026          30  P4   EQU  1026H
>1027          31  P5   EQU  1027H         ;****
>1028          32  VP11 EQU  1028H         ;VP11=VP1*P3
>102A          33  VP22 EQU  102AH         ;VP22=VP1*P4
```

ADDR	OBJECT	STMT	LABEL	OPCD	OPERAND	COMMENT
>103C		34	VV11	EQU	103CH	;VV11=VV1*P3
>103E		35	VY22	EQU	103EH	;VY22=VY2*P4
>1045		36	V11	EQU	1045H	;INTERMEDIATE RESULTS FOR COMPEN...
>1047		37	V22	EQU	1047H	;...;
>1041		38	INTIM1	EQU	1041H	;INTIM1=Y1
>1043		39	INTIM2	EQU	1043H	;INTIM2=YP2,VY2
F		40				;*********************************
F		41				;CONTROL DECLARATIONS*
F		42				;*********************************
F		43				;
F		44				;
F		45				;****
F		46				;OUTPUT DECLARATION
F		47				;*,**
>0002		48	OROLL	EQU	02H	
>0003		49	OPITCH	EQU	03H	
>0004		50	OYAW	EQU	04H	
>0005		51	OCONT	EQU	05H	
>0006		52	STCON	EQU	06H	
F		53				;****

MOSTEK XFOR-80 CROSS ASSEMBLER   PAGE 2

ADDR	OBJECT	STMT	LABEL	OPCD	OPERAND	COMMENT
F		54				;INPUT DECLARATION
F		55				;****
>0000		56	ADCM	EQU	00H	;INPUT REG. ADDRESS
>0001		57	ADCL	EQU	01H	;INPUT REG. LEAST
>000A		58	ADCC	EQU	0AH	;MUX. REG. ADDRESS
>0090		59	ADROL	EQU	90H	
>00FF		60	ADPIT	EQU	0FFH	
>0030		61	ADYAW	EQU	30H	
>13FF		62	STACK	EQU	13FFH	

```
                 63  ;
                 64  ;*********************************************************
                 65  ;*********************************************************
0000             66  START:  ORG     0000H
0000  31FF13     67          LD      SP,STACK        ;INITIALIZE STACK POINTER
                 68                                  ;ROLL LOOP INITIAL CONDITIONS.
0003  3E27       69          LD      A,27H
0005  320610     70          LD      (C1),A          ;C1=-0.154 DPA GAIN
0008  3EB0       71          LD      A,0B0H
000A  320710     72          LD      (A1),A          ;A1=0.6887775 GAIN OF SIMPLE POLE
000D  3E06       73          LD      A,06H
000F  320810     74          LD      (A2),A          ;A2=0.02334
0012  3EF2       75          LD      A,0F2H
0014  320910     76          LD      (B1),A          ;B1=0.94625
0017  210000     77          LD      HL,0000H
001A  220010     78          LD      (VR1),HL        ;ZERO STATE VARIABLES OF ROLL LOOP
001D  220410     79          LD      (VSPF),HL
0020  220210     80          LD      (VR2),HL
                 81                                  ;STATE VARIABLES INITIAL CONDITIONS.
0023  210000     82          LD      HL,0000H        ;****
0026  222010     83          LD      (VP1),HL
0029  222210     84          LD      (VP2),HL
002C  222810     85          LD      (VP11),HL
002F  222A10     86          LD      (VP22),HL
0032  224110     87          LD      (INTIM1),HL
0035  224310     88          LD      (INTIM2),HL
0038  224510     89          LD      (VI1),HL
003B  224710     90          LD      (VI2),HL
003E  221C10     91          LD      (VY1),HL
0041  221E10     92          LD      (VY2),HL
0044  223C10     93          LD      (VYI1),HL
0047  223E10     94          LD      (VYI2),HL
                 95  ;
                 96  ;*********************************************************
                 97  ;END OF INITIAL CONDITIONS*
                 98  ;*********************************************************
```

```
            99
F F  0Ø4A DBØ1   1ØØ  CKFIR:  IN   A,(ADCL)       ;CHECK IF FIRED
     0Ø4C 47     1Ø1          LD   B,A
     0Ø4D E6Ø2   1Ø2          AND  Ø2H
     0Ø4F C25DØØ 1Ø3          JP   NZ,CKSYN
                 1Ø4
F    0Ø52 3E8Ø   1Ø5          LD   A,8ØH           ;** NOT FIRED **
                 1Ø6
```

MOSTEK XFOR-8Ø CROSS ASSEMBLER   PAGE   3
ADDR OBJECT STMT LABEL OPCD OPERAND   COMMENT

```
F F F 0Ø54 D3Ø3   1Ø7          OUT  (OPITCH),A
      0Ø56 D3Ø4   1Ø8          OUT  (OYAW),A
      0Ø58 D3Ø2   1Ø9          OUT  (OROLL),A
      0Ø5A C34AØØ 11Ø          JP   CKFIR          ;CHECK IF FIRED AGAIN
                  111                              ;********
                  112                              ;FIRED.*
                  113                              ;********
      0Ø5D 3E8Ø   114  CKSYN:  LD   A,8ØH
      0Ø5F D3Ø5   115          OUT  (OCONT),A       ;RESET OVF FLAG ON CONT. DAC
      0Ø61 DBØ1   116          IN   A,(ADCL)        ;CHECK 6ØHZ SYNCHRONIZATON.
      0Ø63 47     117          LD   B,A
      0Ø64 E6Ø4   118          AND  Ø4H
      0Ø66 CA72ØØ 119          JP   Z,ROLL          ;TIME INTERVAL LESS THAN TS
```

```
0069 78     120       LD    A,B
006A E601   121       AND   01H
006C CA5D00 122       JP    Z,CKSYN
006F C30000 123       JP    START        ;FOR OPERATOR CONTROL.
            124
            125                           ;START CONVERTING
            126                           ;****
            127  ROLL:
0072 3E90   128       LD    A,ADROL
0074 D30A   129       OUT   (ADCC),A
0076 D306   130       OUT   (STCON),A
0078 CD3B01 131       CALL  GTINP         ;DE=XIN
            132       ;*****************************************
            133       ;CONNECT PITCH CHANNEL TO ADC  *
            134       ;*****************************************
007B 3EFF   135       LD    A,ADPIT
007D D30A   136       OUT   (ADCC),A
            137
            138  DPA:                     ;DE=XIN  ,STACK(1)=XIN
007F D5     139       PUSH  DE            ;****
            140
            141                           ;DIRECT PATH Y(1)=C1*XIN
            142
            143                           ;****
0080 3A0610 144       LD    A,(C1)        ;ON ENTRANCE DE=XIN ,L=C1
0083 6F     145       LD    L,A           ;ON EXIT DE=XIN*C1
0084 CD2B01 146       CALL  MULT
0087 42     147       LD    B,D           ;****
0088 4B     148       LD    C,E
            149
            150                           ;SIMPLE POLE
            151                           ;Y(2)=XIN*2**(-1)*(A1/(1+B1*Z**(-1)))
            152                           ;****
            153
            154
0089 D1     155       POP   DE            ; ** DE =XIN,STACK(0) **
```

```
008A CB2A      156        SRA   D          ; ** DE =XIN*2**(-1)
008C CB1B      157        RR    E          ; **STACK(1)=0.5*XIN**
008E D5        158        PUSH  DE         ; **HL =VSPF          **
008F 2A0410    159        LD    HL,(VSPF)
```

```
MOSTEK XFOR-80 CROSS ASSEMBLER                                    PAGE    4
ADDR OBJECT    STMT LABEL  OPCD OPERAND     COMMENT

0092 A7        160        AND   A           ;RESET  CY (CY=0)
0093 EB        161        EX    DE,HL       ; ** HL =0.5*XIN,DE=VSPF **
0094 ED52      162        SBC   HL,DE       ;HL=HL-DE+CY  VRI=0.5*XIN-VSPF,P/V=V
               163                          ;ADDER (IN SOFTWARE)
0096 EC1801    164        CALL  PE,OVFC
               165                          ; ** HL=VRI,DE=DONT CARE **
0099 EB        166 NOOVF1: EX    DE,HL      ;DE=VRI,HL=DONT CARE
009A ED530010  167        LD    (VRI),DE    ;SAVE VRI FOR FURTHER USE
009E 3A0710    168        LD    A,(A1)
00A1 6F        169        LD    L,A
00A2 CD2B01    170        CALL  MULT
               171                          ;ON ENTRANCE DE=VRI,L=A1
                                            ;ON EXIT  DE=A1*VI1
00A5 EB        172        EX    DE,HL       ; ** HL=Y(2)
00A6 A7        173        AND   A           ;CY=0
00A7 ED42      174        SBC   HL,BC       ;HL=Y(1)+Y(2)+CY
00A9 EC1801    175        CALL  PE,OVFC     ;IF OVF (PE=1) USE SATURATION ADDER
00AC 44        176        LD    B,H
```

```
00AD 4D    177            LD   C,L          ;** BC =Y(1)+Y(2)  **
           178  INTG:                       ;****
           179
           180                              ;   INTEGRATOR LOOP
           181                              ;Y(3)=2**(-3)*XIN*(A2/(1-Z**(-1)))
           182                              ;****
           183                              ;
00AE D1    184            POP  DE           ; ** DE =0.5*XIN,STACK(0) **
00AF CB2A  185            SRA  D
00B1 CB1B  186            RR   E
00B3 CB2A  187            SRA  D
00B5 CB1B  188            RR   E
00B7 CB2A  189            SRA  D
00B9 CB1B  190            RR   E            ; ** DE=2**(-3)*XIN  **
00BB 2A0210 191           LD   HL,(VR2)     ; ** HL=VR2 **
00BE A7    192            AND  A            ;CY =0
00BF ED5A  193            ADC  HL,DE        ;XIN*0.125+VR2=VR2
00C1 EC1801 194           CALL PE,OVFC      ;IF OVERFLOW (PE=1),USE SATURATION ADDER
00C4 220210 195           LD   (VR2),HL     ;UPDATE STATE VARIABLE
00C7 EB    196            EX   DE,HL        ; ** DE=VR2 **
00C8 3A0810 197           LD   A,(A2)
00CB 6F    198            LD   L,A
00CC CD2B01 199           CALL MULT         ;ON ENTRANCE DE =VR2,L=A2
           200                              ;ON EXIT DE =A2*VR2=Y(3)
00CF EB    201            EX   DE,HL        ;HL=Y(3)
00D0 A7    202            AND  A            ;CY=0
00D1 ED4A  203            ADC  HL,BC        ;Y(1)+Y(2)+Y(3)+CY=HL
00D3 EC1801 204           CALL PE,OVFC      ;OUT1=HL=Y(DPA)+Y(SIPOLE)+Y(INTG)
           205                              ;****
           206
           207                              ;OUT=2**4*OUT1  TRUNCATED TO 8 BITS
           208                              ;****
           209
           210
00D6 7C    211            LD   A,H          ;CHECK IF ROTATION RIGHT IS
00D7 B4    212            OR   H            ;POSSIBLE WITHOUT OVERFLOW.
```

```
MOSTEK XFOR-80 CROSS ASSEMBLER                                    PAGE 5
ADDR OBJECT    STMT LABEL    OPCD OPERAND       COMMENT

00D8 FAE500     213          JP   M,NEGN        ;POSITIVE NUMBER LOOK FOR 0000XXXX
00DB E6F8       214          AND  0F8H          ;OVF,A=LARGEST POSSIBLE NUMBER
00DD CAF100     215          JP   Z,ROT
00E0 3EFF       216          LD   A,0FFH
00E2 C30401     217          JP   WRROL
00E5 2F         218 NEGN:    CPL               ;NEGATIVE NUMBER,LOOK FOR 0000XXXX
00E6 E6F8       219          AND  0F8H
00E8 7C         220          LD   A,H
00E9 CAF100     221          JP   Z,ROT
00EC 3E01       222          LD   A,01H
00EE C30401     223          JP   WRROL
                224 ROT:                       ; **HL =OUT1 **
00F1 CB15       225          RL   L
00F3 CB14       226          RL   H            ;HL =2*HL
00F5 CB15       227          RL   L
00F7 CB14       228          RL   H
00F9 CB15       229          RL   L            ;IT IS SHORTER THAN HL+HL
00FB CB14       230          RL   H
00FD CB15       231          RL   L
00FF CB14       232          RL   H            ; **HL =16*OUT1 **
0101 7C         233          LD   A,H
0102 C680       234          ADD  A,80H
0104 D302       235 WRROL:   OUT  (OROLL),A
                236          ;************************************
                237          ;OFF LINE COMPUTATIONS             *
                238          ;************************************
                239 UPDATEC:                   ;1.UPDATE VSPF
0106 ED5B0010   240          LD   DE,(VR1)
010A 3A0910     241          LD   A,(B1)
010D 6F         242          LD   L,A
010E CD2B01     243          CALL MULT          ;ON ENTRANCE  DE=VR1,L=B1
                244                             ;ON EXIT DE=VSPF=VR1*B1
0111 ED530410   245          LD   (VSPF),DE
```

```
0115 C35D00    246        JP   CKSYN
               247 ;**** **** **** **** **** **** **** **** **** ****
               248 ;**********************************************************
               249 OVFC:            ;ARRIVED HERE ONLY IF OVF. OCCUR.THEREFORE
               250              ;IF THE RESULT OF SUMMATION IS POSITIVE
               251              ;THE REAL RESULT IS GT.THE MOST NEGATIVE
               252              ;NUMBER.ELSE IT IS GT.THE MOST POSITIVE
               253              ;NUMBER WHICH IS REPRESENTABLE.
0118 F22301    254        JP   P,NGOV
011B 21FF7F    255        LD   HL,7FFFH
011E 3E00      256        LD   A,00H
0120 D305      257        OUT  (OCONT),A    ;INDICATE POSITIVE OVERFLOW
0122 C9        258        RET
0123 210180    259 NGOV:  LD   HL,8001H
0126 3EFF      260        LD   A,0FFH
0128 D305      261        OUT  (OCONT),A    ;INDICATE NEGATIVE OVERFLOW.
012A C9        262        RET
               263 ;**********************************************************
               264 MULT:            ;MULT-ON ENTRANCE  DE =MULTIPLICAND(16 BIT
               265                  ;L=MULTIPLIER(8 BITS)
```

```
MOSTEK XFOR-80 CROSS ASSEMBLER                    PAGE   6
ADDR OBJECT  STMT LABEL OPCD OPERAND    COMMENT

               266                      ;H =COMMAND
```

```
267  012B  2691          LD   H,91H       ;NO SIGN,WITH ROUNDING
268  012D  73            LD   (HL),E      ;X*YL
269  012E  7E            LD   A,(HL)      ;A=(X*YL) MOST PART
270  012F  24            INC  H           ;SIGNED MULT,WITH ROUNDING
271  0130  72            LD   (HL),D      ;X*YH
272  0131  56            LD   D,(HL)      ;D=(X*YH) MOST
273  0132  CBA4          RES  4,H         ;ADDRESS OF LEAST SIGNIFICANT PART
274  0134  86            ADD  A,(HL)      ;A=(X*YH)MOST + (X*YH) LEAST
275  0135  D23901        JP   NC,SOF
276  0138  14            INC  D
277  0139  5F     SOF:   LD   E,A
278  013A  C9            RET
279
280  ;*****************************************************************
281  ;GTINP FUNCTION:
282  ;READ THE ADC INPUT,ADJUST THE FORMAT FOR TWOS COMPLEMENT
283  ;AND PUT THE RESULT IN DE REGISTER.
284  ;NOTICE THAT THE ADC IS 12BIT AND THE RESULT IS IN 16BIT
285  ;REPRESENTATION .
286         GTINP:
287  013B  DB01   CEOC:  IN   A,(ADCL)
288  013D  CB5F          BIT  3,A
289  013F  CA3B01        JP   Z,CEOC      ;IF NOT FINISHED GO BACK,
290                                       ;CONVERSION IS FINISHED.
291  0142  DB00          IN   A,(ADCM)
292  0144  2F            CPL              ;TWO'S COMPLEMENT FORMAT
293  0145  C580          ADD  A,80H
294  0147  57            LD   D,A         ;SET SIGN FLAG ACCORDING TO ADCM
295  0148  B7            OR   A
296  0149  DB01          IN   A,(ADCL)
297  014B  F25301        JP   P,XINP      ;XIN IS NEGATIVE
298  014E  F60F          OR   0FH
299  0150  C35501        JP   XINRE
300  0153  E6F0   XINP:  AND  0F0H        ;CANCEL 4 LSB.
301  0155  5F     XINRE: LD   E,A         ;XIN READY IN ACC
302                                       ;** DE= XIN **
```

```
0156 C9    303        RET
           304     ; ********************************
0157       305        END
```

TOTAL ASSEMBLER ERRORS = 87

MOSTEK XFOR-80 CROSS ASSEMBLER   PAGE 7

SYMBOL TABLE

A1	1007	A2	1008	ADCC	000A	ADCL	0001
ADCM	0000	ADPIT	00FF	ADROL	0090	ADVAW	0030
B1	1009	C1	1006	CEOC	013B	CKFIR	004A
CKSYN	005D	DPA	0080	GTINP	013B	INTG	00AE
INTIM1	1041	INTIM2	1043	MULT	012B	NEGN	00E5
NGOV	012	3NOOVF	1 00	990CON T	0	005OPITCH.	

003

OROLL	0002	OVFC	0118	OYAW	0004	P1	1024
P3	1025	P4	1026	P5	1027	ROLL	0072
ROT	00F1	SOF	0139	STACK	13FF	START	0000
STCON	0006	UPDATE	0106	V11	1045	V22	1047
VP1	1020	VP11	1028	VP2	1022	VP22	102A
VR1	1000	VR2	1002	VSPF	1004	VY1	101E
VY11	103C	VY2	101C	VY22	103E	WRROL	0104
XINP	0153	XINRE	0155				

6.7.4 Implementation

In Fig. 6.23 a possible implementation is depicted which uses the Z80 micro-processor. Obviously this implementation includes channels for pitch and yaw stabilization (see the program printout on pages 203–213).

Notice that to increase the computational rate an external multiplication unit (MM1-67558) was incorporated in the system. This unit multiplies an eight bit number by a sixteen bit number in 40 μs.

The computational time for the roll stabilization is 210 μs. Memory storage required approximately 272 bytes.

EXERCISES

6.1 Find the two's-complement representations for the following numbers: $\frac{3}{4}, -\frac{3}{4}, \frac{7}{8}, -\frac{7}{16}$.

6.2 Calculate the quantization noise propagation for the discrete filter $D(z)$.

$$D(z) = \frac{0.1}{(1 - 0.9z^{-1})(1 - 0.95z^{-1})}$$

6.3 The input to an ADC is in the range ± 10 V.
Find the number of bits required for 80 dB signal to noise ratio.

6.4 Calculate the multiplication noise generation of $D(z)$, where

$$D(z) = \frac{0.1}{(1 - 0.9z^{-1})(1 - 0.95z^{-1})}$$

(i)   Use parallel realization.
(ii) Use direct form 1 realization.

Compare your answers.

6.5 Find the noise output for a compensator given by $D(z)$, where

$$D(z) = \frac{1}{(1 - 0.5z^{-1})(1 - 0.9z^{-1})}$$

Find the section ordering which minimizes the output noise for cascade representation.

6.6   Suppose $D(z)$ given in Sec. 6.6 is implemented in direct form 1 using an 8 bit computer. Assuming the input is zero

  (i)   Find the deadband.
  (ii) If the initial conditions are $u_0 = 0$ and $u_1 = 1$, calculate the output u until a steady-state pattern emerges.
  (iii) Repeat for $u_0 = 0, u_1 = 10$.
  (iv) Repeat for $u_0 = 10, u_1 = 10$.

6.7   Find the limit cycle in a direct form realization for $D(z) = 1/(1 - 0.9z^{-1})^2$.

6.8   For the discrete controller $D(z)$ given in Sec. 6.7.3:

  (i)   Plot the location of the poles and zeros and estimate the stability.
  (ii) Sketch the system response to a step function.
  (iii) What is the DC gain of $D(z)$?
  (iv) Consider the factor which represents a simple pole. Why does this factor not cause limit cycle behavior when the arithmetic includes truncation of the least significant bit?
        [*Hint*: Consider v_{i-1} and $Q(v_{i-1})$, where Q is the truncation of 2's-complement. What will happen if the sign of the pole is changed?]

6.9   Consider the frequency response $D(z)|_{z=e^{j\omega T}}$ of the digital filter given by eqn. (6.68) (Fig. 6.15).

  (i)   Trace the frequency response (amplitude and phase) of $D(z)$ in the range $0 \leqslant \omega \leqslant 5\pi$.
  (ii) What will be the significance of 100 Hz frequency noise on the incoming signal from the gyro (see Fig. 6.14).

6.10   The following question deals with fixed point arithmetic.

  (i)   Numbers in fixed point representation have M bits where the most significant bit is the sign.
        What kind of error may you expect in the case of the addition of two numbers, subtraction of two numbers? How may the probability of this error be decreased?
  (ii) For an additive operation on two numbers you may use a microcomputer which has the following set of commands: addition, verification of sign bit, verification of sign bit and conditional jump. Trace the flow chart of addition operation for any two numbers including saturation.
  (iii) Do the same for a set of commands which includes the operation 'NOT', where $NOT(A) = \bar{A}$.

7

Selection of Sampling Rate

7.1 INTRODUCTION

It is rather difficult to formulate a uniform method for the selection of an appropriate sampling rate. The well known Nyquist criterion, which says 'sample twice as fast as the highest frequency contained in the signal' is not always applicable for digital control systems. Using this theorem it is indeed possible to reconstruct a sampled signal, but the theorem does not say that it can be done in real time, generally some lag is generated before enough sampling points are accumulated. The second point to consider is that the signal is not accurately defined, we have to consider the bandwidth of the closed loop and measurement noise. Furthermore, an input step function to the system has an infinite frequency content. For these reasons, the question of sampling rate will be subdivided into several topics which have a close interaction with the behavior of the discretely controlled system.

Towards the end of this chapter two new concepts related to sampling rate will be introduced. The first is the 'roughness function', which is a quantitative measure of the influence of discrete inputs on a continuous plant. The second concept is Peled's (PE-1) 'fidelity of response', which measures the influence of discrete control on the frequency response.

216

7.2   UNMODELLED STATES AND PREFILTERING OF UNWANTED
FREQUENCIES

7.2.1   Formulation of the Problem

The controlled plant is represented by a mathematical model formulated as a
transfer function or as a state space system. Some of the states are only estimates
and for some of them we do not want control. As a rule, we prefer to use a simple
model of the plant and to design a simple controller which fulfils the control
criteria. Verification of our design may be accomplished with a more detailed
model using a digital simulation.

Example:

Let us consider the pitch control of an aircraft as described in Fig. 7.1.

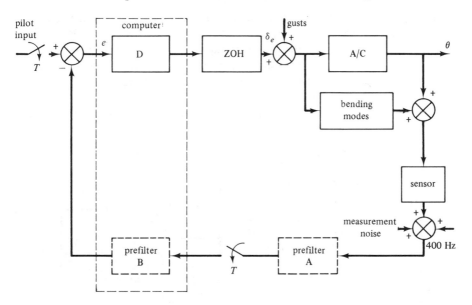

Fig. 7.1   Pitch stabilization of an aircraft

The external noise (gusts) and the measurement noise may be modelled as colored
noise in order to avoid mathematical difficulties (infinite energy of white noise).

The noise, the bending frequency and the 400 Hz of the electrical supply,
may be classified as unwanted frequencies. We do not want to control these
frequencies but they may interfere with our control system. On the frequency
chart, the frequencies are distributed as shown in Fig. 7.2.

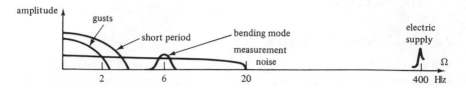

Fig. 7.2 Frequency distribution of aircraft pitch mode

As seen from Fig. 7.2, the gusts, which are acting directly on the controlled plant, cannot be filtered out. Their influence on the plant has to be controlled.

7.2.2 Unmodelled States and Prefilters

There are various physical phenomena accompanying the controlled plant and these have to be regarded as inevitable nuisances. For example, the 50 or 60 Hz of the electrical supply contaminates sensitive medical instruments, bending modes and sloshing in large missiles are picked up by inertial sensors. These unwanted frequencies are usually filtered by notch filters. Sometimes they may be modelled, sensed and controlled using schemes like the Kalman filter. Our aim here is to relate this complicated situation to the selection of sampling rates. The relevant scheme is depicted in Fig. 7.3.

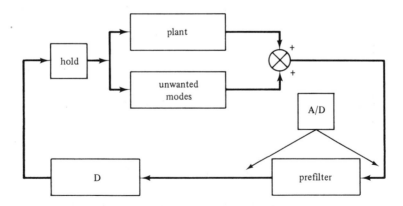

Fig. 7.3 A controlled plant including unwanted modes

We may classify the scheme into three distinct cases.

Case (i)   The frequencies of the unwanted modes (ω_b) are far from the bandwidth of interest. The design solution is shown in Fig. 7.4.

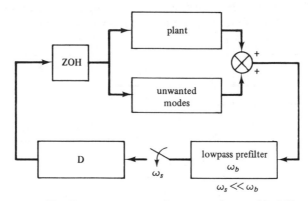

Fig. 7.4 Control configuration for $\omega_b \gg \text{BW}$

The time constants of the analog prefilter are short and we may or may not incorporate the filter in the plant. The unwanted frequencies are not included. The sampling rate is chosen according to the bandwidth and the time response requirements.

Case (ii)   The frequencies of the unwanted modes are stable but near the desired bandwidth. The design solution is given in Fig. 7.5.

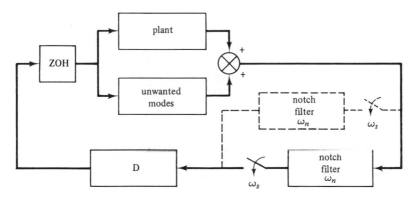

Fig. 7.5 Control configuration $\omega_s > \omega_n$

The sampling rate is chosen according to the bandwidth and the time response requirements. The resonant frequency of the sharp analog or digital notch filter (ω_n) does not interfere too much with the control design and the sampling rate.

Case (iii) The resonant frequencies of the unwanted modes move close to the bandwidth. One design solution is shown in Fig. 7.6.

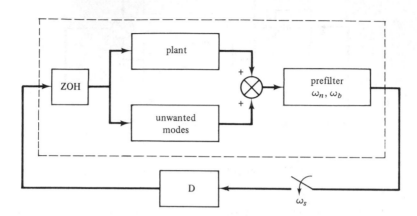

Fig. 7.6   Control configuration $\omega_s < \omega_n$, ω_b

The long time constants of the lowpass prefilter, or the wide band notch filter have to be incorporated in the control design. The prefilter structure increases the complexity of the plant. Therefore the control design has to take it into account. An alternative design solution is shown in Fig. 7.7.

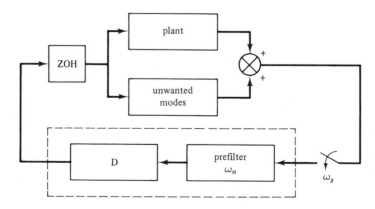

Fig. 7.7   Control configuration, $\omega_n < \omega_s$

In this case, all the prefiltering and averaging of the data is implemented discretely in the digital computer. The sampling rate has to be faster than the time constants of the prefilter, but the computation rate may be much lower. The main advantage of this approach lies in the possibility of adjusting parameters of the prefilter or the notch filter to allow for changes in the dynamics of the unwanted modes. This may be done in an open loop or by using an adaptive control scheme.

As an example let us consider the slender supersonic missile modelled in Fig. 7.8.

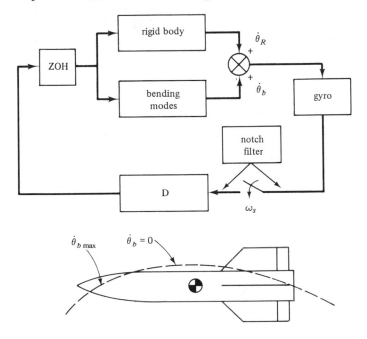

Fig. 7.8 A slender body missile including bending modes

A rate gyro measures the pitch rate $\dot{\theta}$. The value of $\dot{\theta}_b$ detected by the gyro depends on its location and on the shape of the bending. The fastest short period open loop frequency is 13 rad/s and the bending mode frequency migrates from 25 rad/s to 30 rad/s during the flight. The neutral position of the instrument ($\dot{\theta}_b = 0$) changes its location during the flight.

We shall consider a prefilter solution. Obviously the filtered spectrum is wide for low prefilter time constants. Low time constants have a strong influence on the dynamics and consequently it is necessary to incorporate the prefilter as a part of the plant in the control design. There is a mutual interdependence between the sampling rate, the measurement noise and the time constant of the prefilter.

The rms value of the output (θ) is high for low sampling rates. Quantitative results are obtained by simulation and computation of the rms values for different sampling rates. The bending frequency is fairly close to the short period

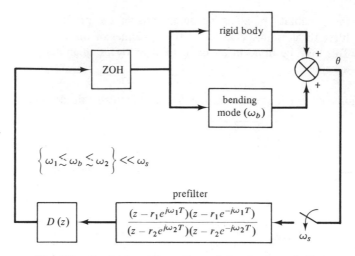

Fig. 7.9   Control configuration of the slender missile

mode. The sampling rate will be chosen according to the time response requirement and far away from the bending frequency. The prefilter chosen has a digital
notch filter characteristic with coefficients varying as a function of time. The
result is shown in Fig. 7.9.

7.2.3   Prefilters and Measurement Noise

Measurement noise tends to be distributed on a wide spectrum, similar to a
white noise characteristic. Consequently, if the rms value of the noise is too
high, it is necessary to filter out the noise using a continuous lowpass prefilter.

As an example we shall consider the system studied by Peled (PE-1) which
we discussed in Sec. 4.6.3. The scheme is repeated in Fig. 7.10 for convenience.

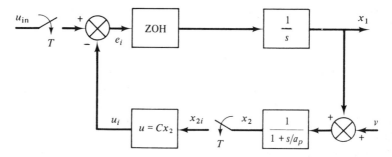

Fig. 7.10   Example of prefilter and measurement noise

The continuous measurement noise is modelled as a first order colored noise with a correlation time of 0.005 s.

The rms response of the plant ($\bar{x}_i$), excited by the nearly white measurement noise, is calculated by the procedure described in Sec. 4.5. However, in this example, the plant includes the integrator and the prefilter, and the external disturbance is the measurement noise.

The combined plant is given by:

$$
\begin{bmatrix} \dot{x}_1 \\ \dot{x}_2 \end{bmatrix} = \begin{bmatrix} 0 & 0 \\ a_p & -a_p \end{bmatrix} \begin{bmatrix} x_1 \\ x_2 \end{bmatrix} + \begin{bmatrix} 1 \\ 0 \end{bmatrix} u + \begin{bmatrix} 0 \\ a_p \end{bmatrix} v \tag{7.1}
$$

$$u = Cx_2$$

Discretized we obtain

$$
\begin{bmatrix} x_1 \\ x_2 \end{bmatrix}_{i+1} = \begin{bmatrix} 1 & 0 \\ 1 - e^{-a_p T} & e^{-a_p T} \end{bmatrix} \begin{bmatrix} x_1 \\ x_2 \end{bmatrix}_i + \begin{bmatrix} T \\ T - \dfrac{1 - e^{-a_p T}}{a_p} \end{bmatrix} u_i + \begin{bmatrix} 0 \\ 1 - e^{-a_p T} \end{bmatrix} v_i \tag{7.2}
$$

After closing the loop we obtain

$$
x_{i+1} = \Phi_c x_i + [\Gamma_v\, v]_i = \Phi_c x_i + v_{d_i} \tag{4.40 repeated}
$$

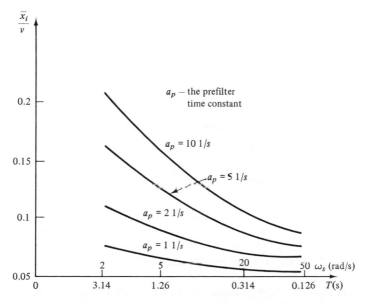

Fig. 7.11   Measurement noise response vs sampling interval

and calculating

$$Q_d = \int_0^T \Phi_c(\tau)\, G_v\, Q_v\, G_v^T\, \Phi_c(\tau)^T d\tau \qquad\qquad \text{(4.41 repeated)}$$

the rms response is the square root of the main diagonal of x where x is the solution of

$$X = \Phi_c X \Phi_c^T + Q_d \qquad\qquad \text{(4.46 repeated)}$$

The results for different values of a_p and different sampling rates are plotted in Fig. 7.11.

7.3   THE TIME RESPONSE AND THE RESPONSE TO AN EXTERNAL NOISE — RELATION TO THE SAMPLING RATE

7.3.1   The Time Response and the Sampling Rate

As mentioned in the beginning of this chapter the Nyquist (or Shannon) rule is difficult to apply for real time control systems, therefore another approach has to be used instead of the sampling theorem. The easiest method to apply is a simulation which checks the time response for different sampling rates.

The major problem is the time delays. It may be visualized by observing Fig. 7.12.

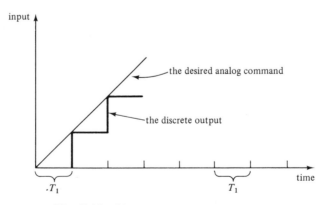

Fig. 7.12   Discrete vs continuous command

The time interval, T_1, is the maximum delay caused by sampling and it is rather difficult to reduce.

As an example we shall consider the system described in Fig. 7.13, which is concerned with pilot input in pitch control of an aircraft.

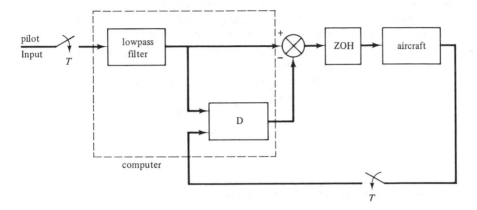

Fig. 7.13   Pitch control of an aircraft

The lowpass filter is necessary in order to provide for a smooth input from the stick with a time constant in the range 0.4 to 0.6 s, and to help to reduce the pitch rate overshoot.

The way in which the pilot command is actually processed by the system will now be explained.

The time $t = 0$ will be defined as the instant when the pilot executes the δ_{s_0} stick input (a step function). The information of this command will reach the computer within T seconds (T sampling interval). In order to be on the safe side, we have to assume a full delay $T_1 = T$ between the δ_{s_0} and the time the computer receives this command (δ_{s_1}). The mechanization of the first order filter on the aircraft computer will generate the signal (u_{δ_e}) which causes a further delay ($T = T_2$). The corresponding signals are shown in Fig. 7.14.

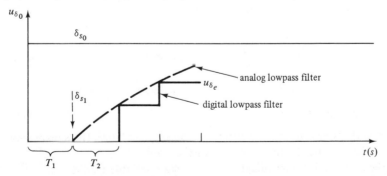

Fig. 7.14   The input timing diagram

One of the delay intervals, T_2, can be eliminated if the analog lowpass filter is implemented. However, in this case, we lose the option of changing the time constant of the lowpass filter for different flight conditions using the digital computer. We shall assume that the lowpass filter (as in BO-1 and SU-1 is mechanized on the digital computer and is part of the discrete control system. The control configuration described in Fig. 7.13 is closed by an additional feedback loop — the pilot, who is sensing θ, the pitch angle. The pilot's transfer function includes a pure delay, $\Delta t = 0.3$ s, and together with the delay caused by the digital system the loop may be unstable. Research undertaken by Stapleford (STA-1) shows that by lowering the sampling rate to the range 10 to 15 Hz, the pilot rejects this sampling rate before instability occurs. The reason for this rejection is the roughness of control.

7.3.2 The Response to External Noise and the Sampling Rate

The response to external disturbances is a function of the closed loop dynamics, the disturbance correlation time, and the sampling interval.

In a discrete control system the commands are executed at discrete instants of time, and during the intervals between sampling instants the system is exposed to uncontrolled disturbances.

In Chapter 4 we considered the discretization of a continuous system driven by white noise, w, and from eqn. (4.18), which is repeated here for convenience, we derived the discrete equations for the system

$$\dot{x} = Fx + Gw \qquad \text{(4.18 repeated)}$$

We showed that eqn. (4.18) may be represented at sampling points by eqn. (4.40).

$$x_{i+1} = \Phi x_i + w_{d_i} \qquad w_{d_i} = N(0, Q_d) \qquad \text{(4.40 repeated)}$$

where

$$Q_d = \int_0^T \Phi(\tau) G_w Q G_w^T \Phi^T(\tau) d\tau \qquad \text{(4.41 repeated)}$$

Note: T — sampling interval
Φ^T — transpose of Φ.

The steady state rms reponse is the solution of the matrix equation

$$\overline{X} = \Phi \overline{X} \Phi^T + Q_d \qquad \text{(4.46 repeated)}$$

where $\overline{X}$ is the steady state covariance matrix of the states. The square roots of the main diagonal are the rms responses of the states.

If the system, F, is controlled by discrete state variable feedback the relationships for the system are

$$x_{i+1} = \Phi x_i + \Gamma_1 u_i + w_i \qquad w_i \to (0, Q_d)$$

$$u_i = C x_i$$

Q_d reflects the accumulation of the influence of the noise between two samples, therefore Q_d does not depend on the control, but the covariance matrix of the states is influenced by the control

$$\overline{X} = (\Phi + \Gamma_1 C) \overline{X} (\Phi + \Gamma_1 C)^T + Q_d$$

As an example let us consider a first order system, driven by continuous white noise, and controlled by a discrete controller.

The system equation is

$$\dot{x} = ax + gu + w \qquad w \to N(0, q) \qquad (a < 0)$$

discretized we obtain

$$x_{i+1} = e^{aT} x_i + \gamma u_i + w_i \qquad w_i \to N(0, q_d)$$

The covariance is

$$q_d = \int_0^T e^{a\tau} q e^{a\tau} d\tau = \frac{q}{2a} (e^{2aT} - 1)$$

closing the loop by $\gamma u_i = b x_i$ yields

$$x_{i+1} = (e^{aT} + b) x_i + w_i \qquad w_i \to N \left[0, \frac{q}{2a} (e^{2aT} - 1) \right]$$

The rms response is the solution of

$$\sigma_x^2 = (e^{aT} + b) \sigma_x^2 (e^{aT} + b) + \frac{q}{2a} (e^{2aT} - 1)$$

$$\sigma_x^2 = \frac{q/2a (e^{2aT} - 1)}{1 - (e^{aT} + b)^2}$$

and the maximum control available is the dead beat controller $b = -e^{aT}$, which yields

$$\sigma_x^2 = \frac{q}{2a} (e^{2aT} - 1)$$

The last relation shows that σ_x^2 is always finite and that zero response to noise can be achieved only by limiting $T \to 0$.

A more realistic frequency distribution of external noise should be modelled as white noise shaped by a linear filter (Gauss-Markov process). For an analysis and simulation, the model of the shaping filter is incorporated in the model of the plant.

In order to decide the minimum sampling rate value only from the influence of the external noise, the rms response should be plotted against the sampling interval.

A short period dynamics of an aircraft will be considered as an example to illustrate the approach. The model of the system is

$$
\begin{bmatrix} \dot{q} \\ \dot{\alpha} \\ \dot{w}_g \end{bmatrix} = \begin{bmatrix} F & \vdots & G_w \\ - & + & - \\ 0 & \vdots & 1/\tau_w \end{bmatrix} \begin{bmatrix} q \\ \alpha \\ w_g \end{bmatrix} + \begin{bmatrix} G \\ - \\ 0 \end{bmatrix} \delta_e + \begin{bmatrix} 0 \\ - \\ 1 \end{bmatrix} \eta
$$

where

q	is the pitch rate
α	angle of attack
F, G	short period dynamics
w_g	gust disturbance
τ_w	correlation time of the disturbance
G_w	the influence of gust on the dynamics
η	white noise $\eta \to N(0, \sqrt{2\tau_w}\sigma/\tau_w)$
σ^2	is the average power of the gusts

On closing the loop with proper control and using a simulation scheme the behavior of the short period mode can be investigated. By plotting the rms response of q against the sampling interval T, we obtain the results shown in Fig. 7.15.

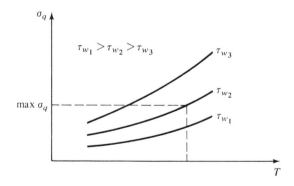

Fig. 7.15 External disturbances vs sampling interval

There are other factors which influence the choice of the sampling interval, but in this example the influence of the gust is probably not the most limiting factor.

7.4 THE ROUGHNESS OF CONTROL CAUSED BY SAMPLING

Most of the digital systems which control continuous plants use the zero order hold (ZOH) as the reconstruction hold. The abrupt action of the ZOH for high sampling rates is reduced and further smoothed by the filtering properties of the various electro-mechanical actuators. The tendency is to shorten the actuator time constants as much as possible in order to satisfy various time response criteria. Consequently the action of the control becomes more abrupt at low sampling rates.

The purpose of this section is to formulate and analyze a criterion which enables us to compare the roughness of control for different sampling rates and for different control laws.

The basic concepts in this section are the definitions of the various 'roughness functions'. The fundamental *Roughness Function*, RF, will be defined as the weighted sum of the squares of the abrupt changes in the state derivatives or in the control inputs.

The expected properties of the roughness function are:

(i)   the RF should be related to the difference of numbers in the discrete input sequence,

(ii) the RF should be related to the derivative discontinuities of the states,

(iii) for $T = 0$ the RF is zero,

(iv) the RF should be represented by a positive function,

(v)   the RF should be user oriented and should have a convenient computation form.

7.4.1 Definition of Roughness Function (RF)

When a step function is applied to a system the derivates of some of the states x_i change their magnitude from $\dot{x}_{-i}$ to $\dot{x}_{+i}$. The expression given by eqn. (7.3)

$$|\dot{x}_{+i} - \dot{x}_{-i}| \triangleq \Delta\dot{x}_i \qquad (7.3)$$

is the basic building block of the RF.

The RF is defined as:

$$RF \triangleq \sum_{i=0}^{N} \Delta\dot{x}_i^T W \Delta\dot{x}_i \qquad (7.4)$$

where W is the weighting matrix.

For a first order system given by

$$\dot{x} = -ax + gu$$

we may write in discretized form

$$x_{i+1} = e^{-aT}x_i + \Gamma u_i$$

where,

$$\Gamma = (1 - e^{-aT})\frac{g}{a}$$

$$u_i = Cx_i$$

The behavior of this system is depicted in Fig. 7.16.

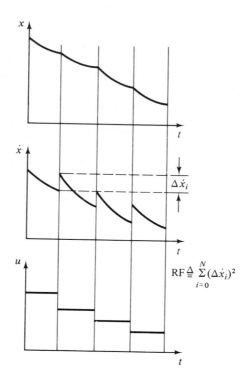

Fig. 7.16 Roughness behavior of a first order system

The RF is considered in detail in Appendix B, where it is shown that RF may be expressed as a function of x_i as given by eqn. (7.5.).

$$RF = \sum_{i=0}^{N} x_i^T R x_i \tag{7.5}$$

where

$$R \triangleq [(\Phi + \Gamma C) - I]^T C^T G^T W G C [(\Phi + \Gamma C) - I] \qquad (7.6)$$

The RF of short period mode of an aircraft controlled by a discrete controller will be considered as an example.

The open loop poles of the short period mode are located at $s = -2.6 \pm j13.5$.

The closed loop poles are relocated to $s = -15 \pm j10$. The simplified equations of motion are

$$\begin{bmatrix} \dot{\alpha} \\ \dot{q} \end{bmatrix} = [F] \begin{bmatrix} \alpha \\ q \end{bmatrix} + Gu$$

where u is a discrete input $u_i = Cx_i$. The position of the poles for different sampling rates is depicted in Fig. 7.17.

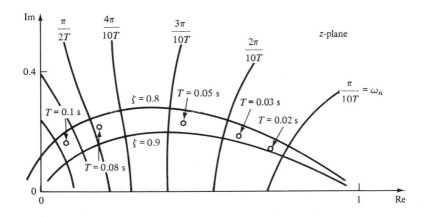

Fig. 7.17   The location of the short period poles

For $\quad W = \begin{bmatrix} 1/q_0^2 & 0 \\ 0 & 0 \end{bmatrix}$, the RF is given by

$$RF = \frac{1}{q_0^2} \sum_{i=1}^{\infty} \Delta \dot{q}_i^2$$

The plot of RF as a function of T is given in Fig. 7.18.

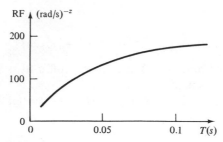

Fig. 7.18 Short period mode RF vs sampling interval

The time responses of q and $\dot{q}$ are plotted in Fig. 7.19.

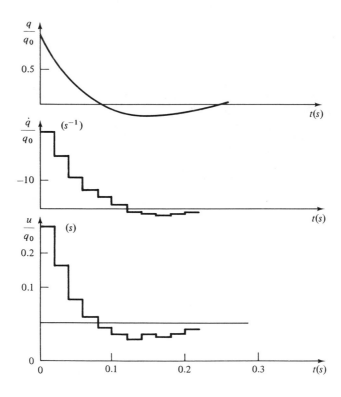

Fig. 7.19 The abrupt behavior of the short period mode

7.4.2   The Mean RF of a Closed Loop System Disturbed by an External Noise

For the discretely controlled system we have

$$\dot{x} = Fx + Gu + w \qquad w \rightarrow N(0, Q)$$

$$u_i = Cx_i$$

$$x_{i+1} = \Phi_C x_i + w_i \qquad w_i \rightarrow N(0, Q_d)$$

where, Φ_c is the closed loop transition matrix.

The mean RF (RF_m) is defined as

$$RF_m \triangleq T_r E\left\{(\dot{x}_{i+1} - \dot{x}_{-i})(\dot{x}_{+i} - \dot{x}_{-i})^T W\right\}_{i \rightarrow \infty} \tag{7.7}$$

$(T_r - \text{Trace})$

Example:

The short period mode of an aircraft augmented by a model of an external disturbance (wind) was described in Sec. 2.3. Repeated here in a discrete form we have

$$\begin{bmatrix} q \\ \alpha \\ w_g \end{bmatrix}_{i+1} = \begin{bmatrix} \phi & \Gamma_w \\ 0 & \phi_w \end{bmatrix} \begin{bmatrix} q \\ \alpha \\ w_g \end{bmatrix}_i + \Gamma_1 u_i + \begin{bmatrix} 0 \\ 0 \\ \eta_i \end{bmatrix} \qquad \eta_i \rightarrow N(0, Q_d)$$

Keeping the sampling interval constant ($T = 0.05$ s), the RF_m will be investigated for different pole locations.

The short period poles are relocated by state variable feedback, see Fig. 7.20.

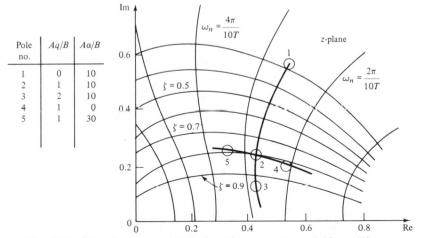

Pole no.	Aq/B	$A\alpha/B$
1	0	10
2	1	10
3	2	10
4	1	0
5	1	30

Fig. 7.20   The short period pole locations vs state variable weights

Moving the short period poles on the lines A_α or A_q the RF_m will be plotted (qualitatively only) on graphs in Fig. 7.21.

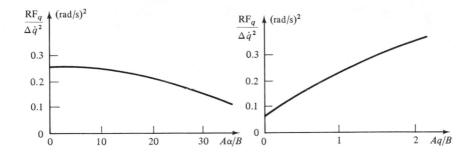

Fig. 7.21 RF_m vs state weights (short period mode)

The explanation of the RF_m behavior is obvious. An increase in A_α keeps nearly the same damping but decreases the natural frequency. This means that the system responds slowly and there are less abrupt actions in the control. On the other hand, an increase in A_q yields more stiff dynamics, more control and an increase in RF_m.

7.5   FIDELITY OF THE RESPONSE AND SAMPLING RATE

This section is based on the concept of fidelity ratio as proposed by Peled and described in his dissertation (PE-1).

The frequency response of a specific discrete controller depends on the ratio of the input frequency, ω_{in}, to the sampling frequency, ω_s. As ω_{in}/ω_s goes from 0 to 0.5, the amplitude of the output at ω_{in} drops, and the amplitude of other harmonics increases. The result is a distortion between input and output.

Fidelity of response is based on r, the ratio between the amplitude of the largest harmonic and the amplitude of the output at the basic frequency. The fidelity of response will be defined as

$$f_r \triangleq \frac{1}{1+r} \tag{7.8}$$

The fidelity is best when this relation is 1.

Example 1.

Sampler and zero order hold in series as shown in Fig. 7.22.

Fig. 7.22   Sampler and ZOH

For a sinusoidal input with a frequency $\omega_{in} = 0.4\,\omega_s$ the output is summarized in the following table:

output frequency/ω_s	output amplitude/input amplitude
0.4	0.74
0.6	0.49
1.4	0.21
1.6	0.175
2.4	0.13
2.6	0.1

The amplitude of the basic (input) frequency component at the output is 0.74. The amplitude of the next highest harmonic is 0.49, thus the fidelity ratio of the response is $1/(1 + 0.49/0.74) = 0.6$.

For $\omega_{in}/\omega_s > 0.5$ the highest output component is no longer at the input frequency.

Example 2.

Lowpass filter.

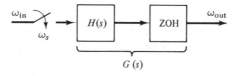

Fig. 7.23   The lowpass filter

Let us assume that the primary modes are below the desired bandwidth. By folding the transfer function around $\omega_s/2$, the output at $\omega_s - \omega_{in}$ can be determined. In low pass systems this output is second in magnitude after the output at ω_{in} in the input frequency range from 0 to 0.5 ω_s. Following Peled (PE-1), the ratio

$$r = \frac{|H[j(\omega_s - \omega)]|}{|H(j\omega)|}\Bigg|_{\omega = \omega_p} \tag{7.9}$$

$$f_r = \frac{1}{1 + r}$$

where ω_p is the breakpoint frequency

may serve as the fidelity ratio. The relationship between ω_s/ω_p and f_r for different transfer functions is depicted in Fig. 7.24.

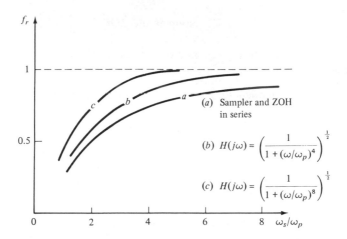

Fig. 7.24   Peled's results for fidelity ratio as a function of the sampling rate

Specifying the highest f_r determines the lowest ω_s.

7.6 PRACTICAL SELECTION OF THE SAMPLING RATE

The practical selection of the sampling rate is related to the word length. In order to keep the same computing accuracy, for a higher sampling rate we need a longer computational word, otherwise all the changing information is concentrated in the least significant bits.

In practice we have a choice between an eight or sixteen bit microprocessor. Therefore, for controlling processes with short time constants we will probably need a higher sampling rate and therefore we shall choose the sixteen bit word length.

The practical choice of the sampling rate is based on the required transient characteristic which should be translated to a closed loop bandwidth. We then choose a sampling rate ten times larger than the bandwidth.

The selection of the sampling rate for digital stabilization of an artillery rocket launcher will be considered as an example.*

The closed loop control system is described in Fig. 7.25.

*Design by Y. Sharoni

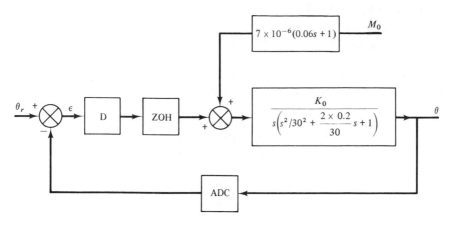

Fig. 7.25   Control system of an artillery rocket launcher

The objective is to design a digital controller which will satisfy an aiming accuracy of

$$2 \text{ mrad, i.e. } e(t) < 2 \text{ mrad for } t > 0$$

The disturbing moment M_o is given by:

$$M_o(t) = 5 \text{ KGm } \frac{t}{50 \text{ ms}} \qquad 0 \leqslant t \leqslant 50 \text{ ms}$$

$$= 0 \qquad\qquad 50 \text{ ms} < t$$

The frequency content of the disturbing moment is described in Fig. 7.26.

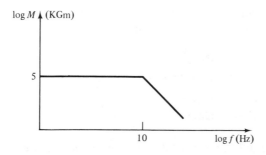

Fig. 7.26   Frequency contents of the disturbing moment

The bandwidth of the disturbing moment is approximately twice as large as the bandwidth of the open loop. Using a compensation network, the closed loop bandwidth is reduced to $f = 4$ Hz and the damping coefficient is increased from 0.2 to 0.5.

Using an explicit solution of $\epsilon(t)$ as a function of the disturbing moment, the error, ϵ, never exceeded the 2 mrad limitation.

Before arriving at the discrete processor, the disturbing signal frequency is attenuated by the plant, therefore the sampling rate for the digital implementation is based on the bandwidth of the closed loop and not the disturbing signal. Accordingly the sampling rate was selected to be ten times larger than the closed loop bandwidth, i.e. $f_s = 40$ Hz. A different controller and different sampling rate will be necessary if the control loop is required to follow an input signal with frequency contents similar to the disturbance.

EXERCISES

7.1   Discretize

$$G(s) = \frac{1}{s + 3}.$$

    (i)   Using an 8-bit computer, plot the behavior of the noise output, caused by quantization, as a function of sampling time.

    (ii)   Generalize (i) for a C-bit computer.

7.2   Repeat 7.1 for $G(s)$ in a closed loop with a unity feedback.

7.3   The time to rise to 80% of the steady state value of $G(s)$ in problem 7.1 should be decreased by a factor of 2. No overshoot is allowed. Design the controller and select an appropriate sampling time.

7.4   Using an 8-bit computer, design a position servo for a double integrator plant. The control requirements are:

$$BW = 10 \text{ Hz} \quad \zeta = 0.5$$

Select the sampling rate and calculate:

    (i)   ADC noise amplification.

    (ii)   Parameter variations.

7.5   For problem 7.3, calculate the multiplication noise. Plot the influence of sampling rate and word length on the output noise.

8

Design Example 1

8.1 INTRODUCTION

We shall consider the estimation of the computing capacity required for an all digital tactical missile*.

The objective is to replace all analog networks in a small tactical missile by a digital avionics implementation using one or more microcomputers.

The model of the missile belongs to a class of small homing missiles and includes a tracking system with a single sensor, an optional communication link, a proportional navigation system with a gravity correction and an autopilot.

8.2 THE ANALOG SCHEME

In order to characterize a general class of small tactical missiles, the model contains:

(i)   Homing missile with an optional midcourse guidance.
(ii)   Tracking system based on a single target sensor.
(iii) Stabilized homing system with two degrees of freedom in which stabilization is based on a heavy rotating mass.
(iv)   Optional communication, wire or wireless link.
(v)   Automatic pilot for roll stabilization and for improving the pitch and yaw dynamics.
(vi)   Proportional navigation, g-bias correction.
(vii) Aerodynamic steering.

*This example is based on the M.Sc. thesis of F. Berkowitz (BER-1).

The various missile functions needed to be implemented onboard are described in Sec. 8.2.1 through 8.2.4.

8.2.1   Homing and Tracking System

This system includes the electronics and data processing for the homing sensor. The sensor may be based on laser, TV, infra-red or millimeter radar detection. The target position is translated to a two-dimensional analog or digital signal. The target signal is usually enclosed in a gate which reduces unwanted background noise.

The tracking system controls the gate and activates the directional movement of the stabilized homing sensor. The homing sensor is stabilized by a rotating mass and an electronic system controls the angular acceleration, the rate of rotation and the precession motion of the stabilizing gyro.

8.2.2   The Guidance and Navigation System

This system generates the proportional navigation law. The navigation system also includes parameter variations such as changes in mass, changes in navigation constant, and g-bias correction. Initial conditions are inserted through the launch system computer.

8.2.3   Automatic Pilot and the Servosystem

The automatic pilot stabilizes the missile in roll, and augments the yaw and pitch aerodynamic damping. The aerodynamic coefficients are constant but there is a limited dynamic range and some non-linearities in the actuator servosystems. The inputs to the system are signals from the gyros and feedback from the servos. The outputs are commands (through a resolver) to four fin actuators.

8.2.4   Additional Functions

Additional computing capacity is required for the operation of the missile as a complex logical system. The additional functions are as follows:

  (i)   Firing sequence which includes activation of various subsystems.
 (ii)   Self test of operational capability of the missile.
(iii)   Safe and arm logic.
(iv)   Encoding and decoding of the optional communication link.

The model of the tracking, guidance and autopilot control system is depicted in Fig. 8.1.

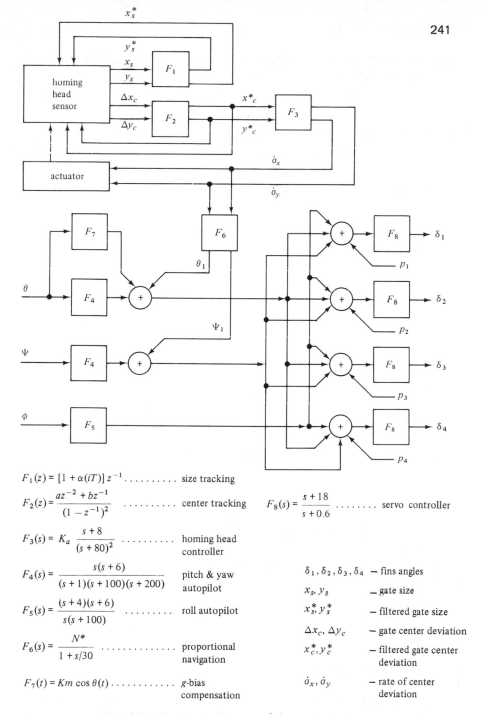

$F_1(z) = [1 + \alpha(iT)]\, z^{-1}$ . . . . size tracking

$F_2(z) = \dfrac{az^{-2} + bz^{-1}}{(1 - z^{-1})^2}$ . . . . center tracking

$F_3(s) = K_a\, \dfrac{s + 8}{(s + 80)^2}$ . . . . homing head controller

$F_4(s) = \dfrac{s(s + 6)}{(s + 1)(s + 100)(s + 200)}$ pitch & yaw autopilot

$F_5(s) = \dfrac{(s + 4)(s + 6)}{s(s + 100)}$ . . . . roll autopilot

$F_6(s) = \dfrac{N^*}{1 + s/30}$ . . . . proportional navigation

$F_7(t) = Km \cos \theta(t)$ . . . . g-bias compensation

$F_8(s) = \dfrac{s + 18}{s + 0.6}$ . . . . servo controller

$\delta_1, \delta_2, \delta_3, \delta_4$ — fins angles

x_s, y_s — gate size

x_s^*, y_s^* — filtered gate size

$\Delta x_c, \Delta y_c$ — gate center deviation

x_c^*, y_c^* — filtered gate center deviation

$\dot{\sigma}_x, \dot{\sigma}_y$ — rate of center deviation

Fig. 8.1 The block diagram of the control system

8.3   DISCRETE MODEL OF THE SYSTEM AND AN ESTIMATION OF THE REQUIRED COMPUTING CAPABILITY

8.3.1   Homing and Tracking System

There are three basic functions F_1, F_2, F_3 (see Fig. 8.1). F_1 feeds the target into a gate, F_2 keeps the center of the gate on the target and F_3 controls the angular direction of the homing stabilized sensor. Only F_1 will be explicitly described.

(i) F_1 is the gate size tracker. The gate magnitude x_s is inversely proportional to the distance from the target, i.e.

$$x_s(t) \simeq K_0 \, \frac{1}{R_0 - V_m t} \tag{8.1}$$

where V_m is the missile velocity, and t is time of flight.
    The magnitude rate is given by eqn. (8.2)

$$\dot{x}_s(t) \simeq \frac{K_0 V}{(R_0 - Vt)^2} = [x_s(t)]^2 \, \frac{V}{K_0} \tag{8.2}$$

The function F_1 has to predict the gate size for the next sensor sample. By linear approximation the discrete equation becomes

$$x_{s_{i+1}} = x_{s_i} + \frac{TV}{K_0} x^2_{s_i} \tag{8.3}$$

Equation (8.3) is calculated for the x-axis and the y-axis of the homing sensor.
    There are two more logic states:

(a)   Search

$$x_{s_{i+1}} = 0 \tag{8.4}$$

and

(b)   Ready and locked on target

$$x_{s_{i+1}} = x_{s_i} \tag{8.5}$$

The complete flow chart of the gate size tracker is depicted in Fig. 8.2.

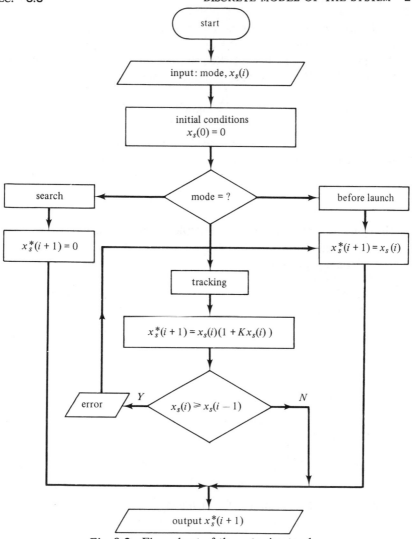

Fig. 8.2   Flow chart of the gate size tracker

We will estimate the computing capacity required for each axis of the gate size tracker:

— Number of arithmetical operations during one computing cycle

        2 multiplications

        4 simple operations (additions, shift. . .)

— Memory   ROM ~ 40 words

                 RAM ~ 10 words

— Sampling time for TV, radar or laser tracker, about $T = 20$ ms.

— Input word length (M), the sensor resolution is not better than 0.5%, 8 bit word $(M = 8)$ will satisfy (0.4%).

— Arithmetic unit word length; the gain for eqn. (8.3) is nearly unity. For the ratio of 40 dB output signal to noise we obtain

$$M = C + 1 = \frac{40}{6} + 0.8 + \frac{10}{6} \log_{10} 103 \leqslant 8 \qquad (8.6)$$

(ii) F_2 — center of the gate tracker. The algorithm chosen for this function is a fading memory polynomial predictor.

$$F_2(z) = \frac{az^{-2} + bz^{-1}}{(1 - z^{-1})^2}$$

The computing requirements for its implementation (each axis) are:

  2 multiplications
  7 simple operations
  ROM $\sim$ 40 words
  RAM $\sim$ 10 words
  $C + 1 \leqslant 8$ bits

(iii) Attitude control of the stabilized homing sensor. Its transfer function (each axis) is given by

$$F_3 = \frac{s + 8}{(s + 80)^2} \qquad (8.7)$$

Using bilinear transformation and frequency prewarping $(T = 0.02$ s) we obtain the discrete transfer function

$$F_3(z) = \frac{0.0026 \, (1 - 0.85z^{-1}) \, (1 + z^{-1})}{(1 - 0.0148z^{-1})^2} \qquad (8.8)$$

— Computing capacity required (for each cycle):

  4 multiplications
  7 simple operations
  ROM $\sim$ 70 words
  RAM $\sim$ 20 words

— Coefficient word length. 10% accuracy in the zero locations.

$$\left. \begin{array}{l} N \leqslant - \log_2 \, (8 \times 0.02)e^{-8 \times 0.02} - \log_2 \, (2 \times 0.1) = 5.2 \\[2mm] N \simeq 6 \text{ bits} \end{array} \right\} \qquad (8.9)$$

— Arithmetic unit word length, for 40 dB signal to quantization noise $(K_\epsilon \simeq 1)$:

$$C + 1 \geqslant \frac{40}{6} + 0.8 = 7.5$$

$$M = 8 \text{ bits.}$$

$$\left.\begin{matrix} \\ \\ \end{matrix}\right\} \qquad (8.10)$$

8.3.2 The Navigation System

In small tactical missiles, the navigation system usually incorporates a proportional navigation term and sometimes gravity correction and midcourse guidance.

In our model there is gravity correction given by

$$F_7(t) = K \times m \times \cos \theta \qquad (8.11)$$

and a proportional navigation term of the form

$$\theta_1(z) = F_6(z)\, \dot{o}_y(z) + F_7 \qquad (8.12)$$

$$\psi_1(z) = F_6(z)\, \dot{o}_y(z) \qquad (8.13)$$

where $\qquad F_6(z) = K_d^* \dfrac{1 - 0.54\, z^{-1}}{1 + z^{-1}} \qquad (8.14)$

Discrete values of parameters m, K, K_d^*, $\cos\theta$, are stored in the memory and used at the appropriate points on the trajectory.

The computing capacity required is:

pitch	5 multiplications
	11 simple operations
yaw	2 multiplications
	5 simple operations
memory	RAM ~ 30 words
	ROM ~ 100 words

Coefficient word length may be estimated by considering the implementation accuracy of the required navigation pole. In this case it is about 1% ($T = 0.02$ s), hence

$$N = -\log_2 (30 \times 0.02)\, (e^{-30 \times 0.02}) - \log_2 \frac{2 \times 0.01}{1} = 7.25 \quad (8.15)$$

therefore $\quad M \leqslant 8$ bits

Arithmetic unit word length may be estimated by the following approach. We are asking for a high signal to quantization noise ratio because the signal from the output is further processed by additional compensation networks. Therefore we will choose $F = 60$ dB hence

$$C + 1 \geqslant \frac{60}{6} + 0.8 = 10.8 \tag{8.16}$$

therefore $M \simeq 10$ bits.

8.3.3   The Automatic Pilot and the Servo Compensation Network

The pitch and yaw transfer function is given by

$$F_4(s) = \frac{s(s + 6)}{(s + 1)(s + 100)(s + 200)} \tag{8.17}$$

The roll transfer function is given by

$$F_5(s) = \frac{(s + 4)(s + 6)}{s(s + 100)} \tag{8.18}$$

The servo compensation network is given by

$$F_8(s) = \frac{s + 18}{s + 0.6} \tag{8.19}$$

The sampling rate chosen was based on the requirement for a ZOH phase lag smaller than 20°.

For a maximum closed loop bandwidth of 10 Hz we get $f_s = 100$ Hz.

$$f_s = f_{max} \frac{180}{20}$$

Using bilinear transformation and frequency prewarping, the discrete transfer functions $F_4(z)$, $F_5(z)$ and $F_6(z)$ may be written as:

$$F_4(z) = \frac{(1 - z^{-1})(1 - 0.9417z^{-1})(1 + z^{-1})}{(1 - 0.99z^{-1})(1 - 0.293z^{-1})(1 + 0.218z^{-1})} \tag{8.20}$$

$$F_5(z) = \frac{(1 - 0.961z^{-1})(1 - 0.9417z^{-1})}{(1 - z^{-1})(1 - 0.2934z^{-1})} \tag{8.21}$$

$$F_8(z) = \frac{1 - 0.8344z^{-1}}{1 - 0.0994z^{-1}} \tag{8.22}$$

The computing capacity required is:
> 20 multiplications
> 52 simple operations
> ROM $\sim$ 400 words
> RAM $\sim$ 120 words

The coefficient word length may be estimated by considering the slowest pole. In this case we are asking for an accuracy of 30%, hence

$$N \geqslant - \log_2 (0.6 \times 0.01)e^{-0.6 \times 0.01} - \log_2 0.6 \times 0.3 \cong 10 \qquad (8.23)$$

therefore $M = 10$ bits

Arithmetic word length may be estimated in the same way as for the navigation system, i.e. $M = 10$ bits.

For the ADC word length we must note that the sensor's dynamic range is not better than $1/1000$, therefore $M = 10$ for the ADC is sufficient.

In the case of the DAC word length, as the dynamic range of the actuators is about $1/100$, this corresponds to $M = 7$ word length.

8.3.4   Additional Functions

Four additional functions are included in the onboard computer tasks. These are:

(i)   A self test and test for all other functions. All these tests are accomplished before the launch and some may be carried out by the launch system computer. Therefore, the computing capability requirements are minimal and are necessary only to ensure a proper interconnection between the computers.

> The memory requirements are estimated as:
> RAM $\sim$ 100 words,
> ROM $\sim$ 200 words.

(ii) Launching procedure. The launching procedure is a supervised timing sequence which includes the activation of different subsystems such as, battery, gyros, rocket engine, etc. The memory requirements are:

> RAM $\sim$ 10 words,
> ROM $\sim$ 100 words.

(iii) Safe and arm logic. The usual practice in small tactical missiles is to use an all-mechanical safe and arm system, but additional reliability may be achieved if the various steps of the arming procedure are controlled or recorded by a computer.

> The computer requirements to include this facility are:
> ROM $\sim$ 20 words,
> RAM $\sim$ 20 words.

(iv) Decoding the information transmitted by the communication link. The optional wire or wireless communication link transmits, besides the steering commands, additional information. For instance it may transmit decision on various tracking modes, changes in navigation constants, and self destruction command.

The computer requirements are covered by 10 simple operations which require:

ROM ~ 50 words,
RAM ~ 10 words.

8.4 THE COMPUTING SYSTEM

8.4.1 Summary of Computing Capacity Requirements

(i) The arithmetic unit. The number of multiplications and simple operations are summarized in Tables 8.1 and 8.2.

Table 8.1 Number of multiplications in one second

Task	Rate samples/s	Multiplications per cycle	Total number of multiplications in one second
Gate size tracker	50	4	200
Center tracker	50	4	200
Sensor direction	50	8	400
Guidance	50	10	500
Autopilot	100	20	2000
Other functions	50		
		Total	3300 mps

Table 8.2 Number of simple operations in one second

Task	Rate samples/s	Number of operations per second	Total number of simple operations per second
Gate size tracker	50	8	400
Center tracker	50	14	700
Sensor direction	50	14	700
Guidance	50	16	800
Autopilot	100	52	5200
Other functions	50	20	1000
		Total	8800 ops

It is good practice to keep about 30% of the capacity for unexpected requirements. In using the additional 30% the CPU is required to perform 4300 mps and 11500 ops.

Assuming that a multiplication is about twenty times slower than a simple operation (twice the word length), we need a microcomputer with a speed of computation of 10 μs for a simple operation and 200 μs for a multiplication. Most of the microcomputers available have this speed of computation.

(ii) The memory. Number of words is summarized in Table 8.3.

Table 8.3 Number of words in the memory

Task	ROM	RAM
Gate size tracker	80	20
Center tracker	80	20
Sensor direction	140	40
Guidance	200	60
Autopilot	400	120
Other functions	370	140
30% spare	400	120
Total	1670	520

(iii) Word length.
      ROM ~ 8 bits, all functions except autopilot.
      RAM ~ 10 bits.
  ADC Tracker: 4 channels, 8 bits, 50 samples per second (sps)
      Autopilot: 7 channels, 10 bits, 100 sps
  DAC Tracker: 5 channels, 8 bits, 50 sps
      Autopilot: 4 channels, 7 bits, 100 sps

8.4.2 Conclusions

The computing system may be subdivided into two weakly connected subsystems which are described below.

(i) The homing subsystem, which should have the following properties:
CPU and I/O word length — 8 bits
1000 mps, 2400 ops ($T = 20$ ms)
      ROM ~ 400 words
      RAM ~ 80 words
  ADC 4 channels (8 bits)
  DAC 5 channels (8 bits)

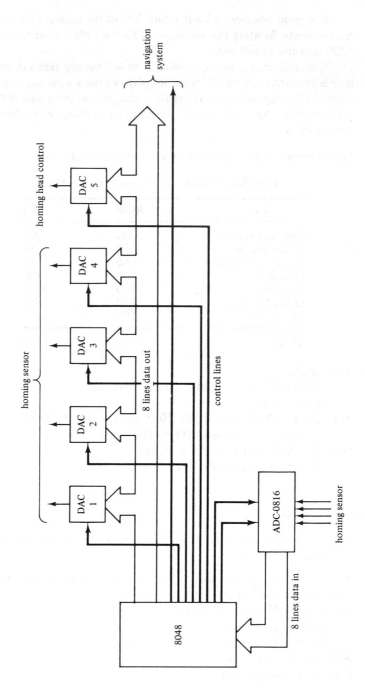

Fig. 8.3 Configuration example for the tracking system

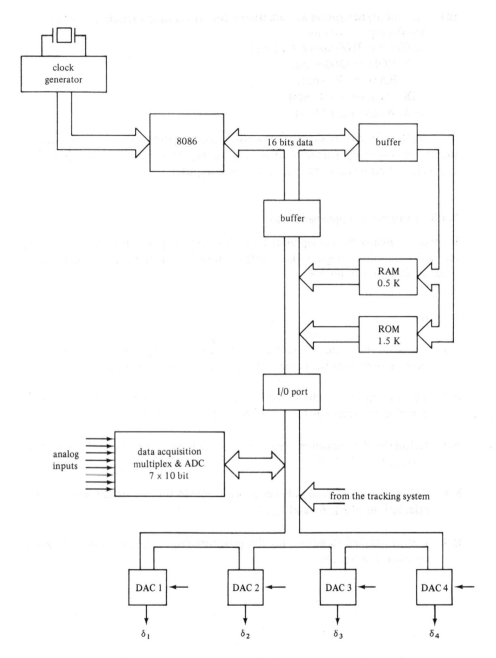

Fig. 8.4 Configuration example for the guidance, autopilot
and additional functions

(ii)   Autopilot, navigation and additional functions which require:
        word length — 10 bits
        3300 mps, 9100 ops ($T = 10$ ms)
                ROM $\sim$ 1300 words
                RAM $\sim$ 440 words
        ADC 7 channels (10 bits)
        DAC 4 channels (7 bits)

The major difficulty is the 10 bit word length requirement. 12-bit microcomputers are not very common so it is probably best to use double precision accuracy or better still to use a 16-bit microcomputer.

8.4.3 Example of Implementation

We may mechanize the system using an 8-bit microcomputer, Intel 8048 or 8748, and a 16-bit microcomputer Intel 8086. These two systems are schematically depicted in Figs. 8.3 and 8.4.

EXERCISES

8.1   Calculate the exact noise transfer function for F_2, taking into account every source of noise. Consider for example an 8-bit word length.

8.2   For the filter F_3, check the influence of T_s on the equivalent transfer function for values of T_s from $(2 \times 8/2\pi)^{-1}$ to 20 ms.

8.3   Calculate the maximum error for a cosine approximation of F_7 if θ is varying from $0°$ to $5°$.

8.4   Why have we checked only the slowest pole in the coefficient word length calculations of F_4, F_5 and F_8?

8.5   Give a detailed flowchart for the programming of F_3, including DC gain, operation order, etc.

9

Design Example 2

9.1   INTRODUCTION

In this chapter we shall consider the digital control of an artificial hand which
has to grasp and transport fragile glass containers of various sizes*. The objective
is to design a digital servosystem which will control the one-dimensional motion
of the holding clamp (Fig. 9.1). For various reasons the drive mechanism is based
on a DC motor, although a stepper motor may serve the same purpose.

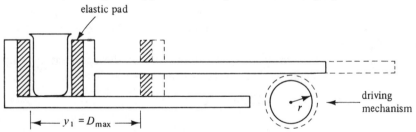

Fig. 9.1   Schematic description of the artificial hand

9.2   THE CONTROL REQUIREMENTS

A pressure sensor detects the gap ΔY as shown in Fig. 9.2. The sensor has an
accuracy of 0.1 mm.

In order to grasp the glass container firmly, but without damage, the elastic

---

*Design carried out by A. Ben-Zwi.

contraction (X) should be at least 5 mm but no more than 6 mm. The weight of the moving clamp is about 1 kg. The weight of the container may be neglected.

The diameter of the container is unknown, but the maximum diameter is 0.2 m. The motion of the closing clamp should be fast and as smooth as possible and the time between start to rest should be about 0.5 s. No mechanical clutch or break is allowed.

9.3   DESCRIPTION OF THE SUBSYSTEMS

9.3.1   The Mechanical Motion

The closing motion of the clamp is carried out through three stages, acceleration, deceleration and position servo stage. We shall consider each stage.

(i)   Acceleration.

During this stage, the driving mechanism will move the clamp with constant acceleration until the pressure sensor contacts the glass container. The container diameter is unknown but a maximum diameter, D_{max}, of 0.2 m is assumed. For small containers this acceleration stage is the most time consuming. The requirement of the design is $t_1 \leqslant 0.5$ s, where t_1 is the time of acceleration. The initial opening of the clamp is equal to the maximum diameter, i.e. $Y_1 = 0.2$ m.

(ii)   Deceleration.

This stage starts with the first contact between the pressure sensor and the container, and ends after the hand stops. The deceleration distance is $X \leqslant 5$ mm. This requirement actually dictates the size of the driving unit.

(iii)   Position servo stage.

The position servo stage starts at the end of the deceleration stage. A constant command is given to the position servo so that

$$\Delta Y_o - \Delta Y_F = 5.22 \text{ mm}$$

where

ΔY_o = the pressure sensor readout at the first contact, and

ΔY_F = the pressure sensor readout after the arm comes to rest.

The overshoot limit will be $\dfrac{6 - 5.22}{5.22} \times 100\% = 15\%$

The low overshoot requirements are caused by the two following constraints:

(a)   the sensor accuracy is 0.1 mm, the A/D resolution is 0.02 mm and the stiffness of the loop 0.1 mm.

This totals 0.1 + 0.1 + 0.02 = 0.22 mm.

This uncertainty adds to the minimum required contraction of $(\Delta Y_o - \Delta Y)_{min}$ = 5 mm, which yields 5.22 mm.

(b) The maximum allowed contraction of the elastic pad is $(\Delta Y_o - \Delta Y)_{max}$ = 6 mm.

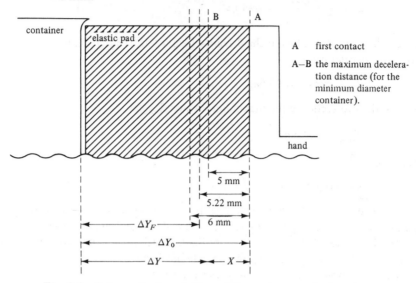

A   first contact

A–B the maximum decelera-
tion distance (for the
minimum diameter
container).

Fig. 9.2 Schematic description of the various control surfaces

9.3.2 Specifications of the Driving Unit, Time Constants, Power Supply and Saturation Limits

The open loop control of the driving unit is schematically described in Fig. 9.3.

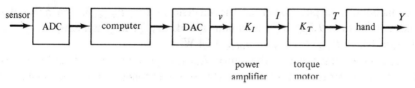

Fig. 9.3 The open loop control of the driving unit

Specifications of the driving unit are:

acceleration

$$a_1 = \frac{2Y_1}{t_1^2} = 1.6 \text{ m/s}^2$$

maximum velocity

$$V_{max} = a_1 t_1 = 0.8 \text{ m/s}$$

deceleration

$$a_2 = \frac{V_{max}^2}{2 \times 5 \text{ mm}} = 64 \text{ m/s}^2$$

Using a direct drive (radius of the driving wheel, $r = 0.015$ m) yields the required torque for deceleration

$$T_1 = rma_2 = 0.95 \text{ Nm}$$

We shall therefore choose the maximum torque T_{max} as

$$T_{max} = 1.2 \text{ Nm}$$

Therefore

$$K_T = 0.3 \text{ Nm/A}$$

We also need to consider some electrical properties. The torque motor is driven by a power (current) amplifier therefore its transfer function is K_T (Nm/A).

The bandwidth of the power amplifier is much larger than the bandwidth of the closed loop hence its dynamics may be neglected.

The saturation of the power amplifier is given by

$$I_{max} = \frac{T_{max}}{K_T} = 4 \text{ A}$$

$$\therefore K_I \cong 1 \text{ A/V}$$

The maximum output power of the electric motor, P_{max}, is the product of maximum torque, T_{max}, and maximum speed, ω_{max}. In this example $\omega_{max/r} = 53$ rad/s, hence $P_{max} = T_{max} \times \omega_{max} = 64$ W.

The ohmic resistance of the motor, R_m is approximately 4Ω, and the resistance of the power transistors, R_{KI}, is 1Ω. Summed together the additional power required is given by

$$\Delta P = I^2 (R_m + R_{KI}) = 80 \text{ W}$$

Therefore the maximum power to be supplied is

$$P_{max} = P_0 + \Delta P = 144 \text{ W}$$

9.4   THE CONTROLLER DESIGN

9.4.1   The Dynamic Model of the Artificial Hand

As

$$T = rm\,\ddot{X}$$
$$X = \Delta Y_0 - \Delta Y$$
$\left.\vphantom{\begin{matrix}a\\b\end{matrix}}\right\}$

(9.1)

the transfer function may be written as eqn. (9.2)

$$\frac{X(s)}{T(s)} = \frac{1}{rms^2}$$

(9.2)

9.4.2   The Closed Loop

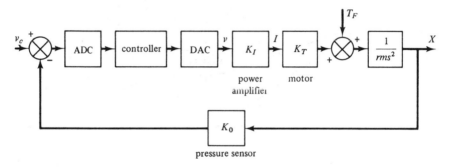

Fig. 9.4   The position servo of the artificial hand

The numerical value of the gain, K_o, of the pressure sensor is $\dfrac{5\ V}{6\ mm} = 0.83\ V/mm$

As constant input corresponds to 5.22 mm, the nominal contraction of the elastic pad, V_c, is given by $V_c = (\Delta Y_o - \Delta Y_F)K_o = 4.33$ V.

9.4.3   The Controller Design

The required DC stiffness, ST, is

$$ST = 0.1\ mm$$

The estimated coulomb friction, T_F, is

$$T_F = 10^{-2}\ Nm$$

The DC gain of the controller is given by eqn. (9.3)

$$K = \frac{T_F}{(ST)(K_o K_I K_T)} = 0.4 \tag{9.3}$$

The open loop transfer function (without the dynamics of the controller) is given by

$$G(z) = \underbrace{\frac{K_o K K_I K_T}{rm}}_{K_1} (1 - z^{-1}) Z\left\{\frac{1}{s^3}\right\}$$

$$G(z) = \frac{K_1 T^2}{2} \frac{z+1}{(z-1)^2} \tag{9.4}$$

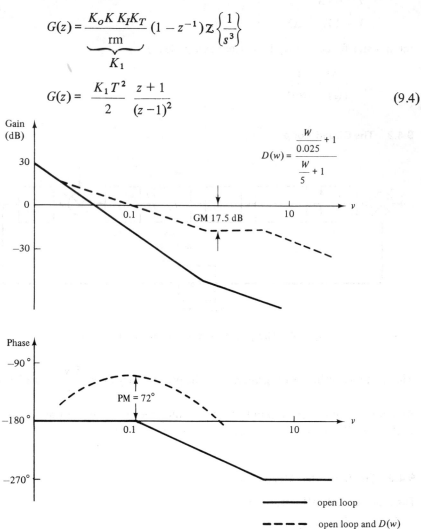

Fig. 9.5 Bode plot of the open loop system with and without compensation

As the design will be carried out on the w-plane we may substitute

$$z = \frac{1 + w}{1 - w}$$

which gives

$$G(w) = \frac{K_1 T^2}{4} \frac{(1 - w)}{w^2} \tag{9.5}$$

The open loop frequency response is obtained from eqn. (9.6) and the results traced in Fig. 9.5.

$$G(jv) = 1660 T^2 \frac{1 - jv}{(jv)^2} \tag{9.6}$$

In this case the pole and zero positions on the w-plane are independent of the sampling interval T, but the DC gain is directly related to T^2. On the Bode plot (Fig. 9.5) one may see that an increase in T requires more effort to stabilize the system. We will select $T = 1.4$ ms.

> *Note:* The transfer function given by eqn. (9.5) is a nonminimum phase type hence the zero contributes a negative phase.

9.4.4 Design of the Compensation Network

The maximum permitted overshoot is 15%, we also require a phase margin, PM, $> 50°$ and a gain margin, GM, > 10 dB.

The closed loop can be approximated as a second order system, so the 15% overshoot corresponds to $M_p = 1.3$ dB on the Nichols diagram (Fig. 9.6). M_p is the maximum gain of the closed loop.

After several trials an appropriate compensation network had the transfer function given by eqn. (9.7).

$$D(w) = 0.4 \frac{\left(\dfrac{w}{0.025} + 1\right)}{\left(\dfrac{w}{5} + 1\right)} \tag{9.7}$$

The Bode plot of the compensated system is depicted in Fig. 9.5.

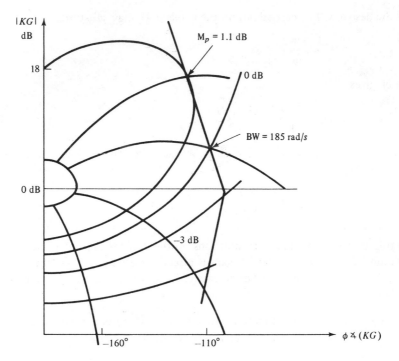

Fig. 9.6   The Nichols diagram of the position servo loop

9.4.5   Frequency Response of the Controller

We may recall that the pole and zero of the controller are expressed in the fictitious frequency domain. The actual frequencies are prewarped, therefore they are:

$$a = \frac{2}{T} \ \tan^{-1} 0.025 = 35.7 \ \text{rad/s}$$

$$b = \frac{2}{T} \ \tan^{-1} 5 \quad\quad = 1960 \ \text{rad/s} \quad\quad\quad (9.8)$$

$$|D(jv)|_{\text{max}} = 20 \left(\log 0.4 + \log \cdot \frac{5}{0.025} \right) = 38 \ \text{dB}$$

The gain of the controller as a function of frequency is traced in Fig. 9.7.

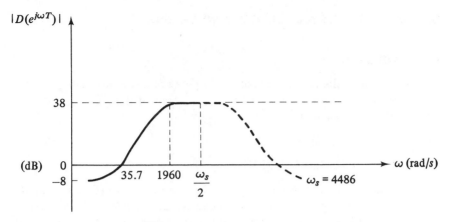

Fig. 9.7 Frequency response of the controller

9.4.6 Properties of the Closed Loop

From inspection of the Bode plot of Fig. 9.5 we can see that

$$PM = 72°$$
$$GM = 17.5 \text{ dB.}$$

The overshoot is 12%, well within the specification, see Fig. 9.8.

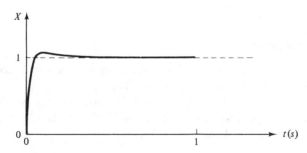

Fig. 9.8 The response to a step function

The bandwidth of the closed loop is 185 rad/s as can be seen from the Bode and Nichols plots

$$BW \cong \frac{2}{T} \tan^{-1} 0.13 \cong 185 \text{ rad/s}$$

9.5   SELECTION OF A/D AND D/A CONVERTERS

9.5.1   A/D Converter

The resolution of the pressure sensor was required to be approximately 0.1 mm. We are asking for about five times better accuracy of the ADC, therefore, its quantization level should be:

$$q = 0.02 \text{ mm}$$

or $q = 0.02 K_0 = 0.0166$ V.

The minimum voltage measured by the ADC corresponds to $(5.22 - 6 \text{ mm}) \times 0.83$ V/mm = -0.65 V. The maximum voltage is 5.22 mm $\times$ 0.83 V/mm = 4.33 V.

These voltages and the quantization level define the range of the ADC.

$$2^C = \frac{4.33 + 0.65}{0.0166} \cong 300 \tag{9.9}$$

$$C = \frac{\log 300}{\log 2} = 8.26 \tag{9.10}$$

$$M = C + 1 = 10 \tag{9.11}$$

Consequently the required number of bits of the ADC is $M = 10$.

9.5.2   D/A Converter

The number of bits of the D/A converter will be calculated using the same approach as for the A/D converter, i.e., $M = 10$.

The quantization noise figure of the A/D converter may be obtained using the approach explained in Chapter 6. Truncation of numbers caused by finite word length generates random noise which gives

$$F = 10 \log \frac{\overline{e}^2}{\overline{e}_T^2} = 10 \log_{10} \frac{2^{2(C+1)}}{3} \tag{9.12}$$

$$F = 10 \log_{10} 2^{2^0} = 55.4 \text{ dB} \tag{9.13}$$

55 dB is a satisfactory noise figure.

9.6   THE CPU

The implemented controller (compensation network) is represented by the transfer function given by eqn. (9.7) which is repeated here.

$$D(w) = 0.4 \; \frac{\left(\dfrac{w}{0.025} + 1 \right)}{\left(\dfrac{w}{5} + 1 \right)} \qquad\qquad \text{(9.7 repeated)}$$

Equation (9.7) will be transformed to the z plane using $w = (z - 1)(z + 1)$. Therefore

$$\frac{u(z)}{e(z)} = D(z) = \frac{13.667 - 13.000z^{-1}}{1.000 + 0.667z^{-1}} \qquad\qquad (9.14)$$

9.6.1   Mechanization of the Controller

Equation (9.14) represents an uncomplicated transfer function and any method of mechanization will be appropriate. The mechanization is charted in Fig. 9.9.

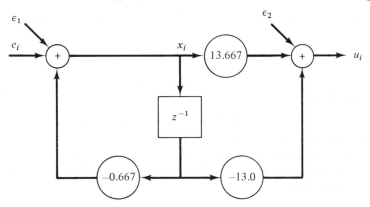

Fig. 9.9   Mechanization of the controller

9.6.2   Required Specifications for the CPU Word Length

The word length of the processing unit will be based on the maximum permitted noise generated by a finite word length truncation. This noise (ϵ_1, ϵ_2) is generated by the multiplication at two points in the system (see the block diagram of Fig. 9.9).

We will first estimate the amplification, $\overset{\prime}{K}$, of the noise (ϵ_1, ϵ_2), propagated through the system

$$\overset{\prime}{K} = \frac{1}{2\pi j} \oint (D_1(z)D_1(z^{-1})z^{-1} + z^{-1})\,dz \tag{9.15}$$

The transfer function, D_1, is identical to D hence

$$\overset{\prime}{K} = \frac{1}{2\pi j} \oint \left[\left(\frac{13.67z - 13}{z + 0.66} \right) \left(\frac{13.67z^{-1} - 13}{z^{-1} + 0.66} \right) + 1 \right] z^{-1}\,dz \tag{9.16}$$

Applying the residue theorem gives

$$\overset{\prime}{K} \cong 1325$$

$F = 40$ dB is a reasonable noise figure.

The corresponding required word length was formulated in Chapter 6.

$$C + 1 = \frac{F\,(\text{dB})}{6} + 0.8 + \frac{10}{6} \log_{10}\overset{\prime}{K} \tag{9.17}$$

which yields, $(C + 1)_{\text{CPU}} = 12.67$, hence the minimum CPU word length should be $C + 1 = 13$ bits.

9.6.3   The Memory Word Length

As can be observed from the Bode plot the accuracy of the transfer function is sensitive to the zero position on the w-plane.

The zero is located on the w-plane at $a = 0.025$ and a maximum shift of 20%, i.e. $\Delta a = 0.005$, will be permitted. This ambiguity will be translated to a minimum word length

$$\frac{w}{a} + 1 \rightarrow \frac{a + 1}{a} \frac{z + \dfrac{a - 1}{a + 1}}{z + 1}$$

$$\frac{a - 1}{a + 1} - \frac{a + \Delta a - 1}{a + \Delta a + 1} = \frac{-2\Delta a}{(a + 1)(a + \Delta a + 1)} \tag{9.18}$$

$$2^{-C} = \left| \frac{2\Delta a}{(a+1)(1+a+\Delta a)} \right|$$

$$C = -3.32 \log_{10} \left| \frac{2\Delta a}{(a+1)(1+a+\Delta a)} \right| \tag{9.19}$$

Inserting $a = 0.025$ and $\Delta a = 0.005$ into eqn. (9.19) yields $C = 6.7$. Consequently the word length memory for coefficient storage will be $C + 1 = 8$ bits.

9.7   THE CONTROLLER PROGRAM

9.7.1   The Combined Tasks of the Computer Control Program

The position servo transfer function on the z-plane is

$$\frac{u(z)}{e(z)} = D(z) = \frac{13.667 - 13.000z^{-1}}{1.000 + 0.667z^{-1}} \tag{9.14 repeated}$$

The numerical algorithm is

$$u_i = -0.667u_{i-1} + 13.667e_i - 13.000e_{i-1} \tag{9.20}$$

The computer program which controls the artificial hand has to include all the three stages described in Sec. 9.2. Recall that the first stage is the stage of constant acceleration therefore the voltage output of the D/A converter for the first stage will be

$$u_a = \frac{(rma_1 + T_F)}{K_T K_I} = 0.11 \text{ V} \tag{9.21}$$

The second stage is the deceleration and the output voltage of the D/A converter for this stage will be

$$u_d = \frac{T_{max}}{K_T K_I} = 4 \text{ V} \tag{9.22}$$

The third stage is the position servo.

9.7.2 The Computer Flow Chart

All the three stages will be combined into a real time computer program. The flow chart is given in Fig. 9.10.

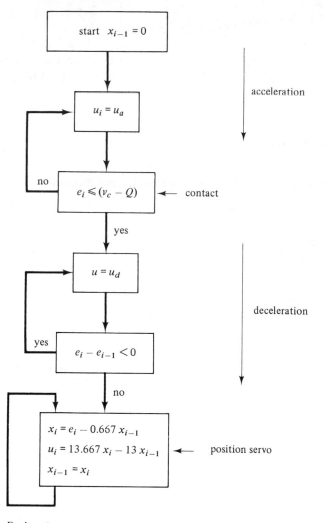

Explanation:

Q = 0.083 V – pressure sensor inaccuracy

v_c = 4.33 V – constant input

Fig. 9.10 Flow chart of the computer control program

EXERCISES

9.1 Plot the frequency response of the controller $D(w) = 0.4(w/0.025 + 1)$ for the fictitious frequency ν and for the actual frequency ω.

9.2 Trace the response to the fictitious frequency ν of the plant including the compensating network of problem 9.1 (open loop).
Estimate:

  (i)   Phase Margin,
  (ii) Gain Margin,
 (iii) Bandwidth.

9.3 Using a Nichols diagram estimate M_p of the system in problem 9.2.

9.4 The closed loop response (problems 9.2, 9.3), using the controller of problem 9.1, is better than the response of the closed loop incorporating the controller given by eqn. (9.7).
     Explain that the pole $w = -5$ is necessary and one has to use the controller given by eqn. (9.7).

9.5 Using the Routh–Hurwitz criterion prove that the closed loop system (problem 9.2) is stable.

Appendix A

Optimal Discrete Control, Some Computational Tools

A.1 DISCRETIZATION OF A CONTINUOUS COST FUNCTION

A continuous quadratic cost function $J(x, u, t)$ may be written as

$$J = \int_0^t (x^T A x + u^T B u)\, d\tau \tag{A.1}$$

and this can be transformed to a discrete version

$$J = \sum_{i=0}^{N-1} [x_i^T u_i^T] \begin{bmatrix} A_{11} & A_{12} \\ A_{21} & A_{22} \end{bmatrix} \begin{bmatrix} x_i \\ u_i \end{bmatrix} \tag{A.2}$$

where $N = t/T$. By the procedure shown below eqn. (A.1) can be rewritten as

$$J = \sum_{i=0}^{N-1} \int_{iT}^{(i+1)T} (x^T A x + u^T B u)\, d\tau \tag{A.3}$$

The interval $0 - t$ is subdivided into N equal intervals of value T. The integrals inside the summation expression of eqn. (A.3) can be expressed as functions of x_i and u_i instead of x and u. Using the state space formulation we may write

$$x(\tau)_{i+1} = \Phi(\tau)x_i + \Gamma_1(\tau)u_i$$

$$iT \leqslant \tau < (i+1)\, T$$

therefore,

$$\int_{iT}^{(i+1)T} (x^T A x + u^T B u)\, d\tau = [x_i^T u_i^T] \begin{bmatrix} A_{11} & A_{12} \\ A_{21} & A_{22} \end{bmatrix} \begin{bmatrix} x_i \\ u_i \end{bmatrix} \tag{A.4}$$

where

$$A_{11} = \int_0^T \Phi^T(\tau) A \Phi(\tau) d\tau$$

$$A_{22} = \int_0^T [\Gamma_1(\tau) A \Gamma_1(\tau) + B] d\tau$$

$$A_{21} = \int_0^T \Phi^T(\tau) A \Gamma_1(\tau) d\tau \qquad (A.5)$$

$$A_{12} = A_{21}^T$$

A.2   GENERAL FORMULATION OF THE DISCRETE REGULATOR PROBLEM

In Sec. A.1 it has been shown that a continuous system controlled by a ZOH with an associated continuous cost function, J, can be reformulated into a discrete form given by

$$x_{i+1} = \Phi x_i + \Gamma_1 u_i$$

$$J = \frac{1}{2} \sum_{i=0}^{N-1} [x_i^T u_i^T] \begin{bmatrix} A_{11} & A_{12} \\ A_{21} & A_{22} \end{bmatrix} \begin{bmatrix} x_i \\ u_i \end{bmatrix} \qquad (A.6)$$

The cost function may be rewritten as:

$$J = \frac{1}{2} \sum_{i=0}^{N-1} [(u_i^T + x_i^T A_{12} A_{22}^{-1}) A_{22} (u_i + A_{22}^{-1} A_{21} x_i) + x_i^T (A_{11} - A_{12} A_{22}^{-1} A_{21}) x_i] \qquad (A.7)$$

Here are different A, B, u, namely, A', B', u'

$$J = \frac{1}{2} \sum_{i=0}^{N-1} x_i^T A' x_i + u_i'^T B' u'_i \qquad (A.8)$$

where

$$A' = A_{11} - A_{12} A_{22}^{-1} A_{21}$$

$$B' = A_{22} \qquad (A.9)$$

$$u'_i = u_i + A_{22}^{-1} A_{21} x_i$$

Using the last expression of eqn. (A.9), eqn. (A.6) can be reformed as

$$
\left.\begin{aligned}
x_{i+1} &= (\Phi - \Gamma_1 A_{22}^{-1} A_{21}) x_i + \Gamma_1 u_i' \\
J &= \tfrac{1}{2} \sum_{i=0}^{N-1} x_i^T A' x_i + u'_i{}^T B' u_i'
\end{aligned}\right\}
\tag{A.10}
$$

If linear state feedback is used for the system of eqn. (A.10), i.e.

$$
u_i' = C x_i
\tag{A.11}
$$

then the control u_i for system of eqn. (A.6) will be

$$
u_i = (C - A_{22}^{-1} A_{21}) x_i
\tag{A.12}
$$

This transformation is necessary because the theory of the optimal discrete regulator is solved for the system defined by eqn. (A.10), whilst a discretization of the continuous system yields the cost function of eqn. (A.7).

A.3   SOLUTION OF THE OPTIMAL REGULATOR

It has been shown that most of the control configurations which interest us can be rewritten in the simple form of eqn. (A.10) which we repeat here

$$
x_{i+1} = \Phi x_i + \Gamma u_i
$$

$$
J = \tfrac{1}{2} \sum_{i=0}^{N} x_i^T A x_i + u_i^T B u_i
\tag{A.13}
$$

The optimal linear controller follows a control law

$$
u_i = C(i) x_i
\tag{A.14}
$$

that minimizes the cost function, J, for any initial conditions. If N increases to infinity and a steady state is reached, then $C(i) = C =$ constant, and the controller is called a regulator.

The solution of the optimal linear controller was given by Kalman (KA-1) who used the dynamic programming approach. We will use Bryson's approach (BR-1) which solves the system defined by eqn. (A.10) via the calculus of variation.

For a finite N, the last control u_N is meaningless as it will influence only the state x_{n+1}, which does not interest us. Therefore the cost function J may be written in the form

$$
J = \tfrac{1}{2} \, x_N^T A x_N + \tfrac{1}{2} \sum_{i=0}^{N-1} (x_i^T A x_i + u_i^T B u_i)
\tag{A.15}
$$

In the minimization procedure used in the calculus of variation, we will augment the cost function, J, by the constraints multiplied by a Lagrange undetermined multiplier λ_i^T (vector). The constraints are the equations of motion for eqn. (A.10). The augmented cost function, J, is

$$J = \tfrac{1}{2} x_N^T A x_N - \lambda_N^T x_N + \sum_{i=1}^{N-1} (\mathcal{H}_i - \lambda_i x_i) + \mathcal{H}_0 \tag{A.16}$$

where $\mathcal{H}_i$ is defined as the Hamiltonian sequence:

$$\mathcal{H}_i = \tfrac{1}{2} x_i^T A x_i + \tfrac{1}{2} u_i^T B u_i + \lambda_{i+1}^T (\Phi x_i + \Gamma u_i) \tag{A.17}$$

Using the methods of the calculus of variation, the condition for a stationary value of J is that dJ is zero for arbitrary du_i

$$dJ = (x_N^T A - \lambda_N^T) dx_N + \sum_{i-1}^{N-1} \left\{ \left[\frac{\partial \mathcal{H}_i}{\partial x_i} - \lambda_i^T \right] dx_i + \frac{\partial \mathcal{H}_i}{\partial u_i} du_i \right\}$$
$$+ \frac{\partial \mathcal{H}_0}{\partial x_0} dx_0 + \frac{\partial \mathcal{H}_0}{\partial u_0} du_0 \tag{A.18}$$

We choose λ_i such that

$$\frac{\partial \mathcal{H}_i}{\partial x_i} - \lambda_i^T = 0 \qquad i = 0, \ldots, N-1 \tag{A.19}$$

$$x_N^T A_N - \lambda_N^T = 0 \tag{A.20}$$

For an extremum,

$$\frac{\partial \mathcal{H}_i}{\partial u_i} = 0 \tag{A.21}$$

yields,

$$\frac{\partial \mathcal{H}_i}{\partial u_i} = u_i^T B + \lambda_{i+1}^T \Gamma = 0 \tag{A.22}$$

$$u_i = -B^{-1} \Gamma \lambda_{i+1} \tag{A.23}$$

Combining eqns. (A.10) and (A.23), we obtain

$$x_{i+1} = \Phi x_i - \Gamma B^{-1} \Gamma^T \lambda_{i+1} \tag{A.24}$$

and from eqns. (A.18) and (A.16), we obtain

$$\lambda_i = \Phi^T \lambda_{i+1} + A x_i \tag{A.25}$$

Equations (A.24) and (A.25), called the 'Euler-Lagrange difference equations' formulated in state space notation are:

$$\begin{bmatrix} x \\ \lambda \end{bmatrix}_{i+1} = \begin{bmatrix} \Phi + \Gamma B^{-1} \Gamma^T \Phi^{-T} A & -\Gamma B^{-1} \Gamma^T \Phi^{-T} \\ -\Phi^{-T} A & \Phi^{-T} \end{bmatrix} \begin{bmatrix} x \\ \lambda \end{bmatrix}_i \qquad (A.26)$$

This is a two-point boundary value problem, x_0 is given at $i = 0$. From eqn. (A.19) we get the boundary condition for $i = N$.

$$\lambda_N = A x_N \qquad (A.27)$$

The solution to this problem was accomplished by Bryson using the 'sweep method' (BR-1). The sweep method assumes a solution for λ_i of the form

$$\lambda_i = S_i x_i \qquad (A.28)$$

This solution leads to a matrix Riccati difference equation in S_j, i.e.

$$\left.\begin{array}{l} S_j = \Phi^T (S_{j+1} + \Gamma B^{-1} \Gamma^T)^{-1} \Phi + A \qquad j = N - 1, \ldots, 0 \\ S_N = A \end{array}\right\} (A.29)$$

Determining S_j from the backward recursive relations of eqn. (A.29), and using eqns. (A.23) and (A.28), the optimal control u_i is expressed as a linear combination of the state x_i. If certain conditions are satisfied as N increases, S_j reaches a steady state S_{ss}, and the controller is reduced to a regulator

$$u_i = -B^{-1} \Gamma \Phi^{-T} (S_{ss} - A) x_i \qquad (A.30)$$

which is obtained by combining eqns. (A.23), (A.25), and (A.28). In the steady state, the matrix Riccati difference equation is reduced to a second-order matrix algebraic equation

$$S_{ss} = \Phi^T (S_{ss}^{-1} + \Gamma B^{-1} \Gamma^T)^{-1} \Phi + A \qquad (A.31)$$

During the last two decades a considerable effort has been made to find an efficient solution of the Riccati equation and the steady state matrix equation. The usual method of solution for eqn. (A.31) is a recursive computation of eqn. (A.29) until S reaches a steady state S_{ss}. A completely different approach to solving for S_{ss} is to use the eigenvector decomposition of the transition matrix eqn. (A.26).

A.4   SOLUTION OF THE DISCRETE RICCATI EQUATION BY EIGENVECTOR DECOMPOSITION

In 1966, Potter (PO-1) described a method for the steady state solution of the matrix Riccati differential equation by eigenvector decomposition. Bryson and

Hall (BR-2), using an efficient QR algorithm for eigenvector calculation, constructed a computer program for linear regulators and Kalman filter syntheses. Vaughan (VA-1) extended the Potter method for discrete system control synthesis. The eigenvector decomposition problem has been solved independently of Vaughan, and applied to the discrete filter synthesis problem. This interpretation is given here.

The Euler-Lagrange eqn. (A.26) will be repeated here, but on the z-plane

$$\begin{bmatrix} zx \\ z\lambda \end{bmatrix} = \begin{bmatrix} \Phi + \Gamma B^{-1} \Gamma^T \Phi^{-T} A & -\Gamma B^{-1} \Gamma^T \Phi^{-T} \\ -\Phi^{-T} A & \Phi^{-T} \end{bmatrix} \begin{bmatrix} x \\ \lambda \end{bmatrix} \quad (A.32)$$

The following theorems will be proved.

Theorem 1 If z is an eigenvalue of the system of eqn. (A.26), then $1/z$ is also an eigenvalue.

Proof Defining E as $E \triangleq z^{-1}$ and defining a new variable γ as $\gamma \triangleq z\lambda$. Then directly using eqns. (A.24) and (A.25), the system of eqn. (A.32) can be transformed to an equivalent form,

$$\begin{bmatrix} \Phi - Iz & -\Gamma B^{-1} \Gamma^T \\ A & \Phi^T - T z^{-1} \end{bmatrix} \begin{bmatrix} x \\ \gamma \end{bmatrix} = 0 \quad (A.33)$$

As $\Gamma B^{-1}\Gamma^T$ and A are symmetric, eqn. (A.33) may be rewritten as

$$[\gamma^T x^T] \begin{bmatrix} \Phi - IE & -\Gamma B^{-1} \Gamma^T \\ A & \Phi^{-1} - IE^{-1} \end{bmatrix} = 0 \quad (A.34)$$

Eqns. (A.33) and (A.34) have the same transition matrix, therefore, if z is the solution of the characteristic equation of eqn. (A.33), then E is a solution also.

Conclusion. The eigenvalues of the Euler-Lagrange eqns. (A.32) are reflected symmetrically across the unit circle on the z-plane. See Fig. A.1.

Definition:

$$T \triangleq \begin{bmatrix} X_z & X_E \\ \Lambda_z & \Lambda_E \end{bmatrix} \triangleq [T_z T_E] \quad (A.35)$$

Matrices T_z and T_E are the eigenvectors of the Euler-Lagrange eqns. (A.32), associated with z and E respectively.

Before formulating and proving Theorem 2, a well-known result from linear systems theory will be presented (KW-1).

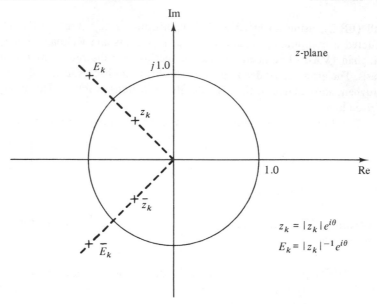

Fig. A.1   Root locations of Euler-Lagrange equations

A homogeneous, linear time-invariant discrete system

$$x_{i+1} = \Phi x_i \tag{A.36}$$

with the initial conditions x_0, has the solution

$$x_i = \Phi^i x_0 \tag{A.37}$$

The solution x_i can be expressed in terms of the individual eigenvector modes as follows. The initial condition x_0 is resolved along the modes of the eigenvectors by the transformation T_r^{-1}

$$\zeta_0 = T_r^{-1} x_0 \tag{A.38}$$

where T_r is the matrix of the eigenvectors of Φ

$$T_r = [l_1, \ldots, l_n] \tag{A.39}$$

The solution x_i is a linear combination of the particular excited modes, i.e.,

$$x_i = \sum_{j=1}^{n} z_j^i \, l_j \, \zeta_0 \tag{A.40}$$

Using this result we can formulate Theorem 2.

Theorem 2   The steady state solution, S_{ss}, of the matrix Riccati difference equation (repeated from eqn. (A.31))

$$S = \Phi^T (zS^{-1} + \Gamma B^{-1} \Gamma^T)^{-1} \Phi + A \tag{A.41}$$

is

$$S_{ss} = \Lambda_E X_E^{-1} \tag{A.42}$$

Proof The homogeneous solution of the Euler-Lagrange equations is

$$\begin{bmatrix} x \\ \lambda \end{bmatrix}_i = \sum_{k=1}^{n} \zeta_0 \begin{pmatrix} x_z(k) \\ \lambda_z(k) \end{pmatrix} z_k^i + \sum_{k=1}^{n} \eta_0 \begin{pmatrix} x_E(k) \\ \lambda_E(k) \end{pmatrix} z_k^{N-i} \tag{A.43}$$

where n = the order of the system,

$$\left. \begin{matrix} \zeta_{0_k} \\ \\ \eta_{0_k} \end{matrix} \right\} = \text{constants expressing boundary conditions,}$$

$$\left. \begin{matrix} z_k \\ \\ E_K \end{matrix} \right\} = \text{eigenvalues of eqn. (A.27).}$$

and $\qquad \begin{pmatrix} x_z^{(k)} \\ \lambda_z^{(k)} \end{pmatrix}$, and $\begin{pmatrix} x_E(k) \\ \lambda_E(k) \end{pmatrix}$

are the eigenvectors of eqn. (A.32) corresponding to z_k and E_k. Equation (A.43) may be formulated in the matrix notation

$$\begin{bmatrix} x \\ \lambda \end{bmatrix}_i = \begin{bmatrix} x_z(1) \dots x_z(n) \\ \lambda_z(1) \dots \lambda_z(n) \end{bmatrix} \begin{bmatrix} \zeta_{01} z_1^i \\ \zeta_{0n} z_n^i \end{bmatrix}$$

$$+ \begin{bmatrix} x_E(1) \dots x_E(n) \\ \lambda_E(1) \dots \lambda_E(n) \end{bmatrix} \begin{bmatrix} \eta_{01} E_1^{-(N-i)} \\ \eta_{0n} E_n^{-(N-i)} \end{bmatrix} \tag{A.44}$$

Defining Z as

$$Z = \begin{bmatrix} z_1 & 0 & \cdot & \cdot & \cdot & 0 \\ 0 & z_2 & \cdot & \cdot & \cdot & 0 \\ \cdot & \cdot & & & & \cdot \\ \cdot & \cdot & & & & \cdot \\ \cdot & \cdot & & & & \cdot \\ 0 & 0 & \cdot & \cdot & \cdot & z_n \end{bmatrix} \tag{A.45}$$

eqn. (A.44) can be further reduced to

$$\left.\begin{array}{l} x_i = X_z \, z^i \, \bar{\zeta}_0 + x_E \, z^{N-i} \, \bar{\eta}_0 \\ \lambda_i = \Lambda_z \, z^i \, \bar{\zeta}_0 + \Lambda_E \, z^{N-i} \, \bar{\eta}_0 \end{array}\right\} \qquad (A.46)$$

As i increases, the stable modes multiplied by the factor ζ_0 attenuate so that eqn. (A.46) becomes

$$\left.\begin{array}{l} x_i = X_E \, z^{N-i} \, \bar{\eta}_0 \\ \lambda_i = \Lambda_E \, z^{N-i} \, \bar{\eta}_0 \end{array}\right\} \qquad (A.47)$$

Solving eqn. (A.47), we get

$$\lambda_i = \Lambda_E X_E^{-1} x_i \qquad (A.48)$$

However $\lambda_i = S_i x_i$ was the assumed solution of the matrix Riccati difference eqn. (A.29). Therefore (repeat of eqn. (A.42))

$$S_{ss} = \Lambda_E X_E^{-1}$$

This concludes the proof of eqn. (4.42).

Having these results, the optimal feedback control of the linear discrete regulator is

$$u_i = -B^{-1} \, \Gamma \Phi^{-T} \, (\Lambda_E X_E^{-1} - A) x_i = C x_i \qquad (A.49)$$

This solution requires nonsingularity of the transition matrix Φ. Made discrete, the linear continuous system always has the property that $|\Phi| \neq 0$. This stems from the fact that a continuous linear system has a unique solution for a given initial condition (KW-1). However, this property ($|\Phi| \neq 0$) is not obvious for a pure discrete system. If, in a pure discrete system Φ is singular, it indicates that some of the states (or the modes) can be expressed as a linear combination of the remaining states (or modes). Hence if state variable feedback is required, the singular system representation can be reduced in dimension until regularity is achieved and the feedback matrix C can be calculated.

Two more results will be given.

(i) The stable eigenvalues of the Euler-Lagrange eqns. (A.32) are identical with the eigenvalues of the closed loop optimal system. This useful property can be proven by analogy to continuous systems (BR-2).

(ii) The expression for S_{ss},

$$S_{ss} = \Lambda_E X_E^{-1} \qquad \text{(eqn. A.42 repeated)}$$

is independent of any rearrangement of the individual eigenvectors in

$$\begin{bmatrix} X_E \\ \Lambda_E \end{bmatrix}$$

The proof is obvious if eqn. (A.42) is rewritten as

$$S_{ss} \Lambda_E = X_E \tag{A.50}$$

Assuming S_{ss} is fixed, then any column j of X_E is a linear combination of S_{ss} and column j of Λ_E. Its values are independent of its relative position with respect to other columns.

A.5 CALCULATION OF THE STEADY STATE OPTIMAL FILTER BY EIGENVECTOR DECOMPOSITION

The steady state optimal (Kalman) filter is an observer which minimizes the steady state error covariance matrix P. The recursive equation for M obtained from the minimization process has the same structure as for S for the optimal control problem. The equations are identical if we consider the following equivalence first recognized by Kalman (KA-1):

Control		Filter
Φ	$\leftrightarrow$	Φ^T
H	$\leftrightarrow$	Γ_2^T
Γ_1	$\leftrightarrow$	H^T
A	$\leftrightarrow$	Q_d
B	$\leftrightarrow$	R

Thus we will replace the matrices of the optimal control problem by the matrices of the filter in Euler-Lagrange eqn. (A.32) which yields the matrix

$$\mathcal{H} = \begin{bmatrix} \Phi^T + H^T R^{-1} H \Phi^{-1} \Gamma_2^T Q_d \Gamma_2 & -H^T R^{-1} H \Phi^{-1} \\ \Phi^{-1} \Gamma_2 Q_d \Gamma_2^T & \Phi^{-1} \end{bmatrix} \tag{A.51}$$

Making direct use of the results from the optimal regulator calculation, the error covariance matrix M is given by

$$M = X_E \Lambda_E^{-1} \tag{A.52}$$

where X_E and Λ_E are defined from

$$T = \begin{bmatrix} X_z & X_E \\ \Lambda_z & \Lambda_E \end{bmatrix} \tag{A.53}$$

T is a matrix of the eigenvectors of the $2n \times 2n$ matrix $\mathcal{H}$,

$$\begin{bmatrix} X_z \\ \Lambda_z \end{bmatrix}$$

are the eigenvectors of $\mathcal{H}$ corresponding to the stable eigenvalues and,

$$\begin{bmatrix} X_E \\ \Lambda_E \end{bmatrix}$$

are the eigenvectors corresponding to the eigenvalues of $\mathcal{H}$ located outside the unit circle.

As in the optimal control problem, the stable eigenvalues are identical with the eigenvalues of the observer error system defined from eqns. (4.23) and (4.24) as

$$\tilde{x} \triangleq \hat{x} - x \tag{A.54}$$

$$\tilde{x}_{i+1} = (\Phi - KH\Phi)x_i + (KH\Gamma_2 - \Gamma_2)w_i + Kv_{i+1} \tag{A.55}$$

A.6   ALGORITHM FOR AN EVALUATION OF THE STEADY STATE RESPONSE TO AN EXTERNAL NOISE

A stable discrete system Φ, disturbed by an external noise with a covariance matrix Q_d reaches a steady state. The average behavior of its states is characterized by a covariance matrix x which is the solution of Bryson and Ho (BR-1).

$$X = \Phi X \Phi^T + Q_d \tag{A.56}$$

Following Bryson, the average behavior of an optimally controlled discrete system, with an external noise disturbance and measurement noise, is characterized by the state covariance matrix X. This is the solution of

$$X - M = (\Phi + \Gamma C)(X - P)(\Phi + \Gamma C)^T \tag{A.57}$$

where C is the optimal gain defined in eqn. (A.49), M and P are the observer error and covariance matrices defined in eqn. (4.45). Equation (A.57) will be rewritten as

$$X - P = (\Phi + \Gamma C)(X - P)(\Phi + \Gamma C)^T + M - P \tag{A.58}$$

Equation (A.58) is now in the form of eqn. (A.56). Equation (A.56) is essentially a linear equation of X. New algorithms for solving eqn. (A.56) appear in the numerical method literature (BER-1). We will present a new numerical solution of eqn. (A.56) which utilizes the algorithm for eigenvector decomposition.

Claim 1 $X = \Lambda_E X_E^{-1}$ (A.59)

where $\begin{bmatrix} X_z & X_E \\ \Lambda_z & \Lambda_E \end{bmatrix}$

is a matrix of eigenvectors of the $2n \times 2n$ system of H', where

$$H' = \begin{bmatrix} \Phi^{-T} & 0 \\ Q_d \Phi^{-T} & \Phi \end{bmatrix}, \text{ and}$$ (A.60)

$$\begin{bmatrix} X_E \\ \Lambda_E \end{bmatrix}$$

is the eigenvectors submatrix corresponding to the eigenvalues of H' outside the unit circle.

Claim 2   If z_k is an eigenvalue of H', then $z_k^{-1} = E_k$ is also an eigenvalue of H'.

Proof   Claim 2 is obvious from inspection. To prove Claim 1, we let

$$H' \begin{bmatrix} X_E \\ \Lambda_E \end{bmatrix} = \begin{bmatrix} X_E \\ \Lambda_E \end{bmatrix} D_E$$ (A.61)

where

$$D = \begin{bmatrix} D_E \\ D_z \end{bmatrix} = \begin{bmatrix} E_1 & \cdot & \cdot & & & 0 \\ \cdot & E_n & \cdot & & \\ \cdot & \cdot & z_1 & \\ \cdot & \cdot & & z_n \end{bmatrix} \qquad |E_k| > 1$$ (A.62)

Using eqns. (A.61) and (A.62)

$$\left.\begin{array}{l} \Phi^{-T} X_E = X_E D_E \\ Q_d \Phi^{-T} X_E + \Phi \Lambda_E = \Lambda_E D_E \end{array}\right\}$$ (A.63)

yields

$$Q_d + \Phi \Lambda_E X_E^{-1} \Phi^T = \Lambda_E X_E^{-1}$$ (A.64)

Defining

$$X = \Lambda_E X_E^{-1}$$ (A.65)

Equation (A.64) is identical to eqn. (A.56), thus proving Claim 1.

Using this result, the average behavior X of the optimally controlled discrete system, including process noise and measurement noise, is given as the solution of eqn. (A.52)

$$X = \Lambda_E X_E^{-1} + P \tag{A.66}$$

where

$$\begin{bmatrix} X_z & X_E \\ \Lambda_z & \Lambda_E \end{bmatrix}$$

is a matrix of eigenvectors corresponding to $2n \times 2n$ matrix H'

$$H' = \begin{bmatrix} (\Phi + \Gamma C)^T & 0 \\ (M - P)(\Phi + \Gamma C)^{-T} & \Phi + \Gamma C \end{bmatrix} \tag{A.67}$$

Appendix B

The Roughness Function

B.1 DEFINITION OF THE ROUGHNESS FUNCTION

A continuous linear system, controlled discretely, has the following form:

$$\dot{x} = Fx + Gu \tag{B.1}$$

where u = constant, $t_i \leqslant t < t_i + T$. Written in a discrete form we have

$$x_{i+1} = \Phi x_i + \Gamma u_i \tag{B.2}$$

When a step function is applied to the system defined by eqn. (B.1) at time t_i, some of the variables $\dot{x}$ abruptly change their magnitude from $\dot{x}_-$ to $\dot{x}_+$. These are all the variables (not states), which are directly influenced by the input u_i. In other words, the abruptly changing variables are the derivatives of the states for which the control distribution matrix, G, has non-zero elements. We shall limit our discussion to the case in which the state variables x are not abruptly changed, i.e., $(x_+)_i = (x_-)_i = x_i$. This is the common case in mechanical systems, where a step input in force changes the acceleration. The requirement that none of the states be abruptly changed is necessary in order to obtain an explicit expression for the RF.

　　If full state variable feedback is implemented eqns. (B.1) and (B.2) can be combined in the following form

$$(\dot{x}_+)_{i+1} - (\dot{x}_-)_{i+1} = GC[(\Phi + \Gamma C) - I]x_i \tag{B.3}$$

Proof:　The input u_i, through the time interval T, $t_i \leqslant t < t_i + T$ is

$$u_i = Cx_i \tag{B.4}$$

281

and

$$(\dot{x}_-)_{i+1} = Fx_{i+1} + G(u_-)_{i+1} \left.\begin{array}{c} \\ \end{array}\right\}$$
$$(\dot{x}_+)_{i+1} = Fx_{i+1} + G(u_+)_{i+1} \quad (B.5)$$

Combining eqns. (B.5) and (B.4) gives

$$(\dot{x}_+)_{i+1} = (\dot{x}_-)_{i+1} + GC(x_{i+1} - x_i) \tag{B.6}$$

By using eqn. (B.2) we obtain the desired form eqn. (B.3). This concludes the proof.

The quantity $|(\dot{x}_+)_i - (\dot{x}_-)_i|$ indicates the roughness of control in the instant t_i. We will define the RF of a closed loop system as a scalar non-negative number.

$$\mathrm{RF} \triangleq \sum_{i=0}^{N} \Delta\dot{x}_i^T \, W \, \Delta\dot{x}_i \tag{B.7}$$

where,

$$\Delta\dot{x}_i \triangleq (\dot{x}_+)_i - (\dot{x}_-)_i$$
$$t = N \times T$$
$$W \geqslant 0$$

In the definition of eqn. (B.7), RF = RF(N) and by using eqn. (B.3), we may express RF as a function of x_i.

$$\mathrm{RF} = \sum_{i=0}^{N} x_i^T \, [(\Phi + \Gamma C - I]^T C^T G^T WGC \, [(\Phi + \Gamma C) - I] x_i \tag{B.8}$$

If x_0 is given, the RF is a function of x_0 and N

$$\mathrm{RF} = \sum_{i=0}^{N} x_0 (\Phi + \Gamma C)^{iT} \, [(\Phi + \Gamma C) - I]^T C^T G^T WGC \, [(\Phi + \Gamma C) - I] \, (\Phi + \Gamma C)^i x_0 \tag{B.9}$$

Obviously, the expression of eqn. (B.9) is rather difficult to calculate. However, a simple form for RF can be obtained for the limiting case $N \to \infty$. There are two methods for the calculation of $\mathrm{RF}_{N \to \infty}$.

Method 1:   Using z-transforms and Parseval's theorem, we have

$$r \triangleq GC(x_{i+1} - x_i) \tag{B.10}$$

$$r(z) = GC(Iz - I)(Iz - \Phi - \Gamma C)x_0 \tag{B.11}$$

$$RF = \frac{1}{2\pi j} \oint_{\gamma} r^T(z) \, Wr(z^{-1}) \, dz \tag{B.12}$$

where γ is the unit circle.

Method 2: By using a Liapunov function. From eqns. (B.7) and (B.8) we obtain the following set of equations:

$$x_{i+1} = (\Phi + \Gamma C) x_i$$

$$RF = \sum_{i=0}^{N} x_i^T R x_i - T_r(x_0 x_0^T P_0) \tag{B.13}$$

where x_0 is given and,

$$R \triangleq [(\Phi + \Gamma C) - I]^T C^T G^T WGC[(\Phi + \Gamma C) - I] \quad (R \geqslant 0) \tag{B.14}$$

and P_0 is obtained by a backward sweep from eqn. (B.15),

$$\left. \begin{array}{l} P_j = (\Phi + \Gamma C)^T P_{j+1} \, (\Phi + \Gamma C) + R \\ P_N = R, \qquad j = N - 1, \ldots, 0 \end{array} \right\} \tag{B.15}$$

For $N \to \infty$, the solution for the RF reduces to the simple form.

$$RF = \sum_{i=0}^{N} x_i^T \, R x_i = T_r(x_0 x_0^T P) \quad_{N \to \infty} \tag{B.16}$$

where P is the solution of

$$P = (\Phi + \Gamma C)^T P \, (\Phi + \Gamma C) + R \tag{B.17}$$

The easiest way to obtain the limiting case $RF_{N \to \infty}$ is to use Method 2 which involves the solution of the linear matrix equation given by eqn. (B.17). This type of equation is extensively treated in Appendix A. The solution we proposed there was to use the eigenvector decomposition algorithm. This algorithm, directly applicable to eqn. (B.17), can be solved for P.

B.2 THE MEAN ROUGHNESS FUNCTION OF A CLOSED LOOP SYSTEM DISTURBED BY AN EXTERNAL NOISE

We are also interested in estimating the average roughness of a continuous system controlled discretely and disturbed by a random noise.

The disturbed system is

$$\dot{x} = Fx + Gu + w \qquad\qquad w \to N(0, Q)$$
$$x_{i+1} = \Phi_c\, x_i + w_i \qquad\qquad w_i \to N(0, Q_d) \qquad\Big\} \qquad (B.18)$$

where Φ_c is the closed loop transition matrix. Q_d is the covariance matrix of the discretized white noise with a power spectral density matrix Q.

The mean roughness function, $\mathrm{RF_m}$, of this system will be defined as

$$\mathrm{RF_m} = T_r E\left\{ [(\dot{x}_+)_i - (\dot{x}_-)_i][(\dot{x}_+)_i - (\dot{x}_-)_i]^T W \right\}_{i \to \infty} \qquad (B.19)$$

where $W \geqslant 0$. Using eqn. (B.6), we have

$$\Delta\dot{x}_{i+1} \overset{\Delta}{=} (\dot{x}_+)_{i+1} - (\dot{x}_-)_{i+1} = G(u_{i+1} - u_i)$$

Therefore,

$$E\left\{\Delta\dot{x}_{i+1}\right\} = E\left\{GC(x_{i+1} - x_i)\right\} \qquad (B.20)$$

Combining eqns. (B.18) and (B.20), we get

$$E\left\{\Delta\dot{x}_{i+1}\right\} - E\left\{GC(\Phi_c x_i - x_i + w_i)\right\} \qquad w_i \to N(0, Q),$$

where E is a linear operator. Furthermore, x_i and w_i are uncorrelated by definition. Therefore

$$E\left\{\Delta\dot{x}_{i+1}\right\} = E\left\{GC(\Phi_c - I)x_i\right\} \qquad (B.21)$$

where x_i is a Gaussian-Markov random process with a covariance matrix X_i. $\Delta\dot{x}_i$ is a linear combination of x_i, thus $\Delta\dot{x}_i$ is also a Gaussian-Markov process with a covariance matrix, X_{r_i} given by

$$X_{r_i} = GC(\Phi_c - I) X_i (\Phi_c - I)^T C^T G^T + GCQ_d C^T G^T \qquad (B.22)$$

where $X_i = E(x_i x_i^T)$. The steady state value of the covariance matrix X_i is the solution of

$$X = \Phi_c\, X\, \Phi_c + Q_d \qquad (B.23)$$

By combining eqns. (B.19) and (B.22) we have the final expression for $\mathrm{RF_m}$

$$\mathrm{RF_m} = T_r(X_r W) \qquad (B.24)$$

where

$$X_r = GC(\Phi_c - I) X (\Phi_c - I)^T C^T G^T + GCQ_d C^T G^T \qquad (B.25)$$

As with the RF for an impulse response, the $\mathrm{RF_m}$ involves the solution of a linear matrix equation of the form given by eqn. (B.23).

Appendix C

Table of z-transforms and s-transforms

$f(t)$	$F(s)$	$f(iT)$	$F(z)$
$\delta(t)$	1	$1, i = 0;$ $0, i \neq 0$	1
1	$\dfrac{1}{s}$	1	$\dfrac{1}{1 - z^{-1}}$
t	$\dfrac{1}{s^2}$	iT	$\dfrac{Tz^{-1}}{(1 - z^{-1})^2}$
e^{-at}	$\dfrac{1}{s+a}$	e^{-aiT}	$\dfrac{1}{1 - e^{-aT}z^{-1}}$
te^{-at}	$\dfrac{1}{(s+a)^2}$	iTe^{-aiT}	$\dfrac{Te^{-aT}z^{-1}}{(1 - e^{-aT}z^{-1})^2}$
$1 - e^{-at}$	$\dfrac{a}{s(s+a)}$	$1 - e^{-aiT}$	$\dfrac{(1 - e^{-aT})z^{-1}}{(1 - z^{-1})(1 - e^{-aT}z^{-1})}$
$\sin at$	$\dfrac{a}{s^2 + a^2}$	$\sin aiT$	$\dfrac{(\sin aT)z^{-1}}{1 - (2\cos aT)z^{-1} + z^{-2}}$
$\cos at$	$\dfrac{s}{s^2 + a^2}$	$\cos aiT$	$\dfrac{1 - (\cos aT)z^{-1}}{1 - (2\cos aT)z^{-1} + z^{-2}}$
$e^{-at}\sin bt$	$\dfrac{b}{(s+a)^2 + b^2}$	$e^{-aiT}\sin biT$	$\dfrac{e^{-aT}(\sin bT)z^{-1}}{1 - 2e^{-aT}(\cos bT)z^{-1} + z^{-2}e^{-2aT}}$
$e^{-at}\cos bt$	$\dfrac{s+a}{(s+a)^2 + b^2}$	$e^{-aiT}\cos biT$	$\dfrac{1 - z^{-1}e^{-aT}\cos bT}{1 - 2e^{-aT}(\cos bT)z^{-1} + z^{-2}e^{-2aT}}$

References

BA-1   Barna, A. and Porat, D. I., *Introduction to Microcomputers and Microprocessors*, Wiley, 1975.

BE-1   Beauchamp, K. G., *Signal Processing*, George Allen, 1973.

BEN-1   Ben-Zwi, A. and Preiszler, M., *Comparison of Discretization Methods*, Rafael, Israel MOD, 1979 (in Hebrew).

BER-1   Berkowitz, F., *Estimation of the Computing Capacity Required from all Digital Tactical Missiles*, M.Sc. thesis, Technion, Israel Inst. of Techn., Faculty of Electr. Eng., 1978.

BI-1   Bishob, A. B., *Introduction to Linear Discrete Control*, Academic Press, 1975.

BIB-1   Bibbero, R. J., *Microprocessors in Instrumentation and Control*, Wiley, 1977.

BL-1   Blakelock, J. H., *Automatic Control of Aircrafts and Missiles*, Wiley, 1965.

BLA-1   Blaschke, W. S. and McGill, J., *The Control of Industrial Processes by Digital Techniques*, Elsevier, 1976.

BO-1   Borow, M. S., *et al.*, 'Navy Digital Flight Control System Development', *Honeywell Document No. 21857-FR*, Honeywell Inc., Minneapolis, Minn., Dec. 1972.

BOG-1 Bogner, R. E. and Constantinides, A. G., *Introduction to Digital Filtering*, Wiley, 1975.

BR-1   Bryson, A. E. and Ho, Y. C., *Applied Optimal Control*, Wiley, 1975.

BR-2   Bryson, A. E. and Hall, W. E., 'Optimal Control and Filter Synthesis by Eigenvector Decomposition', *SUDAAR Report No. 436*, Stanford University, Dept. Aeronautics & Astronautics, Stanford, Calif., Nov. 1971.

BU-1   Bucy, R. S. and Joseph, P. D., *Filtering for Stochastic Processes with Application to Guidance*, Wiley-Interscience, 1968.

CA-1   Cadzow, J. A. and Martens, H. R., *Discrete-Time and Computer Control Systems*, Prentice-Hall, 1970.

CA-2   Cadzow, J. A., *Discrete-Time Systems*, Prentice-Hall, 1973.

DA-1   Dazzo, J. J. and Houpis, C. H., *Linear Control System Analysis and Design*, McGraw-Hill, 1975.

JU-1   Jury, E. I., *Theory and Application of the z-Transform Method*, Wiley, 1964; revised by Robert E. Krieger, 1973.

KA-1   Kalman, R. E., 'A New Approach to Linear Filtering and Prediction Problems', *Trans. ASME, J. Basic Eng.*, Mar. 1960.

KAI-1   Kaiser, J. F. and Kuo, F. F., *System Analysis by Digital Computer*, Wiley, 1960.

KAT-1   Katz, P., *Sample Rate Selection for Digital Control of Aircraft*, Ph.D dissertation, Stanford University, Dept. of Aeronautics & Astronautics, Stanford, Calif., Sept. 1974.

KW-1   Kwakernaak, H. and Sivan, R., *Linear Optimal Control Systems*, Wiley-Interscience, New York, 1972.

OP-1   Oppenheim, A. V. and Schafer, R. W., *Digital Signal Processing*, Prentice-Hall, 1975.

OS-1   Osborne, A., *An Introduction to Microcomputers*, SYBEX, 1979.

PE-1   Peled, U., 'Design Methods with Application to Prefilters and Sampling-rate Selection in Digital Flight Control Systems', *SUDAAR Report No. 512*, Stanford University, Dept. of Aeronautics & Astronautics, Stanford, Calif., May 1978.

PO-1   Potter, J. E., 'Matrix Quadratic Solution', *SIAM J., Applied Math.*, *Vol. 14, No. 3*, May 1966.

RA-1   Ragazzini, S. P. and Franklin, G. F., *Sampled Data Control Systems*, McGraw-Hill, 1958.

RA-2   Rabiner, L. R. and Gold, B., *Theory and Application of Digital Signal Processing*. Prentice-Hall, 1975.

SH-1   Shenberg, I., 'The Design and Implementation of Digital Compensation Networks'. *IEEE Israel Tenth Conference*, Tel-Aviv, 1977.

SH-2   Shenberg, I., 'Implementation of digital controllers'. *Summary of lectures, Israel M.O.D.*, 1978.

SU-1   Sutton, M. L. *et al.*, 'Feasibility Study for an Advanced Digital Flight Control System', *LSI Tech. Rept. No. ADR-773*, Lear Siegler, Inc., Santa Monica, Calif., Oct. 1972.

TR-1   Truxal, J. G., *Automatic Feedback Control Synthesis*, McGraw-Hill, N.Y., 1955.

VA-1   Vaughan, D. R., 'A Non-Recursive Solution of the Discrete Matrix Riccati Equation', *IEEE Trans. on Automatic Control*, Oct. 1970.

WH-1   Whitback, R. F. and Hoffman, L. C., 'Digital Control Law Synthesis
            in the w' domain'. *J. Guidance and Control, Vol. 1, No. 5*, Sept.-
            Oct. 1978.
ZI-1   Zissos, D., *System Design with Microprocessors*, Academic Press,
            1978.

Index

abscissa, 96
acceleration, 114
  stage, 254
accelerometer, 114
ASCII characters, 147
actual measurements, 114
actuator, 29
ADC, 143, 262
adders, 136
additive function, 175
addresses, 146
aerodynamic steering, 239
aiming accuracy, 237
aircraft, 217
algorithm, 87, 135
aliasing, 44
all-digital missile, 239
amplification of noise, 178
amplitude
  response, 41
  scaling, 54
analog
  control loop, 38, 57
  filter, 48
  network, 239
  signals, 144
  switch, 148
analysis of algorithms, 163
analytical
  design, 71
  expression, 4
angular
  acceleration, 240
  attitude, 64
  direction, 242
  position servo, 96
antenna dish, 148
arithmetic
  devices, 145
  operations, 243

arming procedure, 247
artificial
  hand, 253
  hold, 48
  zeros, 56
artillery rocket, 237
assembly, 146
asymptotes, 81, 90
asymptotic solution, 184
attitude control, 244
autocorrelation, 172
autopilot, 195, 239
average roughness, 283
avionics, 239

background noise, 240
backward
  difference, 50
  sweep, 283
bandpass filter, 66
bandstop filter, 66
bandwidth, 48, 86, 219
Basic, 146
battery, 247
bending
  frequencies, 217
  mode, 46, 221
Ben-Zwi, A., 47, 253
Bibbero, R., 286
bilinear transformation, 25,
  51
  and frequency pre-warping,
  53, 151, 244
binary
  arithmetic, 164
  fraction, 66, 167
  point, 165
bipolar ADC, 148
block diagram, 13
  for sampled systems, 20

bode diagram, 86, 89
boundary
  conditions, 275, 289
  problems, 122
break, 254
breakpoints, 130, 235
Bryson, A., 122, 286
Bucy, R., 126, 287
buffers, 145
building blocks, 144
bus, 145

Cadzow, J., 15, 287
calculus of variation, 122, 270
canonical, 136
cascade
  controller, 82
  realization, 139, 181
Cauchy's residue theorem, 14,
  35
causality, 72
center of gravity, 81
center tracker, 248
characteristic equation, 8
  polynomial, 79
clock, 144
coefficient errors, 167, 179
coefficients, 123
closed loop
  poles, 82
  system, 13, 105
  zeros, 82
colored noise, 126, 217
command guidance, 239
communication link, 239
compensation, 79, 82
compensator, 130
compiler, 147
complex form, 56
computational algorithm, 19

computing cycle, 19
conditional jump, 215
Constantinides, A., 66, 286
constraints, 122
continuous design, 38
  compensator, 39
contour integration, 14
control
  algorithm, 135
  distribution matrix, 281
  objectives, 110
  sequence, 111
controllability
  condition of, 112
  definition of, 111
convolution, 3, 20, 171
correction factor, 114
correlation time, 126, 226
cost function, 122, 268
coulomb friction, 257
covariance matrix, 125, 227,
  277, 284
CPU, 263
critical frequencies, 62
cross assembler, 147
crossover frequencies, 62
CRT, 146
cutoff frequency, 48, 55

DAC, 144, 262
damping coefficients, 28,
  91, 240
data acquisition, 251
DC
  gain, 47
  motor, 253
deadband, 152, 183, 197
deadbeat, 75
debugging, 146
decade, 89
deceleration, 254
decibel, 89
decoders, 145
decoding, 240
degree of freedom, 112
delay, 26
  elements, 136
  in observers, 125
denominators, 112
derivative control, 82
derivatives, 229
design example, 148, 195,
  239, 253
desired plant, 72
destruction command, 248
development system, 145
difference
  backward, 50
  equation, 7
  forward, 7, 51

digital
  hardware, 136
  noise, 152
  range, 54
  to analog, 18
Dirac delta function, 33
direct
  drive, 256
  form, 136
  realization, 177
discontinuities, 229
discrete
  design, 70
  equation, 5
  processing, 16
  time, 4
discretization
  of continuous system, 15
  of compensation network,
    39
display, 143
disturbance
  external, 116
  random, 125
disturbing
  moment, 237
  signal, 238
dither, 185
dividers, 145
dominant poles, 80, 82
double integrator, 238
down counter, 149
drivers, 149
driving unit, 254
dynamic
  programming, 122
  range, 191, 247

editor, 140
eigenvector decomposition,
  123, 272
elastic
  contraction, 253
  deflection, 114
electric
  motor, 256
  supply, 217
elementary operations in
  matrices, 113
elevator angle, 123
encirclement rule, 94
encoding, 240
equation of motion, 113
equivalence, 126
equivalent voltage, 150
error
  covariance matrix, 126
  equation, 116
  estimator, 125
  in truncation, 166, 169
  multiplication, 168

error (cont'd)
  numerical, 167
  of observer, 116
  roundoff, 167, 170
Euler-Lagrange equation,
  122, 272
exact methods, 70
excess poles, 56
explicit model following, 129
external
  disturbance, 116
  noise, 127, 226, 278
extremum, 271

factorized form, 56
fading memory, 244
feedback loop, 79, 82
feedforward gain, 129
fidelity
  of response, 234
  ratio, 235
filter
  bandpass, 66
  bandstop, 66
  digital, 41
  FIR, 41
  highpass, 56
  Kalman, 116
  lowpass, 66
  moving average, 41
  notch, 218
  optimal, 126
  transversal, 41
fictitious frequency, 86
final value theorem, 13, 171
finite
  difference, 5
  polynomial in z^{-1}, 77
  settling, 75
  word length, 164, 179
firing sequence, 240
first order
  element, 139
  hold, 31
  system, 110
fixed point, 164
flight conditions, 123
floating
  bridge, 5
  point, 167
flow chart, 242, 266
folding of frequencies, 44
forcing function, 5
Fortran, 146
forward loop gain, 80
Fourier series, 34
frequency
  content, 224
  prewarping, 53, 82
  response, 32, 41
friction rod, 112

gain margin, 47
gate, 240
  center tracker, 244
  size tracker, 242
Gauss-Markov process, 227, 284
Gaussian signal, 191
glass container, 253
Glick, B., 195
gravity correction, 239
group delay, 41
guard filter, 48
guidance, 240
gusts, 217

Hall, W., 273, 286
Hamiltonian sequence, 271
heat dissipation, 150
high level language, 146
highpass filter, 56
Ho, Y., 125, 286
holds, 29
homing, 239
homogeneous equation, 9

ICE, 147
implementation of algorithms, 163
implicit model following, 129
impulse invariant transformation, 48
impulse response
  definition of, 3
  for RF, 284
  train, 19, 33, 291
inertial
  element, 64
  sensor, 218
infra-red, 240
initial states, 111
initial value theorem, 13
input commands, 128
instability, 226
instrument noise, 125
integral control, 82, 109
integrator, 23, 201
Intel, 252
interface, 145
interrupts, 143
inverse z-transform, 14
I/O ports, 145

Joseph, P., 126, 287
Jury, E., 25, 287

Kaiser, J., 179, 287
Kalman, R., 116, 270
keyboard, 146
Kuo, F., 179, 287
Kwakernaak, H., 273, 287

lag compensation, 82
Lagrange multipliers, 122
language, 146, 271
Laplace transformation, 10
laser, 240
latches, 145
launch system, 240
launcher, 237
launching procedure, 247
lead-lag, 132
lead network, 91
least significant bit, 164
Liapunov function, 283
limit cycle, 183, 186, 197
limiter, 66
linear
  approximation, 242
  function, 3
  range, 123
  system, 2
  time invariant discrete system, 3
log magnitude, 89
logarithmic
  scale, 81
  spiral, 28
logic
  intervention, 145
  states, 242
long division, 14
loop
  gain, 80
  stiffness, 72
lowpass filter, 48
LSI, 144

M-circles, 94
machine language, 146
magnetic tape, 146
magnitude, 89
main diagonal, 226
mapping of differentials, 50
matched z-transform, 55
matrix
  co-factor of, 106
  covariance, 125, 284
  inverse of, 111
  power spectral density, 125
  rank of, 113
  singular, 112, 276
  transition, 23, 272
  variance, 125
maximum
  likelihood, 125
  overshoot, 72, 104
mean, 125, 170
mean RF, 233, 283
measurement
  error, 102
  noise, 125, 222, 280

mechanical
  clutch, 254
  system, 112
mechanization, 135
medical instruments, 218
memories, 144
microcomputers, 143
microcontrollers, 144
midcourse guidance, 245
minimization procedure, 122
missile, 195, 239
mnemonic language, 146
model following, 128
modes, 274
modulation process, 33
monitor, 147
most significant bit, 215
moving average filter, 41
moving clamp, 254
multi-input/multi-output, 104
multiloop feedback, 82
multiple roots, 9
multiplexer, 145
multiplication error, 168
multipliers, 136
multivariable digital control, 104

N-circles, 94
natural frequency, 234
navigation, 240, 248
Nechemia, N., 148
Nichols
  chart, 91
  diagram, 100, 259
noise, 116, 280
  amplification, 178
nonlinear
  control, 105
  elements, 197
  properties of controller, 183
non-minimum phase, 72
non-unity feedback, 81
non-zero element, 281
normal distribution, 125
notch filter, 218
numerator, 112
numerical
  accuracy, 101
  algorithm, 163
  error, 88
  integration, 111
Nyquist, 16, 92, 216
  frequency, 44
  plot, 96
  stability criterion, 92

object code, 146
observability test, 119
observer design, 105, 113, 115
octave, 89

Ohmic resistance, 256
one's-complement arithmetic, 165
open loop
  poles, 80
  transfer function, 13
  zeros, 80
optimal
  control, 122
  filter, 126, 277
  filtering, 127
  regulator, 123, 270
overflow, 165
overshoot, 225, 255, 259

Padé expansion, 40
paper tape, 141
parallel realization, 140, 174, 181
parameter errors, 167
Parseval theorem, 172, 282
partial fraction expansion, 15
particular solution, 9
Pascal, 146
peak frequency response, 47
Peled, U., 130, 222, 234
periodic signal, 41
peripherals, 145
phase
  lag, 62, 246
  lead, 62
  margin, 47, 58, 104, 259
  response, 41
  shift, 92
pilot command, 225
pitch, 114
  control, 217
  dynamics, 239
  rate, 123, 225
PLM, 146
point connector, 32
Poisson summation rule, 34
polar plot, 92
pole
  location, 125
  placement, 105
polynomial
  extrapolation, 29
  factorization, 79
  predictor, 244
ports, 145
position servo, 57, 254
positive function, 229
potentiometer, 96
Potter, J., 272
power
  amplifier, 96, 255
  series expansion, 14
  spectral density, 125, 284
precession, 240
predictor, 32, 244

prefilter, 130, 217
pressure sensor, 253
primary strip, 27
principal factor, 140
principle of superposition, 3
printer, 146
probability density function, 169
process noise, 125, 280
programming, 145
PROM, 145
propagation of noise, 169
proportional
  control, 81
  navigation, 239
pulse transfer function, 18
  with modulation, 29, 148

quadratic factor, 91
quadratic synthesis, 122
quality
  criterion, 130
  ratio, 130
quantization, 169
  noise, 152, 171
Q-R algorithm, 273

radar tracking, 6
Ragazzini, S., 1, 287
RAM, 145, 243
ramp input, 76
random
  noise, 283
  process, 171
rate gyro, 46, 221
rational
  expression, 40
  function, 15
reader punch, 146
realizability, 72
realization, 136
reconstruction scheme, 33
  of states, 107
recursive equation, 183, 186, 277
reference voltage, 148
register, 146
regulator, 123, 269
reliability, 247
reprogramming, 145
resolution of ADC, 187
resonance peak, 91
RF, 229
Riccati equation, 122, 272
ripple-free response, 75
rocket engine, 247
roll stabilization, 195
ROM, 145, 243
root locus method, 79
roughness function, 229, 281
rotating mass, 239

rounding, 165
roundoff error, 168
Routh-Hurwitz criterion, 25

safe and arm, 240
sampled data theory, 16, 33
sampled sinusoid, 44
sampling
  continuous function, 4
  frequency, 4
  function, 33
  process, 16, 33
  rate, 4
  theorem, 16
scalar, 123
scaling, 66, 165
saturation, 201
  limit, 255
second order element, 139
selection of sampling rate, 217
self test, 240
sensor accuracy, 254
sensors, 187
separation theorem, 116
series realization, 136
servo
  actuators, 187
  compensation, 246
servomechanism, 148
Shannon, C., 16, 224
Shenberg, I., 163, 185, 287
shift theorem, 10
short
  mode, 124
  period, 46
sign magnitude, 164
signal to noise ratio, 191
simple operation, 243
simulation, 114
single sensor, 239
singular matrix, 277
slender missile, 221
sloshing, 218
smoothing, 104
software, 136
space dimension, 109
spectral density matrix, 125
s-plane, 26, 86
stability, 25
  in z-plane, 25, 73
stable region, 102
Stapleford, R., 226
state space, 6
  representation of discrete system, 22, 105, 107
state variable, 105
static friction, 97
stationary noise, 171
statistical error, 169
steady state error, 74
  response, 278

step
  input, 74
  response, 47, 58
stepper motor, 29, 143, 253
stick input, 225
stiffness, 254
summers, 136
superposition, 3
supersonic, 124
sweep method, 123
switching function, 33
system, 2

time
  axis, 115
  between samples, 4
  lag, 39
  response, 222
tracking, 239
trajectory, 245
transfer function, 12, 13
transient response, 80, 128
transistor bridge, 149
transition matrix, 23, 233
transportation lag, 73
transpose, 226
transversal filter, 41

trapezoidal
  integration, 51
  reconstruction, 32
trial-and-error, 123
triangular hold, 32, 49
truncation, 164
  operator, 186
Truxal, J., 71, 287
turbulence, 125
Tustin transformation, 51
two's-complement arith-
  metic, 151, 164
two degrees of freedom, 239
two-point boundary
  problem, 123, 272

uncontrolled disturbance, 226
unit
  circle, 25, 73
  vector, 93
unity feedback, 93
unmodelled states, 217
unrounded quantity, 166

variance, 170
  matrix, 125
variation of coefficients, 182

Vaughan, D., 273, 287
vector, 93
velocity of missile, 242

w-plane, 26, 71, 84
w'-plane, 84
weighting matrix, 122
Whitback, R., 87, 287
white noise, 125, 169, 284
wideband, 55
wide spectrum, 222
word length, 164, 244
  in roundoff, 184
  of ADC, 192
  of memory, 193
  of DAC, 194

z-plane, 25
z-transform
  definition of, 10
  inverse of, 14
  matched, 55
  of state space representation,
    23
z-transforms, table of, 285
zero order
  frequency response of, 31
  hold, 29, 49
zero steady-state error, 74